Site Carpentry and Joinery

The NVQ Construction series titles are:

WOOD OCCUPATIONS by Peter Brett
(covers all wood occupations at Level 1)

A BUILDING CRAFT FOUNDATION (2nd edition) by Peter Brett
(covers the common core units at Levels 1 and 2)

SITE CARPENTRY AND JOINERY (2nd edition) by Peter Brett
(covers the Site Carpentry units at Level 2)

BENCH JOINERY by Peter Brett
(covers the Bench Joinery units at Level 2)

Nelson Thornes Construction NVQ Series

Level 2

Site Carpentry and Joinery

SECOND EDITION

Peter Brett

First published in 1993 by:
Stanley Thornes (Publishers) Ltd

Second edition published in 2002 by:
Nelson Thornes Ltd
Delta Place
27 Bath Road
CHELTENHAM
GL53 7TH
United Kingdom

CORNWALL COLLEGE
STUDY CENTRE

03 04 05 06 / 10 9 8 7 6 5 4 3 2

A catalogue record for this book is available from the British Library

ISBN 0 7487 6532 8

Illustrations in Chapter 6 by Peters and Zabransky (UK) Ltd
Page make-up by Florence Production Ltd, Stoodleigh, Devon

Printed in Great Britain by Scotprint

Contents

Acknowledgements

The author wishes to thank the following:

Richard Burbridge Ltd for their permission to include their stair-part details.

Elizabeth Whiting Associates for the photograph of wet rot.

Rentokil Property Care for the photographs of dry rot.

My sincere thanks go to: my wife Christine for her assistance, support and constant encouragement; my daughter Sarah and my son James for their patience particularly at weekends; my colleagues and associates past and present for their continued support and motivation.

Word-square searches were kindly produced by James Brett.

Finally, all the best for the future to those who use this book.

National Vocational Qualifications – NVQs

The work of a skilled person in the construction industry can be divided into various tasks: build a brick wall; fix plasterboard; prepare and paint surfaces; assemble a door; hang a door, etc. These tasks along with many others are grouped into 'units of competence'. You can consider these units of competence as a menu to select from, according to your own or employers' skill requirements.

Traditional barriers to gaining a qualification such as age, length of training, mode of training, how and where skills are acquired have been removed. Individuals may acquire units of competence, in any order as and when and where they want. Units of competence are accredited individually and may be transferred to any appropriate NVQ award.

Credits for units of competence, which can be accumulated over any period of time, may be built into a full NVQ award at three levels.

NVQ Level 1   Introduction to industry, a 'foundation' common core plus occupational base skills, e.g. Wood occupations, Trowel occupations and Decorative occupations, etc.

NVQ Level 2   A set number of units of competence in a recognisable work role, e.g. Carpentry and joinery, Sitework, Benchwork and brickwork, etc.

NVQ Level 3   A more complex set of units of competence again in a recognisable work role including some work of a supervisory nature.

The Qualification and Curriculum Authority QCA is the accrediting body for NVQ qualifications in the construction industry.

The Construction Industry Training Board CITB establish standards for the units of competence and the qualification structure for the industry.

Collecting evidence

You will need to collect evidence of your satisfactory performance in each element of a unit of competence.

This evidence can be either:

- **Work-based**. This will be evidence from your employers and supervisors, etc. that confirms you have demonstrated the full range of practical skills required for a unit. This should be supported by drawings, photographs and other associated documentation used/produced as part of the activity.

- **Simulation**. Where work-based evidence is not available or appropriate, simulated activities may be undertaken in a training or assessment environment. Again, supporting documentation will be required as with work-based evidence, so that the total provides sufficient evidence to infer that you can repeat the skills competently in a work-based environment.

- **A combination** of **work-based and simulation evidence**. Again with supporting documentation to infer competence.

Introduction

This book you are about to start is one of the Construction NVQ Series, and is aimed at those working, intending to work or undergoing training as a carpenter and joiner. The workplace will be mainly on a building site and include new building work, maintenance, refurbishment and restoration. The completion of this book can be used as evidence towards job knowledge achievement which, coupled with acceptable evidence or a demonstration of practical skills, can lead to the full NVQ Level 2 award.

The following eight units make up the NVQ Level 2 Carpentry and Joinery Sitework option.

Mandatory core units (common to all construction craft options)

Unit No. 07   Store resources ready for work

Unit No. 08   Erect and dismantle working platforms

Unit No. 09   Contribute to efficient working practices

Sitework option units

Unit No. 143   Install first fixing components

Unit No. 144   Install second fixing components

Unit No. 145   Erect structural carcassing components

Additional units

Unit No. 160   Maintain internal and external timber components

Unit No. 161   Produce timber and timber-based products (circular saw)

The mandatory core units are fully covered in the companion book, *A Building Craft Foundation*, to which reference should be made.

All of the sitework option units and both of the additional units are fully covered in this book with a chapter being dedicated to each.

How to use this book

This is a self-study package designed to be supported by:

- tutor reinforcement and guidance
- group discussion
- films, slides and videos
- text books
- practical learning tasks.

You should read/work through each section of a chapter, one at a time as required. Discuss its content with your group, tutor, or friends wherever possible. Attempt to answer the *Questions for you* in that section. Progressively read through all the sections, discussing them and answering the questions and other learning tasks as you go. At the same time you should be either working on the matching practical learning task/assessment set by your college/training centre or, alternatively, be carrying out the practical competence and recording its successful completion in the workplace.

This process is intended to aid learning and enable you to evaluate your understanding of the particular section and to check your progress through the chapters and entire package. Where you are unable to answer a question, further reading and discussion of the section is required.

Throughout this learning package, 'Harry' the General Foreman will prompt you regarding important details.

FOLLOW MY THOUGHTS REGARDING IMPORTANT DETAILS AND THINGS TO DO

The *Questions for you* in this package are either multiple choice or short answer.

Multiple-choice questions consist of a statement or question followed by four possible answers. Only *one* answer is correct, the others are distracters. Your response is recorded by filling in the line under the appropriate letter.

Example

This indicates that you have selected (b) as the answer.

If after consideration you want to change your mind, fill in the box under your first answer and then fill in the line under the new letter.

This changes the answer from (b) to (d).

Short-answer questions consist of a task to which a short written answer is required. The length will vary depending on the 'doing' word in the task, *Name* or *List* normally require one or two words for each item, *State*, *Define*, *Describe* or *Explain* will require a short sentence or two, *Draw* or *Sketch* will require an illustration. In addition sketches can be added to any written answer to aid clarification.

Example

Name the member used around frames to conceal the joint between wall and timber.

Typical answer: Architrave

Example

Define the term 'Herring-bone strutting'.

Typical answer: Diagonal cross-strutting fixed across joists at their mid-span to stiffen the joists and prevent lateral (sideways) movement.

Example

Produce a sketch to show the difference between herring-bone and solid strutting to floor joists.

Typical answer:

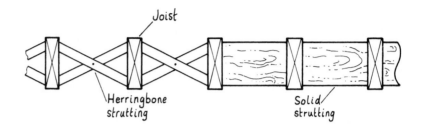

In addition this learning package also contains *Learning tasks*. Follow the instructions given with each exercise. They are intended to reinforce the work undertaken in this package. They give you the opportunity to use your newly acquired awareness and skills before attempting the *Questions for you*.

In common with NVQ knowledge and understanding assessments, the learning exercises in this package may also be attempted orally. You can simply tell someone your answer, point to a diagram, indicate a part in a learning pack or text book, or make sketches, etc.

1 Basic skills

READ THIS CHAPTER, WORKING THROUGH THE 'QUESTIONS FOR YOU'

In order to successfully complete the main practical activities in each Level 2 Unit of Competence, you will require an understanding of a range of enabling skills and supporting job knowledge, e.g. interpretation of drawings and oral/written instructions, adoption of safe working practices, loading and unloading materials, use of tools and general knowledge.

You may have already achieved some or all of these skills and knowledge either in industry or as a result of training at Level 1 or similar. Thus this basic skills chapter has been included in the form of typical questions for you to undertake. Questions are divided into topic areas. Where you cannot answer any particular question, further study should be undertaken using either the information source indicated, other appropriate text books, or talk it through with your tutor or a workmate.

This chapter should be studied on its own, or alongside other chapters according to your need.

Persons with prior achievement may wish to use these questions on basic skills as a refresher to support other chapters as required.

Interpreting instructions and planning own work

These two topics are covered in *A Building Craft Foundation* under 'Communications' and 'Materials'. These should be referred to if you have difficulty in answering the following questions.

Questions for you

1. State the reason why construction drawings are drawn to a scale and not full size.

_____

_____

2. Mark on the scale rule shown below 4.550 m to a scale of 1:50.

| 1:5 | 0 | | 100mm | | 200 | | 300 | | 400 | | 500 | | 600 | | 700mm | |
| 1:50 | | | 1m | | 2 | | 3 | | 4 | | 5 | | 6 | | 7m | |

Metric   **JAKAR**   315 PL.   British Made

| 1:2500 | 360m | 340 | 320 | 300 | 280 | 260 | 240 | 220 | 200 | 180 | 160 | 140 | 120 | 100 | 80 | 60 | 40 | 20m | |
| 1:1250 | 180m | 170 | 160 | 150 | 140 | 130 | 120 | 110 | 100 | 90 | 80 | 70 | 60 | 50 | 40 | 30 | 20 | 10m | |

3. Produce sketches to show the standard symbols used to represent: brickwork, blockwork, concrete, sawn and planed timber.

THE TERMS 'UNWROT' AND 'WROT' ARE SOMETIMES USED INSTEAD OF SAWN AND PLANED TIMBER

4. State what is meant by orthographic projection.

_____

_____

5. Define the terms: plan, elevation and section when applied to a drawing of an object.

_____

_____

_____

6. State the purpose of specifications and schedules.

_____

_____

7. State why messages must be relayed accurately.

_____

_____

8. State the meaning of the following standard abbreviations:

bwk _____   bldg _____

DPC _____   dwg _____

hwd _____   swd _____

9. State the action to be taken when damaged goods are received from a supplier.

_____

_____

10. State **ONE** reason why you as an employee should plan how to carry out work given to you.

_____

_____

11. Name the person you should contact in the event of a technical problem occurring at work.

_____

_____

12. State the reason why dust sheets should be used when working internally in occupied premises.

_____

_____

13. State why it is important to be polite with the customer.

_____

_____

14. State why it is important to be co-operative and helpful with work colleagues.

_____

_____

REFER BACK TO THE INDICATED SOURCES IF YOU HAVE ANY PROBLEMS

Adopting safe working practices

This topic is covered in *A Building Craft Foundation* under 'Health and Safety' and 'Scaffolding'. These should be referred to if you have difficulty in answering the following questions.

———————— Questions for you ————————

15. State **TWO** duties expected of you as an employee under the Health and Safety at Work Act.

_____

_____

16. State **TWO** objectives of the Health and Safety at Work Act.

_____

_____

17. State **TWO** main powers of a Health and Safety Executive Inspector.

_____

_____

18. State **TWO** situations where protective equipment must be used. Name the item of equipment in **EACH** case.

_____

_____

19. State the reason for keeping work areas clear and tidy.

_____

_____

20. Name a suitable fire extinguisher for use on a flammable liquid or gas fire.

_____

_____

21. Describe the correct body position for lifting a large box from ground level.

_____

_____

22. Name the type of safety sign that is contained in a yellow triangle with a black border.

_____

23. Describe the role of a site Safety Officer.

_____

_____

24. State the purpose of a toe board on a scaffold platform.

_____

_____

25. Name **TWO** parts of a ladder.

_____

_____

26. List **THREE** checks that should be made before using a scaffold.

_____

_____

27. State the correct working angle of a ladder.

_____

_____

28. State the immediate action to be taken if a scaffold is found to be defective.

_____

_____

29. State where the flattened end of a putlog is inserted.

_____

REFER BACK TO THE INDICATED SOURCES IF YOU HAVE ANY PROBLEMS

Identifying, maintaining and using hand tools

This topic is covered in *Wood Occupations*. This should be referred to if you have difficulty in answering the following questions.

Questions for you

30. Produce a sketch to show the difference in cutting action between a rip and cross-cut saw.

31. Name the saw best used for cutting down the sides of tenons to a middle rail of a door.

_____

32. Define the difference between a warrington and claw hammer.

_____

_____

33. State an advantage of using a water level over using a spirit level.

_____

_____

34. State the procedure used for sharpening a plane iron.

_____

_____

---

35. When sharpening saws the following operations are carried out: setting, shaping, sharpening and topping. State the order in which these are carried out.

_____

_____

36. Explain the operations carried out when preparing a piece of sawn timber to PAR by hand.

_____

_____

37. State the purpose of using oil when sharpening plane and chisel blades.

_____

_____

38. Name the type of work for which a panel saw is most suitable.

_____

_____

39. Name the type of work for which a bullnose plane is most suitable.

_____

_____

40. Name **THREE** different types of chisel and state a use for **EACH**.

_____

_____

_____

41. State the purpose of a bradawl.

_____

42. Produce a sketch to show a mitre template and state a situation where it may be used.

_____

_____

43. Name a tool that can be used to draw large diameter curves.

_____

44. State the reason for taking off the corners of a smoothing plane iron after sharpening.

_____

_____

REFER BACK TO THE INDICATED SOURCES IF YOU HAVE ANY PROBLEMS

Setting up and using portable power tools

This topic is covered in *Wood Occupations*. This should be referred to if you have difficulty in answering the following questions.

——————— Questions for you ———————

45. State **FOUR** basic safety rules that should be followed when using any powered tool.

_____

_____

_____

_____

46. When using a hand held electric circular saw state **THREE** operations that should be carried out before plugging the tool into the power supply.

_____

_____

_____

47. State the reason why power tools should never be carried, dragged or suspended by their cables.

_____

_____

48. Describe the procedure for plunge cutting with a jig saw.

_____

_____

49. State the reason why the cutters of a portable planer should be allowed to stop before putting the tool down.

_____

_____

50. State how cutters are held in a portable powered router.

_____

_____

51. Describe the **THREE** basic work stages when using a plunging portable powered router.

_____

_____

_____

52. Produce a sketch to show the correct direction of feed for a router in relation to the rotation of the cutter.

53. State the purpose of using 110 volt power tools.

_____

_____

54. What type of power tools does not require an earth wire?

_____

_____

55. State the correct location of an extension cable used in conjunction with a transformer that steps 240 volts mains supply down to 110 volts.

_____

_____

56. Which of the following sanders is best used for fine finishing work: circular, orbital, belt?

_____

57. A cartridge-operated fixing tool is to be used for fixing timber grounds to a concrete ceiling. List **THREE** items of equipment that are recommended for the operator to wear.

_____

_____

_____

58. The cartridge-operated fixing tool you are using on site has been supplied with **THREE** colours of cartridge: red, black and yellow. List them in order of decreasing strength.

_____

_____

_____

59. State the action that the operator should take if a power tool is not working correctly or its safety is suspect.

_____

_____

REFER BACK TO THE INDICATED SOURCES IF YOU HAVE ANY PROBLEMS

Handling timber-based materials and components

This topic is covered in *A Building Craft Foundation* under 'Materials'. This should be referred to if you have difficulty in answering the following questions.

Questions for you

60. State the reason for stacking timber off the ground.

_____

_____

61. State **TWO** reasons why materials storage on site should be planned.

_____

_____

62. State **THREE** personal hygiene precautions that may be recommended by a manufacturer when handling materials.

_____

_____

_____

63. State the reason for using piling sticks or cross-bearers when stacking carcassing timber.

_____

_____

64. Give the reason for stacking sheet materials flat and level.

_____

_____

65. Explain why joinery should be stored under cover after delivery.

_____

_____

66. State the reason why the leaning of items of joinery against walls is not to be recommended.

_____

_____

67. State the reason why new deliveries are put at the back of existing stock in the store.

_____

_____

68. Explain why liquids should not be kept in any container other than that supplied by the manufacturer.

_____

_____

69. Explain why veneered sheets of plywood are stored good face to good face.

_____

_____

REFER BACK TO THE INDICATED SOURCES IF YOU HAVE ANY PROBLEMS

General knowledge

1) Timber and manufactured boards
2) Preservatives
3) Adhesives
4) Fixings
5) Calculations

This topic is covered in *Wood Occupations*. Calculations are covered in *A Building Craft Foundation* under 'Numerical skills'. These should be referred to if you have difficulty in answering the following questions.

———— Questions for you ————

70. Describe **THREE** main differences between softwoods and hardwoods.

_____

_____

_____

71. List **FOUR** common sawn sizes for carcassing timber.

_____

_____

72. Softwood is available in stock lengths from 1.8 m. State the measurement that stock lengths increase by.

_____

73. Produce a sketch to distinguish between multi-ply, blockboard and laminboard.

---

74. Describe what is meant by stress-graded timber and name **TWO** grades.

_____

_____

75. Produce sketches to show the following mouldings: torus, ogee, bullnosed, ovolo, scotia.

76. List the **TWO** initial factors that must be present for an attack of dry rot in timber.

_____

_____

77. Describe the **THREE** stages of an attack of dry rot.

_____

_____

_____

78. State the purpose of using preservative-treated timber.

_____

_____

79. Name **TWO** types of timber preservative and state **TWO** methods of application.

_____

_____

80. Produce sketches to show the following timber defects: cup shake, knot, cupping, waney edge and sloping grain.

81. Name **TWO** common wood-boring insects and for **EACH** state the location and timber they will most likely attack.

_____

_____

82. Define what is meant by conversion of timber and produce sketches to show through-and-through and quarter sawn.

_____

_____

83. Define the term seasoning of timber.

_____

_____

84. State a suitable moisture content when installing carcassing timber and explain how a moisture meter measures this.

_____

_____

_____

85. State **TWO** advantages that sheet material have over the use of solid timber.

_____

_____

86. A sheet of plywood has been marked up WBP grade. Explain what this means.

_____

_____

87. Explain the reason why water is brushed into the mesh side of hardboard prior to its use.

_____

_____

88. Define the following terms when applied to adhesives: storage/shelf life, pot life.

_____

_____

89. Explain the essential safety precaution to be taken when using a contact adhesive.

_____

_____

90. Produce a sketch to show the difference between countersunk, round-head and raised-head screws.

91. Describe a situation where **EACH** of the following nails may be used: wire nail, oval nail, annular nail and masonry nail.

_____

_____

_____

_____

92. Define with the aid of sketches **EACH** of the following types of nailing: dovetail, skew, and secret.

93. Describe a situation where a non-ferrous metal plug would be specified for screwing into rather than a fibre or plastic one.

_____

_____

94. Add together the following dimensions 750 mm, 1.200 m, 705 mm, 4.645 mm.

95. 756 joinery components are produced by a manufacturer. 327 are to be preservative treated, the remainder require painting. State how many are to be painted.

96. Nine pieces of timber are required to make an item of joinery. How many pieces of timber are required to make 17 such items?

97. A rectangular room measures 4.8 m × 5.2 m. Calculate the floor area and the length of skirting required. Allow for **ONE** 900 mm wide door opening.

98. Five semi-circular pieces of plywood are required. Calculate the cost of plywood at £4.55 per square metre if the radius of **EACH** semi-circular piece is 600 mm.

99. A 105 m run of carcassing timber is required for a project. You have been asked to allow an additional 15% for cutting and wastage. Determine the amount to be ordered.

100. A triangular piece of plywood has a base span of 1.4 m and a rise of 500 mm. Determine in metres square the area of five such pieces.

101. A semi-circular bay window has a diameter of 2.4 m. Determine the length of skirting required for this window.

102. A door 1980 mm in height is to have a handle fixed centrally. A security viewer is to be positioned 350 mm above this height. Determine the height of the viewer.

103. A carpenter earns £65.60 per day. The apprentice is paid 30% of this amount. Determine the wage bill for five days, for both people if the employer has to allow an additional 17.5% for on-costs.

104. Use a calculator or tables to solve the following:
(a) 457 divided by 239
(b) 6945 multiplied by 1350
(c) 336 raised to the third power
(d) The square root of 183.

WELL, HOW DID YOU DO?

REFER BACK TO THE INDICATED SOURCES IF YOU HAVE ANY PROBLEMS

2 Carcassing

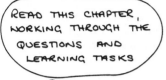
READ THIS CHAPTER, WORKING THROUGH THE QUESTIONS AND LEARNING TASKS

In undertaking this chapter you will be required to demonstrate your skill and knowledge of the following carcassing elements:

● floors, roofs and their finishings.

You will be required practically to:

● Construct an equal pitched roof with hip, valley and gable using trussed rafters and traditional timbers.
● Position and fix fascia board, barge board and soffit.

Floor and flat roof joists

Joist terminology

Floor – the ground or upper levels in a building that provide an acceptable surface for walking, living and working.

Roof – the uppermost part of a building that spans the external walls and provides protection from the elements.

Timber ground floor – the floor of a building nearest the exterior ground level and known as a hollow or suspended floor. Joists are supported at intervals by honeycomb sleeper walls. Air bricks and ventilation gaps in the sleeper walls provide ventilation to the under-floor space to keep the timber dry and reduce the possibility of rot.

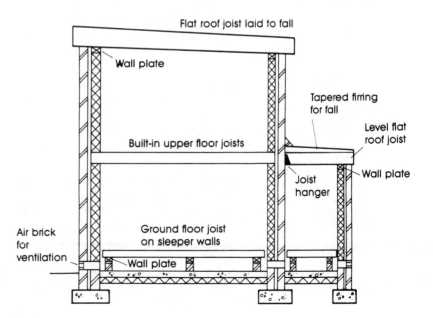

Figure 2.1 *Floor and roof joists*

Timber upper floors – the floor levels of a building above the ground floor. They are known as suspended floors. Bridging joists span between supports. Binders may be incorporated to reduce span; strutting is used in mid-span to reduce tendency to buckle. Openings in floors are framed using trimming, trimmer and trimmed joists.

Timber flat roofs – any roof having an angle or slope that is less than 10 degrees to the horizontal. They are constructed similar to timber upper floors. The slope on the top surface may be formed by either laying the bridging joist to falls (out of level), or by the use of firrings.

Joist – one of a series of parallel timber beams, used to span the gap between walls and directly support a floor surface, ceiling surface or flat roof surface.

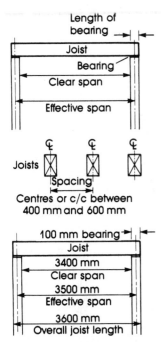

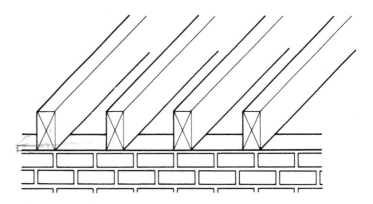

Figure 2.2 *Joists*

The sectional size of a joist depends on its span, spacing, weight or loading placed upon it and the quality of the timber used. The Building Regulations 2000 Approved Documents contain tables of suitable sectional joist size for use in different situations.

Span – Clear span is the distance between joist supports. *Effective span* is the distance between the centres of the joist bearings (see Figure 2.3). The bearing itself is the length of the end of a joist that rests on the support. The overall length of a joist is its clear span plus the length of its end bearings, e.g. a joist with a 3400 mm clear span and 100 mm end bearings will have an effective span of 3500 mm and an overall joist length of 3600 mm.

Joists are commonly laid out to span the shortest distance between the supporting walls of a room or other area. This keeps to a minimum the size of joist required. Once the depth of the joist is determined for the longest span it is normal practice to keep all other joists the same. The shorter span joists will be oversize, but all joist covering and ceiling surfaces will be level.

Spacing – Joist spacing is the distance between the centres of adjacent joists. Commonly called joist centres or c/c (centre to centre). They range between 400 to 600 mm depending on the joist covering material.

Joists should be spaced to accommodate surface dimensions of their covering material. End joists adjacent to walls should be kept 50 mm away from the wall surface, in order to allow an air circulation and prevent dampness being transferred from wall to joist, and thus reduce the risk of rot. In addition this gap helps reduce the transmission of noise at party walls.

Figure 2.3 *Joist span and spacing*

Unventilated and damp timber is open to an attack of rot (dry rot or wet rot) which leads to a loss of strength and possible collapse. For detailed information on timber rots, their prevention and remedial treatment see Chapter 6 Maintenance.

To determine the number of joists required and their centres for a particular area the following procedure, shown in Figure 2.4, can be used:

- Measure the distance between adjacent walls, say 3150 mm.
- The first and last joist would be positioned 50 mm away from the walls. The centres of 50 mm breadth joists would be 75 mm away from the wall. The total distance between end joists centres would be 3000 mm.
- Divide distance between end joists centres by specified joist spacing say 400 mm. This gives the number of spaces between joists. Where a whole number is not achieved round up to the nearest whole number above. There will always be one more joist than the number of spaces so add one to this figure to determine the number of joists.

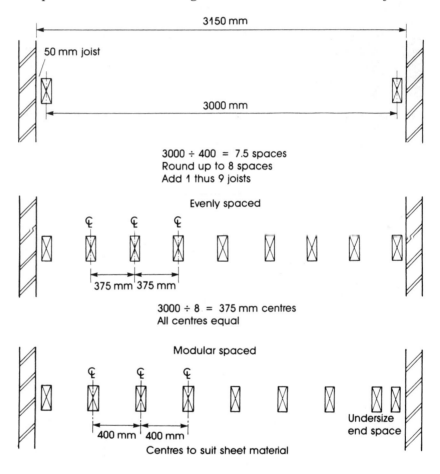

Figure 2.4 *Determining number of joists required*

- Where T & G boarding is used as a floor covering the joist centres may be spaced out evenly, i.e. divide the distance between end joist centres by the number of spaces.
- Where sheet material is used as a joist covering to form a floor, ceiling or roof surface, the joist centres are normally maintained at a 400 mm or 600 mm module to coincide with sheet sizes. This would leave an undersized spacing between the last two joists.

Joist spacing according to covering material used

Table 2.1 *Joist spacing according to covering material used*

Covering material	Finished thickness (mm)	Maximum spacing of joists (mm)
Softwood T & G boarding	16	450
Softwood T & G boarding	19	600
Flooring-grade chipboard	18/19	400–450
Flooring-grade chipboard	22	600
Decking plywood	16	400
Decking plywood	18/19	600

READ THE INSTRUCTIONS AND COMPLETE THE TASK

Preservative treatment – it is recommended that all timber used for structural purposes is preservative treated before use. Any preservative treated timber cut to size on site will require re-treatment on the freshly cut edges/ends. This can be carried out by applying two brush flood coats of preservative. Timber preservatives prevent rot by poisoning the food supply on which fungi feed and grow.

Learning task

Determine the number of 50 mm breadth joists required to be spaced at approximately 400 mm centres, between two walls 4350 mm apart.

Position of floor   Ends of joists

4350 mm

100 mm bearing

Joist

3400 mm

Determine the total amount of timber required in metres run, for all the floor joists. These have a clear span of 3400 mm and a bearing at each end of 100 mm.

TRY TO ANSWER THESE

──────── **Questions for you** ────────

1. State the purpose of a joist.

_____

_____

2. Why do joists normally span the shortest distance?

_____

_____

3. Define a joist's clear span.

_____

_____

_____

4. The total length of joist having an effective span of 3600 mm and end bearings of 100 mm is:
(a) 3500 mm
(b) 3600 mm
(c) 3700 mm
(d) 3800 mm

a	b	c	d

5. A joist spans between two walls 2.8 metres apart and has end bearings of 100 mm, what length of joist is required?

_____

6. Name the regulations that apply to the positioning and fixing of joists.

_____

7. State the reason for treating sawn ends of joists with preservative.

_____

_____

Fixing joists

Section – the breadth and depth of a joist. The strength of a joist varies in direct proportion to changes in its breadth and in proportion to the square of its depth. For example, doubling the breadth of a section doubles its strength.

E.g. a 100 mm × 100 mm joist has double the strength of a 50 mm × 100 mm joist.

Whereas doubling the depth of a section increases its strength by four times.

E.g. a 50 mm × 200 mm joist has four times the strength of a 50 mm × 100 mm joist.

Less material is required for the same strength when the greatest sectional dimension is placed vertically rather than horizontally.

E.g. a 100 mm × 100 mm joist has the same sectional area as a 50 mm × 200 mm joist, but the deeper joist would be twice as strong.

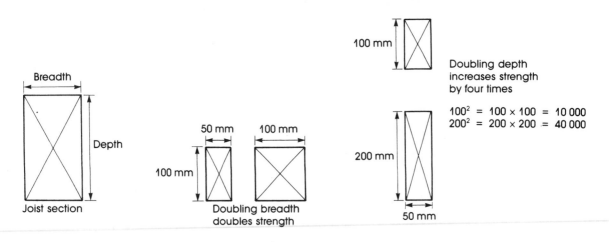

Figure 2.5 *Joist section*

Therefore joists are normally placed so that the depth is the greatest sectional dimension. Joists of the same sectional size and span would clearly have different strengths if their breadths and depths were reversed. Those with the smaller depth would sag under load, possibly leading to structural collapse (see Figure 2.6). When stating the sectional size of a joist the first measurement given is the breadth and the second the depth.

Regularised timber, as shown in Figure 2.7, is preferred for joists as all timber will be a consistent depth. This aids levelling and ensures a flat fixing surface for joist coverings and ceilings. Joists are regularised to a consistent depth by re-sawing or planing one or both edges. A reduction in size of 3 mm must be allowed for timber up to 150 mm in depth and 5 mm, over this width.

E.g., 50 mm × 150 mm may be regularised to 50 mm × 147 mm and 50 mm × 200 mm may be regularised to 50 mm × 195 mm.

Joist supports – any joists which are not straight should be positioned with their camber or crown (curved edge) upwards. When loaded these joists will tend to straighten out rather than sag further if laid the other way. Joists with edge knots should be positioned with the knots on their upper edge. When loaded the knots will be held in position as the joists sag, rather than fall out, weaken the joist, and possibly lead to structural collapse if laid the other way (see Figure 2.8)

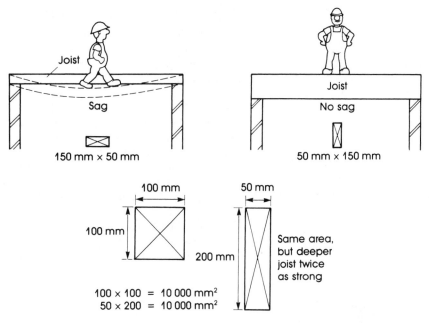

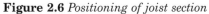

Figure 2.6 *Positioning of joist section*

50 mm × 200 mm joist
regularised to
50 mm × 195 mm
by machining

Figure 2.7 *Regularised joist*

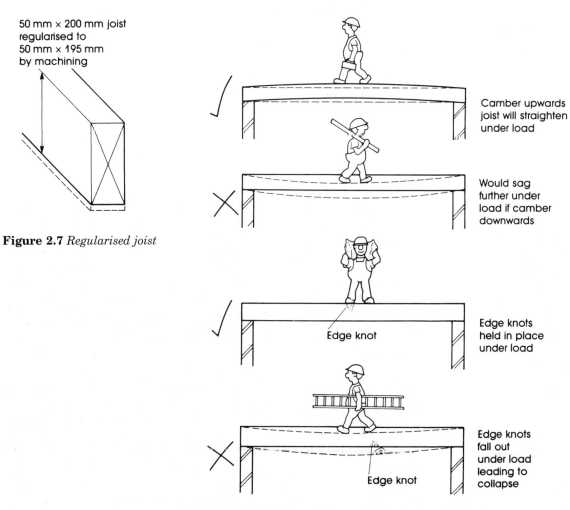

Figure 2.8 *Positioning of joists with camber or edge knots*

The ends of joists may be supported:

- by building in
- on hangers
- on wall plates
- on binders.

Building in – the inner leaf of a cavity wall (see Figure 2.9). The minimum bearing in a wall is normally 90 mm. (Shorter bearings do not tie in the wall sufficiently and can lead to a crushing of the joist end possibly leading to collapse.) A steel bearing bar may be incorporated into the mortar joint where lightweight blocks are used to reduce the risk of the blocks crumbling. The ends of the joists are often splayed but they must not project into the cavity where they could possibly catch mortar droppings during building, leading to dampness in the joist and rotting. The ends of joists that are in contact with the external wall should be treated with a timber preservative to protect them from dampness and subsequent rot.

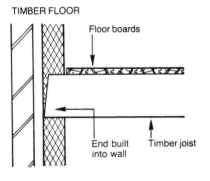

TIMBER FLOOR

Floor boards

End built into wall

Timber joist

Figure 2.9 *Building in a joist*

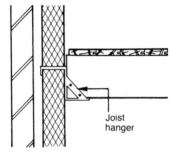

Joist hanger

Figure 2.10 *Use of joist hanger*

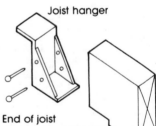

Joist hanger

End of joist recessed over hanger to provide level ceiling

Figure 2.11 *Use of joist hanger*

Hangers – ends of joists may be supported on galvanised steel joist hangers, which are themselves built into or bear on a wall (see Figure 2.10). Double hangers are available which saddle internal walls to provide a support for joists on both sides. An advantage of this method is that the joist can be positioned independently of the building process. Hangers are useful when forming extensions as they are simply inserted into a raked out mortar joint. The bottom edge or bearing surface of the hanger must be recessed into the joist, as shown in Figure 2.11. This ensures that the top and bottom edges of the joists are flush and also prevent hangers obstructing any ceiling covering. Joists should be secured into the hanger using 32 mm galvanised clout nails in each hole provided.

Wall plates – ends of joists may be supported by a wall plate bedded on the top of a wall. This is normally used for ground floor construction, flat roofs and internal load bearing partitions. The minimum bearing required and thus the minimum width of wall plate is 75 mm. Often joists from either side meet over a wall plate; it is usual to nail them together side by side, both overlapping the wall plate by about 300 mm.

The use of wall plates provides a means of securing joists by skew nailing with 75 mm or 100 mm wire nails. In addition, wall plates also spread the loading of a joisted surface evenly over a wide area rather

Floor and flat roof joists

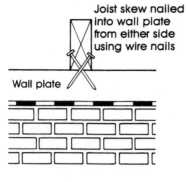

Figure 2.12 *Joist supported on a wall plate*

Figure 2.13 *Fixing joist to wall plate*

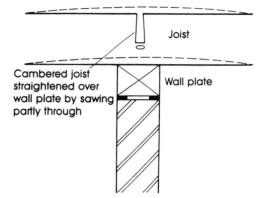

Figure 2.14 *Straightening cambered joist at wall plate*

than a point load. Cambered joists may be straightened over a wall plate by partly sawing through and nailing down. Wall plates are not suitable for use in external walls of upper floor construction. This is due to shrinkage movement and the likelihood of rot.

Wall plates are jointed by the carpenter using halving joints as shown in Figure 2.15. The plates are bedded and levelled in position by the bricklayer using bedding mortar.

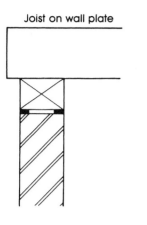

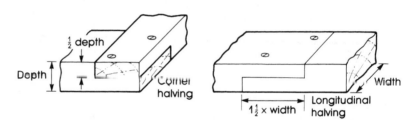

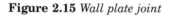

Figure 2.15 *Wall plate joint*

Binders – are introduced into a structure in order to provide an intermediate support for large span joists. These binders may be of: steel (when they are known as a universal beam (UB)), timber (either of solid section, glue laminated section (glulam) or a plywood box beam) or concrete. Depending on the space available binders may be positioned below the joists, or accommodated partly within the joist depth projecting above or below as required. Where joists are fitted to a steel universal beam, a plywood template may be cut to speed the marking out of the joists and ensure a consistent, accurate fit (see Figure 2.17).

Figure 2.16 *Binders*

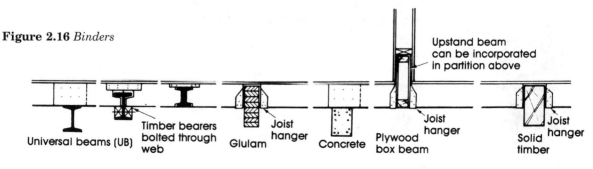

29

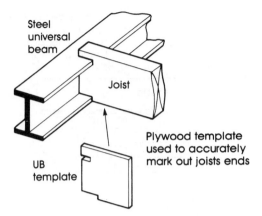

Figure 2.17 *Marking and cutting a joist to fit a universal beam*

Restraint straps – with modern lightweight structures, walls and joisted areas require positive tying together for strength, to ensure wall stability. Galvanised mild steel restraint straps should be used at not more than 2 metre intervals for joists parallel to the wall, at right angles to the wall and those on wall plates.

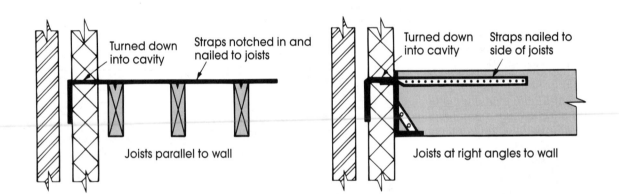

Figure 2.18 *Restraint straps*

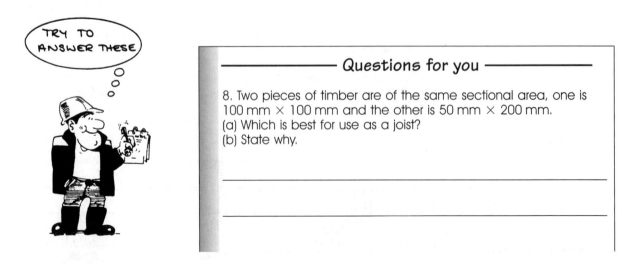

TRY TO ANSWER THESE

———— Questions for you ————

8. Two pieces of timber are of the same sectional area, one is 100 mm × 100 mm and the other is 50 mm × 200 mm.
(a) Which is best for use as a joist?
(b) State why.

9. Use a sketch to define regularised timber.

10. State why joists should not project into wall cavities.

_____

_____

11. State the minimum joist bearing when:
(a) building in
(b) on wall plates.

_____

_____

12. State why regularised joists are preferred.

_____

_____

13. State a reason for recessing joists to receive joist hangers.

_____

_____

14. State the total metres run of timber required for six joists each spanning 3.6 metres and being supported by joist hangers.

_____

_____

15. State the purpose of binders.

_____

_____

16. State the purpose of restraint straps.

_____

_____

17. At what centres should restraint straps be fixed?

_____

18. State the purpose of a template when cutting joists into a steel binder.

_____

_____

19. Produce sketches to illustrate the following:
(a) a joist hanger

(b) a binder

(c) a wall plate lengthening (longitudinal) joint

(d) a restraint strap

WELL, HOW DID YOU DO?

WORK THROUGH THE SECTION AGAIN IF YOU HAD ANY PROBLEMS

Joist restraint

Strutting – where deep joists exceed a span of 2 metres, they tend to buckle and/or sag under load, unless restrained by strutting. Joists spanning between 2 and 3.6 metres should be restrained by strutting at their mid-span; larger span joists should be restrained at about 1.8 metre intervals. There are three main types of strutting in use:

● Galvanised steel strutting
● Solid timber strutting
● Herring-bone timber strutting

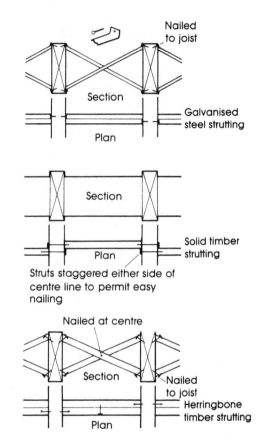

Figure 2.19 *Strutting to joists*

Galvanised steel strutting has a disadvantage in that the depth and centres of the joist must be specified when ordering; different depths and spacings will require different sized struts.

Solid strutting is quick to install but is considered inferior, as it tends to loosen and become ineffective when joists shrink.

Herring-bone timber strutting is considered the most effective as it actually tightens when joists shrink. However, it takes longer to install and thus is more expensive in terms of labour costs.

Herring-bone timber struts can be marked out using the following procedure shown in Figure 2.20.

● Mark across the joists the centre line of the strutting.
● Mark a second line across the joist so that the distance between the lines is 10 mm less than the depth of the joist.

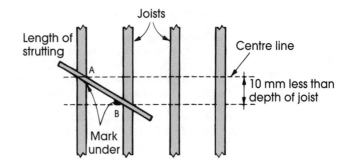

Figure 2.20 *Marking out strutting*

- Place the length of strutting on top of the joists as shown and mark underneath against the joists at A and B.
- Cut two struts to these marks. If all joists are spaced evenly, all the strutting will be the same size and can be cut using the first one as a template. If not, each set of struts will have to be marked individually.
- Fix struts on either side of the centre line using wire nails, one in the top and bottom of each strut and one through the centre.

Whichever method of strutting is used, care should be taken to ensure that they are clear of the tops and bottoms of the joists, otherwise they may subsequently distort the joist covering or ceiling surface.

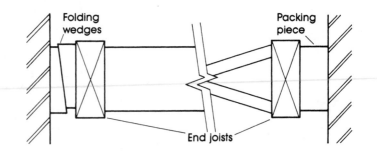

Figure 2.21 *Strutting tightened using a packing piece and folding wedges*

Again, whichever method of strutting is used, the gaps between the end joists and the walls will require packing and wedging to complete the system. Care must be taken not to overtighten the folding wedges as it is possible to dislodge the blockwork.

Trimming – where openings are required in joisted areas or where projections occur in supporting walls, joists must be framed or trimmed around them (see Figure 2.22). Members used for trimming each have their own function and are named accordingly.

Bridging joist – a joist spanning from support to support, also known as a common joist.

Trimmed joist – a bridging joist that has been cut short (trimmed) to form an opening in the floor.

Trimmer joist – a joist placed at right angles to the bridging joist, in order to support the cut ends of the trimmed joists.

Trimming joist – a joist with a span the same as the bridging joist, but supporting the end of a trimmer joist.

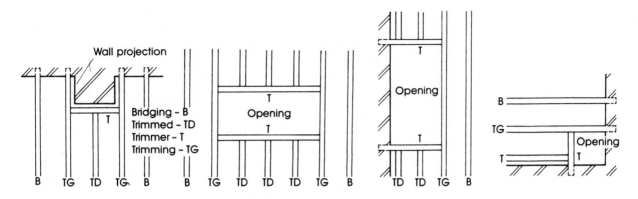

Figure 2.22 *Trimming openings*

As both the trimmer and the trimming joists take a greater load, they are usually 25 mm thicker in breadth than the bridging joists. For example, use 75 mm × 200 mm trimmer and trimming joists with 50 mm × 200 mm bridging joists.

The Building Regulations 2000 Approved Documents restrict the positioning and trimming of timber near sources of heat.

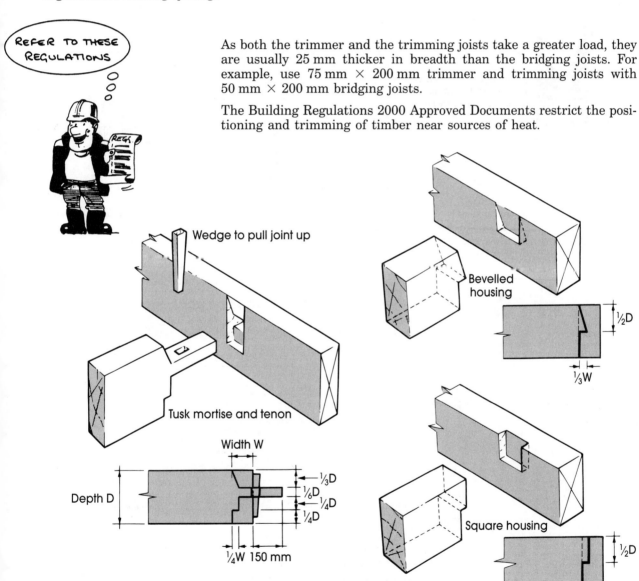

Figure 2.23 *Traditional trimming joists*

Trimming joints – Traditionally, tusk mortise and tenon joints were used between the trimmer and trimming joists, while housing joints were used between the trimmed joists and the trimmer. Once wedged the tusk mortise and tenon joint requires no further fixing. The housing joints will require securing with 100 mm wire nails. The proportions of these joints must be followed. They are based on the fact that there are neutral stress areas in joists (see Figure 2.24). If any cutting is restricted mainly to this area then the reduction in the joist strength will be kept to a minimum. Joist hangers which are a quicker, modern alternative to the traditional joints are now used almost exclusively. As these hangers are made from thin galvanised steel, they do not require recessing in as do the thicker wall hangers but they must be securely nailed in each hole provided with 32 mm galvanised clout nails.

Joints cut in shaded areas will cause the minimum reduction in strength

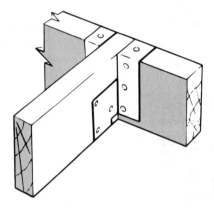

Figure 2.24 *Neutral stress areas*

Figure 2.25 *Trimming using a joist hanger*

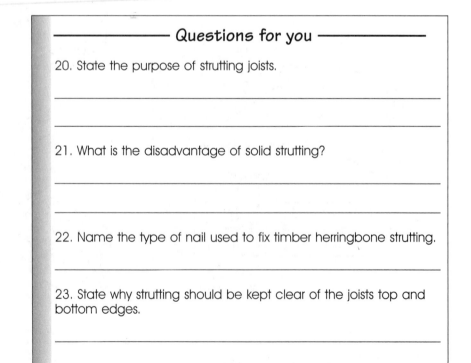

———————— Questions for you ————————

20. State the purpose of strutting joists.

_____

_____

21. What is the disadvantage of solid strutting?

_____

_____

22. Name the type of nail used to fix timber herringbone strutting.

_____

23. State why strutting should be kept clear of the joists top and bottom edges.

_____

_____

24. State the purpose of trimming joists.

_____

_____

25. Name the regulations that apply to the trimming of joists near to sources of heat.

_____

_____

26. What type of nails are used for fixing a thin galvanised steel joist hanger used to connect a trimmed joist to a trimmer?

_____

_____

27. Use a sketch to define the neutral stress areas of a joist.

28. Produce a sketch to illustrate the proportions of a tusk mortise and tenon joint.

WELL, HOW DID YOU DO?

WORK THROUGH THE SECTION AGAIN IF YOU HAD ANY PROBLEMS

2 *Carcassing*

Positioning joists

Layout of joists – the positioning of joists is a fairly simple operation. The first task is to establish their vertical position in the building. (For joists built-in or on wall plates the vertical position will have been fixed by the bricklayer.) Vertical positioning in a building is commonly achieved by either the use of a storey rod, shown in Figure 2.26, which is marked out before work commences and fixed in one corner, or by datum marks/lines which are positioned at a convenient height around the walls of a building and indicated by an arrow and horizontal line as shown in Figure 2.27. A set measurement up from the datum will establish the position of the joists.

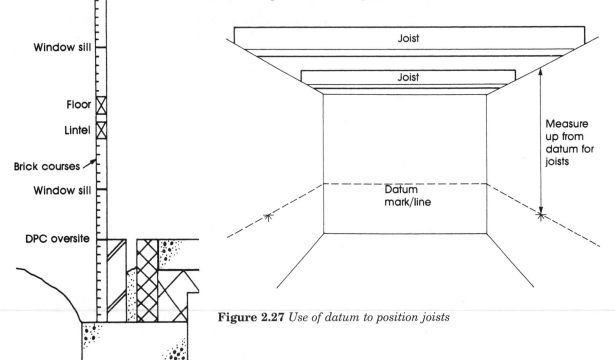

Figure 2.27 *Use of datum to position joists*

Figure 2.26 *Storey rod*

The outside bridging joists are placed in position first, leaving a 50 mm gap between them and the wall. The other joists are then spaced out to the required centres in the remaining area.

However, when openings for fireplaces and stairwells, etc., are required in the joisted area the layout of the joists is governed by these openings. The trimming and outside bridging joists are the first to be positioned, once again leaving a 50 mm gap between all joists and the walls. The other joists are then spaced out to the required centres in the remaining areas as shown in Figure 2.28.

Double joists are required where blockwork partition walls are to be built on a joisted area. These double joists are either nailed or bolted together (depending on specification), and positioned under the intended wall to take the additional load. When laying out a joisted area, double joists are positioned along with the trimming and end bridging joists, before the other joists are spaced.

In order to span the shortest direction it is sometimes necessary to change the direction of joists in a particular joisted area. This is done over a load-bearing wall where the bridging joists from one area are allowed to overhang by 50 mm, the end bridging joist in the other area is simply nailed to the overhanging ends (see Figure 2.30).

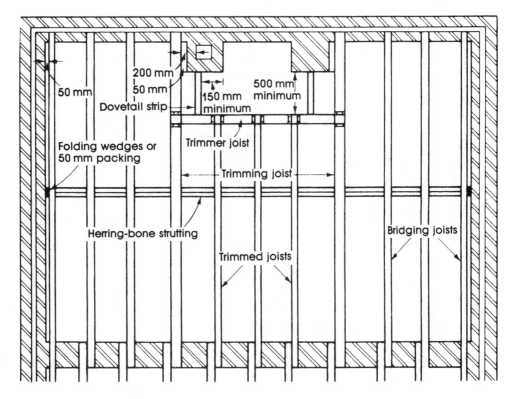

Figure 2.28 *Layout of floor around fireplace*

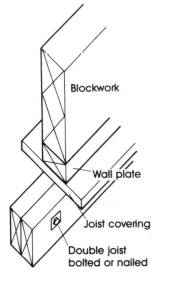

Figure 2.29 *Double joists required to support blockwork partition above*

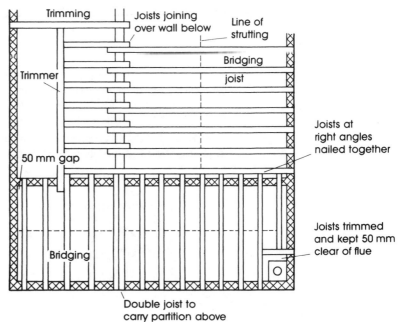

Figure 2.30 *Typical joist layout*

Levelling joists – After positioning, the joists should be checked for line and level. End joists are set using a spirit level; intermediate joists are lined through with a straight edge and spirit level (see Figure 2.31).

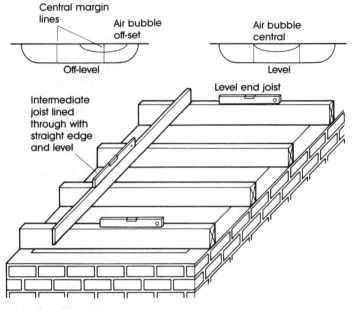

Figure 2.31 *Levelling joists*

Where the brickwork or blockwork course has been finished to a level line by the bricklayer or where wall plates are used and have been accurately bedded level, and where regularised joists have been used, the bearings of the joist should not require any adjustment to bring them into line and level. However, minor adjustments may be required as shown in Figure 2.32. Joists may be housed into or packed off wall plates. Where packings are required for built-in joists, these should be slate or other durable material. Do not use timber packings as these may shrink and work loose and in any case are susceptible to rot. Joists may be recessed, to lower their bearing, providing the reduced joist depth is still sufficient for its span.

Figure 2.34 shows temporary battens which can be nailed across the top of the joists to ensure that their spacing remains constant before and during their 'building in'. Joists fixed to wall plates can be skew nailed to them using 75 mm or 100 mm wire nails.

Notching joists – the position of notches for pipes and holes for cables in joists, should have been determined at the building design stage and

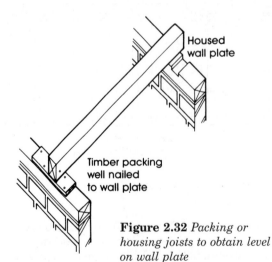

Figure 2.32 *Packing or housing joists to obtain level on wall plate*

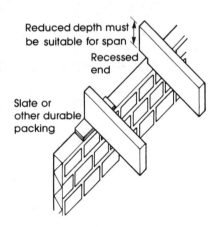

Figure 2.33 *Packing or recessing joists to obtain level when built-in*

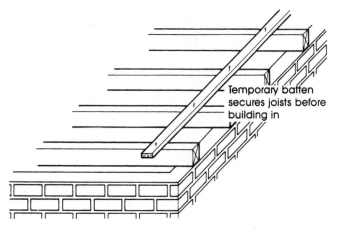

Figure 2.34 *Use of temporary batten to secure joists before building in*

indicated on the drawings, as both reduce the joist strength. Notches and holes in joists should be kept to a minimum and conform to the following (see Figures 2.35 and 2.36):

Notches on the joist's top edge of up to 0.125 of the joist's depth located between 0.07 and 0.25 of the span from either support are permissible.

Holes of up to 0.25 of the joist's depth drilled on the neutral stress line (centre line) and located between 0.25 and 0.4 of the span from either support are permissible. Adjacent holes should be separated by at least three times their diameter measured centre to centre.

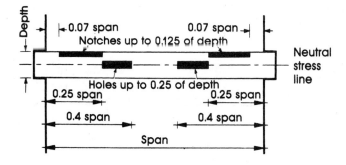

Figure 2.35 *Positions for notches and holes*

Figure 2.36 *Positioning of notches and holes to accommodate services*

Example

The position and sizes for notches and holes in a 200 mm depth joist spanning 4000 mm are:

Notches – between 280 mm and 1000 mm in from each end of the joist and up to 25 mm deep.

Holes – between 1000 mm and 1600 mm in from each end of the joist and up to 50 mm diameter.

Excessive notching and drilling of holes outside the permissible limits will seriously weaken the joist and may lead to structural failure.

Learning task

The plan of the building at upper floor joist bearing level is shown.

Internal walls are to receive a wall plate.

Joists are to be built into the external walls.

The flue is 500 mm square.

Double joists are required where partitions are to be built on the floor.

READ THE INSTRUCTIONS AND COMPLETE THE TASK

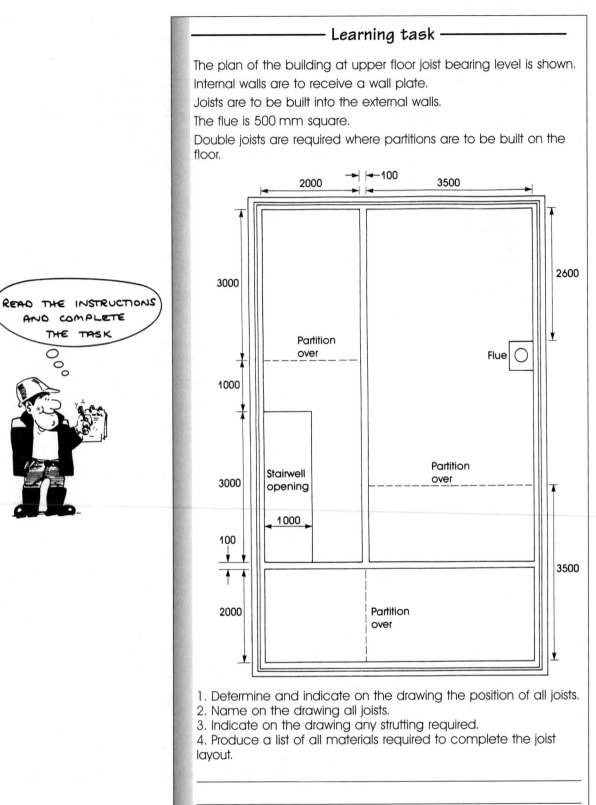

1. Determine and indicate on the drawing the position of all joists.
2. Name on the drawing all joists.
3. Indicate on the drawing any strutting required.
4. Produce a list of all materials required to complete the joist layout.

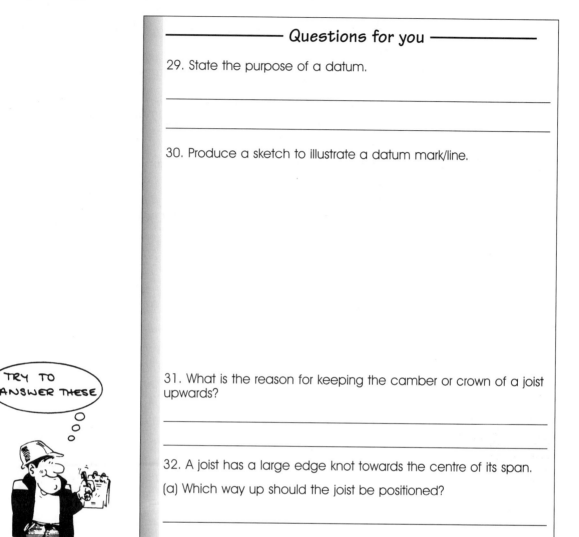

──────── **Questions for you** ────────

29. State the purpose of a datum.

_____

_____

30. Produce a sketch to illustrate a datum mark/line.

31. What is the reason for keeping the camber or crown of a joist upwards?

_____

_____

32. A joist has a large edge knot towards the centre of its span.

(a) Which way up should the joist be positioned?

_____

_____

(b) State the reason for your answer to (a).

_____

_____

33. State the reason why joists adjacent to walls are kept 50 mm away.

_____

_____

34. State the purpose of a trimmer joist used when forming openings.

_____

_____

TRY TO ANSWER THESE

35. State the purpose of notching and boring holes in joists.

_____

_____

36. Why are temporary battens sometimes fixed across the tops of joists?

_____

37. State the maximum diameter hole that can be bored in a 200 mm deep joist.

_____

38. Produce a sketch to show how a notch in the top of a joist could be formed to receive a 25 mm diameter pipe.

39. State the likely effect of excessive or wrongly placed notching to joists.

_____

_____

40. State why timber should not be used when packing joists to line in an external wall.

_____

_____

WELL, HOW DID YOU DO?

WORK THROUGH THE SECTION AGAIN IF YOU HAD ANY PROBLEMS

WORD-SQUARE SEARCH

Hidden in the word square are the following 20 words associated with *'Joists'*. You may find the words written forwards, backwards, up, down or diagonally.

Floor	Binder
Roof	Restraint
Wallplate	Herringbone
Span	Notching
Pitch	Packing
Hanger	Crown
Strutting	Datum
Preservative	Trimmer
Regularised	Trimmed
Building in	Trimming

Draw a ring around the words, or line in using a highlight pen thus:

EXAMPLE

EXAMPLE

COMPLETE THE WORD SQUARE

```
P L A N F O R S T R I M M E D O C S
R U S O L I P H E A D S R R E W O T
E R T T A A M F D N D H O M G P H R
S I C C N D D E R L C P F N M E E U
E A R H O Y A N E T E O I D U H R T
R U O I N G O I G G O M S E T E R T
V A W N E F L O O R M D N S R L I I
A N N G P T S S L I L S A I I M N N
T I T O S N S E R I P O R R M E G G
I G C O C I P T T R E S T A M T B N
V N O R I A O A I M L H O L E S O I
E I N E R R G L O U O A E U R T N W
R D S P E T D P N T S N B G N P E A
O L T V D S S L S A E G O E C C E P
L I R C N E P L E D S E A R I O I D
K U A T I R L A T T E R R O D T N V
F B C T B S B W L A D E D E C S I E
P A C K I N G O C A T S R H G D E L
```

Joist coverings

Joist coverings are often termed decking; the main materials in common use for this are (Figure 2.37):

- Timber floor boards mainly PTG (planed, tongued and grooved) but square-edged boarding may be used for roofing.
- Flooring grade particle board, mainly tongued and grooved or square-edged chipboard, but OSB orientated strand board is also used.
- Flooring grade plywood either tongued and grooved or square-edged.

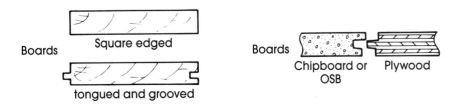

Boards — Square edged

Boards — Chipboard or OSB — Plywood

tongued and grooved

Figure 2.37 *Joist coverings*

Floorboarding is normally carried out after timber carcassing and preferably also after the window glazing and roof tiling is complete so that it is not exposed to the weather. Boarding or decking to flat roofs should be carried out just before they are to be waterproofed. Chipboard roof sheets are available pre-covered with a layer of felt to provide some measure of initial protection.

Softwood flooring

Softwood flooring usually consists of ex 25 mm × 150 mm tongued and grooved boarding.

A standard floorboard section has the tongue and groove offset away from the board's face. This identifies the upper face and also provides an increased wearing surface before exposing the tongue and groove. Boards can be fixed either by floor brads nailed through the surface of the boards and punched in, or by lost-head nails secret-fixed through the tongue as shown in Figure 2.38. Nails should be approximately 2½ times the thickness of the floorboard in length. Figure 2.39 shows square-butted or splayed heading joints, which are introduced as required to utilise offcuts of board and avoid wastage. Splayed heading joints are preferred as there is less risk of the board end splitting. Heading joints should be staggered evenly throughout the floor for strength; these should never be placed next to each other, as the joists and covering would not be tied together properly.

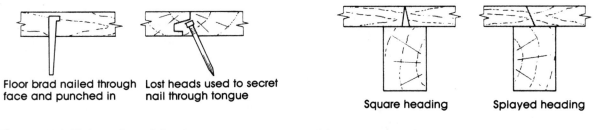

Figure 2.38 *Fixing softwood flooring*

Figure 2.39 *Heading joints for softwood flooring*

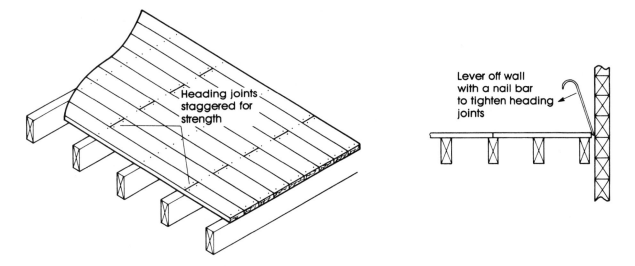

Figure 2.40 *Positioning of heading joints*

Surface fixing

Boards are laid at right angles to the joists. The first board should be fixed at least 10 mm away from the outside wall. This gap which is later covered by the skirting, helps to prevent dampness being absorbed through direct wall contact. In addition, the gap also allows the covering material to expand without either causing pressure on the wall or a bulging of the floor surface. The remainder of the boards are laid four to six at a time, cramped up with floorboard cramps (see Figure 2.41) and surface nailed to the joists. The final nailing of a floor is often termed 'bumping' This should be followed by punching the nail head just below the surface. Boards up to 100 mm in width require one nail to each joist while boards over this require two nails.

Figure 2.42 shows two alternatives to the use of floorboard cramps are folding or wedging, although neither of these is as quick or efficient. Folding a floor entails fixing two boards spaced apart 10 mm less than the width of five boards. The five boards can then be placed with their tongues and grooves engaged. A short board is laid across the centre and 'jumped on' to press the boards in position. This process is then repeated across the rest of the floor. Alternatively, the boards may be cramped, four to six at a time using dogs and wedges.

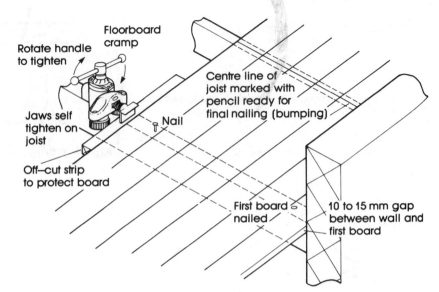

Figure 2.41 *Use of floorboard cramp*

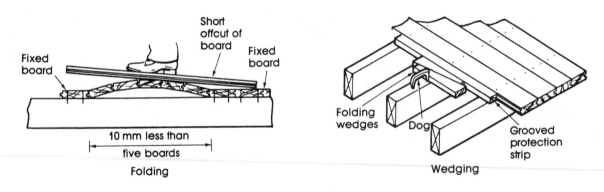

Folding

Wedging

Figure 2.42 *Tightening floorboards*

Secret fixing

Secret-fixed boards (Figure 2.38) must be laid and tightened individually and cramping is therefore not practical. Figure 2.43 shows how they may be tightened by levering them forward with a firmer chisel driven into the top of the joist, or with the aid of a floorboard nailer. This tightens the boards and drives the nail when the plunger is struck with a hard mallet.

Figure 2.43 *Tightening secret-fixed floorboards*

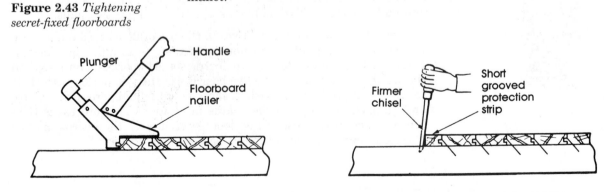

Secret fixing is normally only used on high class work or hardwood flooring, as the increased laying time makes it considerably more expensive.

Services

Where services such as water and gas pipes or electric cables are run within the floor, there is a danger of driving nails into them. They should be marked on saying in chalk or pencil 'PIPES NO FIXING', so that on nailing the danger area is kept clear. The floorboards over services can be fixed with recessed cups and screws to permit easy removal for subsequent access, and also to provide easy recognition of location.

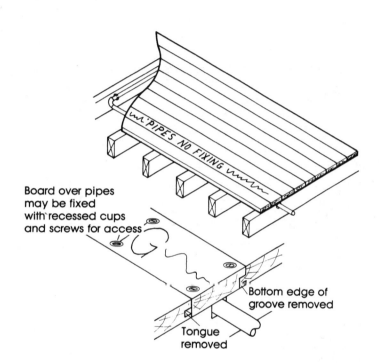

Figure 2.44 *Marking position of services*

Access traps, Figure 2.45, may be required in a floor over areas where water stop cocks or electrical junction boxes are located. Again these can be fixed with recessed cups and screws to permit easy removal.

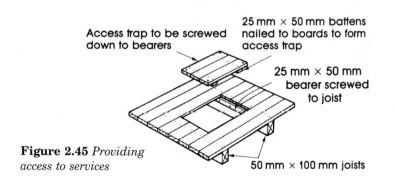

Figure 2.45 *Providing access to services*

49

Chipboard flooring

This is now being increasingly used for domestic flooring. Flooring grade chipboard is available with square edges in 1220 mm × 2440 mm sheets, and with tongued and grooved edges in 600 mm × 2440 mm sheets. Square-edged sheets are normally laid with their long edges over a joist. Noggins must be fixed between the joists to support the short ends. Tongued and grooved sheets are usually laid with their long edges at right angles to the joists and their short edges joining over the joist. Both types require noggins between the joists where the sheet abuts a wall. See Figure 2.46. Joists should be spaced to accommodate the dimensions of the sheet flooring.

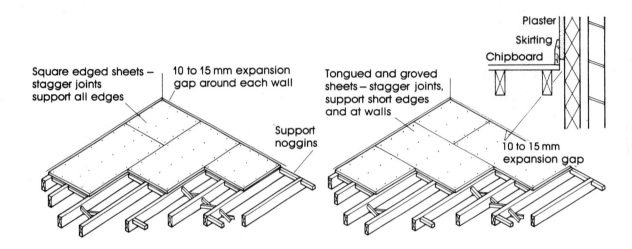

Figure 2.46 *Layout of chipboard floors*

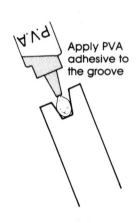

Figure 2.47 *Gluing joints in chipboard flooring*

Fixing

Sheets are laid staggered and fixed at 200 mm to 300 mm centres with 50 mm lost-head nails or, for additional strength, annular ring shanked or serrated nails. A gap of 10 mm must be left along each wall to allow for expansion and prevent absorption of dampness from the wall. Manufacturers of chipboard often recommend the gluing of the tongues and grooves with a PVA adhesive to prevent joint movement and stiffen the floor. See Figure 2.47.

For protection it is recommended that the floor be covered with building paper after laying and that this is left in position until the building is occupied.

Plywood flooring is laid using the same procedures as chipboard flooring.

Flat roof decking

The choice of materials and method of laying decking can be likened to floors with the exception that where timber boards are used they should be laid either with, or at a diagonal to, the fall of the roof's surface. Cupping or distortion of the boards can lead to pools of water being trapped in hollows formed on the roof's surface, where boards are laid at right angles to the fall. See Figure 2.48.

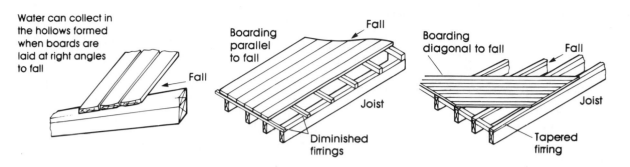

Figure 2.48 *Timber boards for flat roof decking*

Determining materials

Simple calculations are used in order to determine the amount of joist covering materials required for an area.

To determine the area of a simple rectangular room multiply its width by its length.

Example

Calculate the floor area of a room 3.6 m wide by 4.85 m long.

Area of floor = 3.6 × 4.85
            = 17.46 m²

To determine more complex floor areas, divide them into a number of rectangles or other recognisable shapes and work out the area of each in turn.

Example

Calculate the floor area of the room shown in Figure 2.49. This can be divided into two rectangles, A and B, each being solved separately then added together. (As an area in square metres, m², is required change all dimensions to metres before starting.)

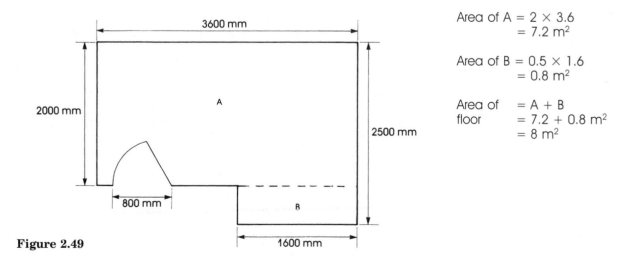

Area of A = 2 × 3.6
         = 7.2 m²

Area of B = 0.5 × 1.6
         = 0.8 m²

Area of   = A + B
floor   = 7.2 + 0.8 m²
             = 8 m²

Figure 2.49

Example

The area of the room shown in Figure 2.50 is equal to area A plus area B minus area C.

Area A $= (9 + 10.5) \div 2 \times 6.75$
(Trapezium) $= 65.813 \text{ m}^2$

Area B $= 0.75 \times 5.5$
              $= 4.125 \text{ m}^2$

Area C $= 0.9 \times 3$
              $= 2.7 \text{ m}^2$

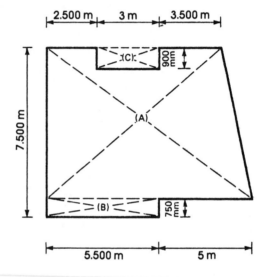

Figure 2.50

Total area of floor $= A \times B - C$
                    $= 65.813 + 4.125 - 2.7$
                    $= 67.238 \text{ m}^2$

In order to determine the metres run of floorboards required to cover a room, the floor area is divided by the board's covering width.

Example

Calculate the metres run of floorboards required to cover a floor area of 4.65 m², if the floorboards have a covering width of 137 mm. (Change 137 mm to metres before starting by moving its imaginary point (behind the 7) three places forward to become 0.137 m. This is because all the units in a calculation must be the same.)

Metres run required $=$ Area $\div$ Width of board
                    $= 4.65 \div 0.137$
                    $= 33.94 \text{ m}$
                    say 34 m run.

It is standard practice to order an additional amount of flooring to allow for cutting and wastage. This is often between 10% and 15%.

To calculate the metres run of floor boarding required plus an additional percentage, turn the percentage into a decimal,

e.g. 5% = 0.05; 10% = 0.1; 25% = 0.25

Place a one in front of the point (to include original amount) and use this number to multiply the original amount e.g. for 5% increase use 1.05 to multiply, for 10% increase use 1.1, for 25% increase use 1.25.

Example

If 34 m run of floorboarding is required to cover an area, calculate the amount to be ordered including an additional 12% for cutting and wastage. (For 12% increase multiply by 1.12.)

$$\text{Amount to be ordered} = 34 \times 1.12$$
$$= 38.08$$
say 38 m run.

In order to determine the number of sheets of plywood or chipboard required to cover a room either:

Divide area of room by area of sheet, or

Divide width of room by width of sheet, divide length of room by length of sheet. Convert these numbers to the nearest whole or half and multiply them together.

Example

Calculate the number of 600 mm $\times$ 2400 mm chipboard sheets required to cover a floor area of 2.05 m $\times$ 3.6 m.

Area of room	$= 2.05 \times 3.6$
	$= 7.38 \text{ m}^2$
Area of sheet	$= 0.6 \times 2.4$
	$= 1.44 \text{ m}^2$

$$\text{Number of sheets required} = \frac{\text{Area of room}}{\text{Area of sheet}}$$
$$= 7.38 \div 1.44$$
$$= 5.125$$
say 6 sheets

or alternatively,

Number of sheet widths in room width	$= 2.05 \div 0.6$
	$= 3.417$
	say 3.5
Number of sheet lengths in room length	$= 3.6 \div 2.4$
	$= 1.5$
Total number of sheets	$= 3.5 \times 1.5$
	$= 5.25$
	say 6 sheets.

READ THE INSTRUCTIONS AND COMPLETE THE TASK

─── Learning task ───

The bungalow shown below is to have a timber suspended hollow ground floor to all rooms except the garage. The overall internal measurements are 10 950 mm × 6650 mm, the garage is 2750 mm × 4550 mm.

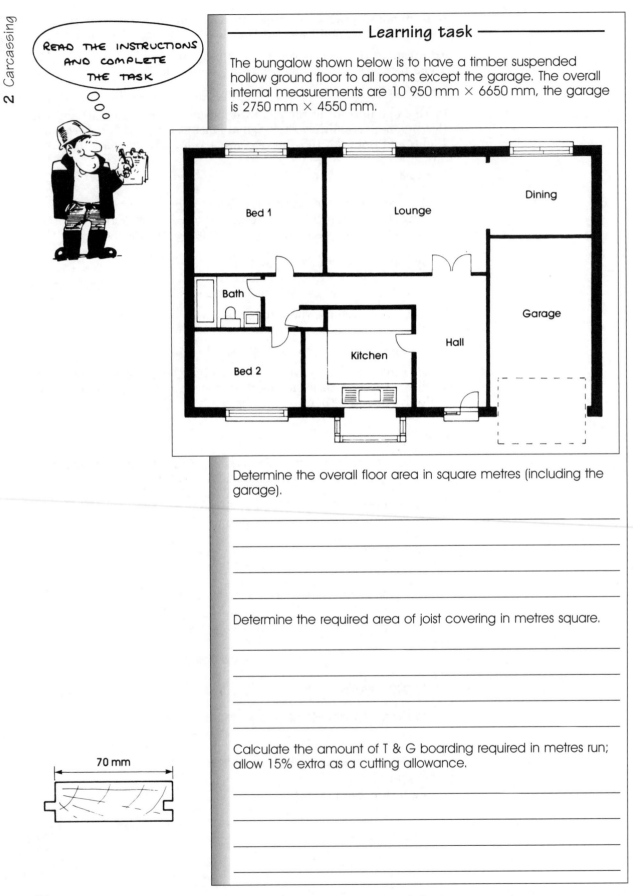

Bed 1

Lounge

Dining

Bath

Garage

Bed 2

Kitchen

Hall

Determine the overall floor area in square metres (including the garage).

_____

_____

_____

_____

Determine the required area of joist covering in metres square.

_____

_____

_____

_____

Calculate the amount of T & G boarding required in metres run; allow 15% extra as a cutting allowance.

_____

_____

_____

_____

_____

70 mm

TRY TO ANSWER THESE

━━━━━━━━ Questions for you ━━━━━━━━

41. Produce a sketch to show the section of a tongued and grooved floorboard.

42. State the purpose of heading joints in timber boarded floor surfaces and explain why they should be staggered.

_____

_____

43. State a reason why an access trap may be required in joist covering.

_____

_____

44. State the reason why a gap is left between joist coverings and adjacent walls.

_____

_____

45. Name a nail and state its length which is suitable for the surface fixing of a 20 mm finished thickness floorboard.

_____

_____

46. Explain **ONE** method that can be used to cramp up tongued and grooved floorboards in the absence of flooring cramps.

_____

_____

47. Explain the purpose of noggins when using sheet joist coverings.

_____

_____

48. Explain the purpose of gluing the tongues and grooves of sheet joist coverings.

_____

_____

49. Name one nail suitable for fixing sheet joist coverings.

_____

50. Produce a sketch to show what is meant by secret fixing when applied to tongued and grooved floorboards.

WORD-SQUARE SEARCH

Hidden in the word square are the following 20 words associated with 'Fixing joist coverings'. You may find the words written forwards, backwards, up, down or diagonally.

Fixing	Secret
Joist	Softwood
Coverings	Tongue and groove
Floor	Square edge
Ground	Chipboard
Upper	Strand board
Roof	Plywood
Timber	Noggins
Boarding	Cramp
Services	Bumping

Draw a ring around the words, or line in using a highlight pen thus:

EXAMPLE

EXAMPLE

```
E F G H C H I P B O A R D I R K C C
V E X J E B C A D K I G H F E E D O
O H G I O D O O W Y L P A E B K F V
O B F D G I E B A C S I C K M E D E
R A C E E D S G O G E O S T I R C R
G G N D E E F T R E C G F K T O P I
D R X O F J R G H E I C I T F Y X N
N E G B G K E A B C V R X A W O N G
A E G O H G C U E R U I P O O N S
E D R T I C I E D Q E M N S O D O E
U K O T G A F N S F S B G E S E E D
G A U O N E R F S G O P G G O E G A
N E N M I B O O N K E D N I G S F E
O B D E D O O H I K M O I N L E A N
T H K D R U L E C R A M P F H C E H
C D A U A T F G D K O N M G K R K F
E F F D O R O O R E P P U I J E E K
D R A O B D N A R T S E B M O T O D
```

Timber pitched roofs

Roof terminology

Roof – the uppermost part of a building that spans the external walls and provides protection from the elements. Roofs may be classified as either pitched or flat and further variously named according to their shape.

Pitched roof – any roof having a sloping surface in excess of 10 degrees pitch. Those with a single sloping surface are known as mono pitch and those with two opposing sloping surfaces are known as double pitched.

Gable roof – a double pitched roof with one or more gable ends.

Gable – the triangular portion of the end wall of the building with a pitched roof.

Hipped roof – a double pitched roof where the roof slope is returned around the shorter sides of the building to form a sloping triangular end.

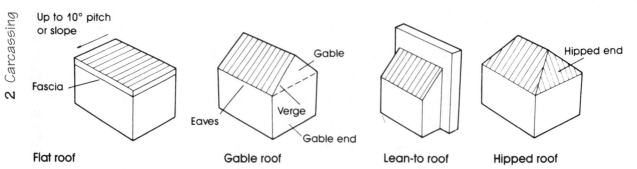

Figure 2.51 *Types of roof*

Flat roof – any roof having a pitch or slope of up to 10 degrees to the horizontal.

Pitch – the angle of a roofs inclination to the horizontal, or the ratio of rise to span, e.g. a one third pitch roof with a span of 6 metres will rise 2 metres.

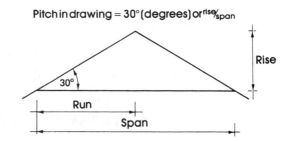

Figure 2.52 *Roof pitch*

Verge – the termination or edge of a pitched roof at the gable end or a flat roof at the sloping edge. Both often overhang the wall and are finished with a barge board and soffit.

Eaves – the lowest part of a pitched roof slope where the ends of the rafters terminate, or the level edge of a flat roof. Both usually overhang the wall and are finished with a fascia board and soffit.

Valley – the intersection of two pitched roof surfaces at an internal corner.

Figure 2.53
Roof terminology

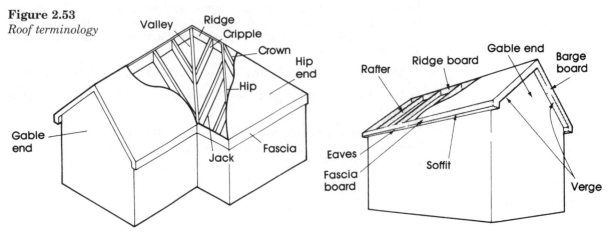

Construction terminology

Timber pitched roofs may be divided into two broad but distinct categories.

Traditional framed cut roofs – entirely constructed in situ from loose, sawn timber sections and utilising simple jointing methods.

Prefabricated trussed rafters – normally manufactured in factory conditions from prepared timber butt-jointed and secured using nail plates.

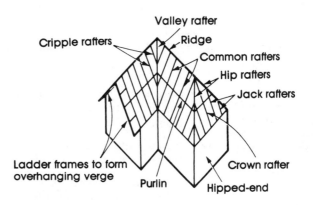

Figure 2.54 *Terminology for traditional framed cut roof*

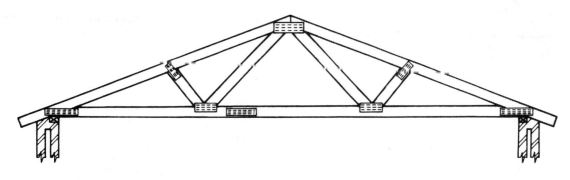

Figure 2.55 *Trussed rafter*

Cut roofs

Cut roofs may be constructed as either single or double roofs, according to their span.

Single roofs – The rafters of single roofs do not require any intermediate support (see Figure 2.56). They are not economically viable when the span of a roof exceeds about 5.5 m. This is because very large sectioned timber would have to be used. A central binder may be hung from the ridge to bind together and prevent any sagging when ceiling joists are used in a close coupled single roof.

Double roofs – The rafters of double roofs are of such a length that they require an intermediate support (see Figure 2.57). This is normally given by purlins to support the rafters in mid span.

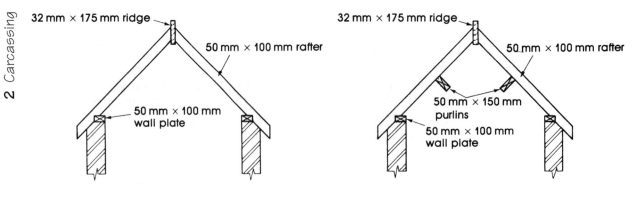

Figure 2.56 *Section through a single roof*

Figure 2.57 *Section through a double roof*

Common rafters – the main loadbearing timbers in a roof, which are cut to fit the ridge and birdsmouthed over the wall plate (see Figure 2.58).

Ridge – the backbone of the roof which provides a fixing point for the tops of the rafters, keeping them in line.

Jack rafters – span from the wall plate to the hip rafter, like common rafters that have had their tops shortened.

Hip rafter – used where two sloping roof surfaces meet at an angle. It provides a fixing point for the jack rafters and transfers their loads to the wall.

Cripple rafters – span from the ridge to the valley, like common rafters that have had their feet shortened (the reverse of jack rafters).

Valley rafter – like the hip rafter but forming an internal angle (see Figure 2.63).

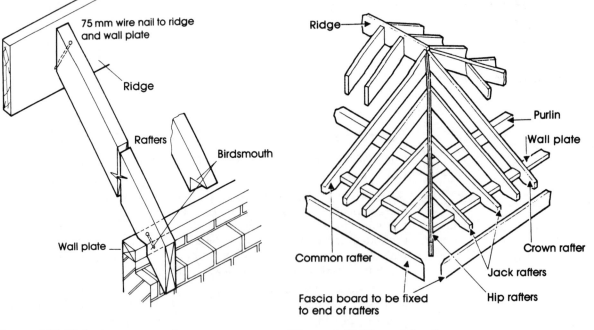

Figure 2.58 *Fixing a common rafter*

Figure 2.59 *Hip-end detail*

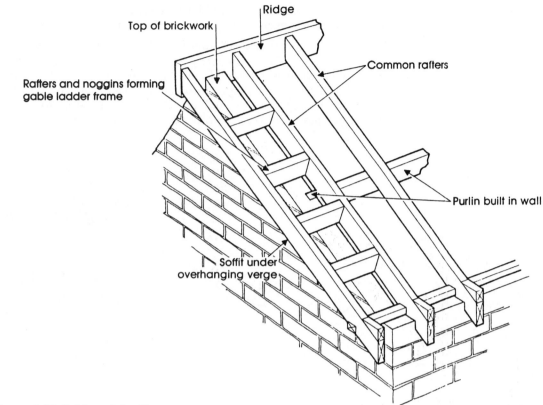

Figure 2.60 *Gable-end detail*

Purlin – a beam that provides support for the rafters in their mid-span.

Ladder frame – This is also known as a gable ladder and is fixed to the last common rafter to form the overhanging verge on a gable roof. It consists of two rafters with noggins nailed between them.

Wall plate – This transfers the loads imposed on the roof, uniformly over the supporting brickwork. It also provides a bearing and fixing point for the feet of the rafters.

Ceiling joists – As well as being joists on which the ceiling is fixed, they also act as ties for each pair of rafters at wall plate level.

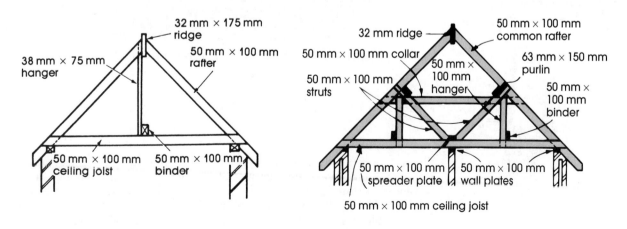

Figure 2.61 *Close-couple roof*

Figure 2.62 *Double roof for spans up to 7.2 m*

Binders and hangers – These stiffen and support the ceiling joists in their mid-span, to prevent them from sagging and distorting the ceiling.

Valley – Where two pitched roofs intersect a valley is formed between the two sloping surfaces. This valley may be constructed in one of two ways. Either a valley rafter is used and the feet of the common rafters (cripple rafters) of both roofs are trimmed into it, as shown in Figure 2.63, or the rafters of one roof are run through and lay boards are used to take the feet of the cripple rafters of the other roof as shown in Figure 2.64.

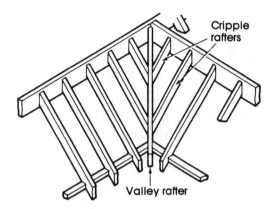

Figure 2.63 *Valley using valley rafter*

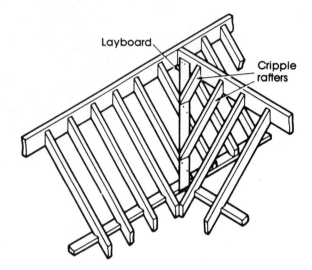

Figure 2.64 *Valley using lay board*

Trimming – Where openings occur in roofs, in either the rafters or ceiling joists or both, these have to be trimmed (see Figures 2.65, 2.66). Framing anchors or housing joints are used to join the trimmers, trimmings and trimmed components together.

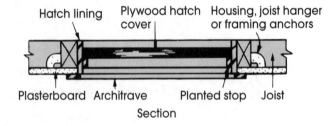

Figure 2.65 *Trimming to loft hatch*

When trimming around a chimney stack in order to comply with Building Regulations, no combustible material, including timber is to be placed within 200 mm of the inside of the flue lining; or, where the thickness of the chimney surrounding the flue is less than 200 mm, no combustible material must be placed within 40 mm of the chimney.

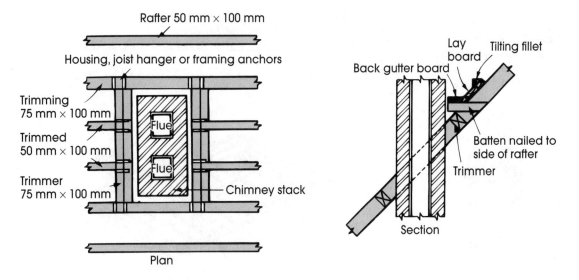

Figure 2.66 *Trimming to chimney stack*

Anchoring roofs – rafters can be skew nailed to the wall plates or, in areas noted for high winds, framing anchors or truss clips where appropriate can be used.

Wall plates must be secured to the wall with straps at 2 m centres.

The rafters and ceiling joists adjacent to the gable end should also be tied into the wall with metal restraint straps at 2 m centres.

Thermal insulation in pitched roofs – can be achieved by placing insulation between the ceiling joists and incorporating a vapour check, such as foil-backed plasterboard, at ceiling level.

Care must be taken not to block the eaves with the insulating material, as the roof space must be ventilated.

Roof erection

The procedure for roof erection is similar for most untrussed types of roof. The procedure of erection for a hipped-end roof would be as follows:

1) The wall plate, having been bedded and levelled by the bricklayer, must be tied down.
2) Mark out the position of the rafters on the wall plate.
3) Make up two temporary A-frames. These each consist of two common rafters with a temporary tie joining them at the top, leaving a space for the ridge and a temporary tie nailed to them in the position of the ceiling joists.
4) Fix ceiling joists in position.
5) Stand up the A-frames at either end of the roof in the position of the last common rafter (half span of roof from corner of wall plate to centre line of rafter).
6) Fix temporary braces to hold the A-frames upright.
7) Mark out the spacing of the rafters on the ridge and fix in position (see Figure 2.67).

8) Fix the crown and hip rafters.
9) Fix the purlins, struts and binders.
10) Fix the remaining common rafters and jack rafters.
11) Fix the collars and hangers.
12) Finish the roof at the eaves with fascia and soffit as required.

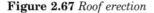

Figure 2.67 *Roof erection*

Roofing lengths and bevels

Geometry or the use of a roofing square are the two methods mainly used to determine the lengths and bevels required for a traditional cut roof.

Roofing geometry

In this section the geometry required for hipped-end roofs, double roofs and roofs with valleys is covered.

Figure 2.68 is a scale drawing of a part plan and section of a hipped-end roof with purlins. The drawing shows all the developments, angles and true lengths required to set out and construct the roof.

Note: Common abbreviations, which may be used, have been included in brackets.

The geometry for each of these developments, angles and true lengths are considered separately in the following figures.

Angles and true lengths for the common and hip rafters – shown in Figure 2.69. The method used is as follows:

Draw to a suitable scale, the plan and section of the roof.

Note: On regular plan roofs, the hip rafters will be 45 degrees. On irregular plan roofs the angle will have to be bisected.

Indicate on the section the following:
(a) the true length of the common rafter (TLCR)
(b) the plumb cut for the common rafter (PCCR)
(c) the seat cut for the common rafter (SCCR)
At right angles to one of the hips on the plan, draw line A^1B^1 and mark on it the rise of the roof AB taken from the section.

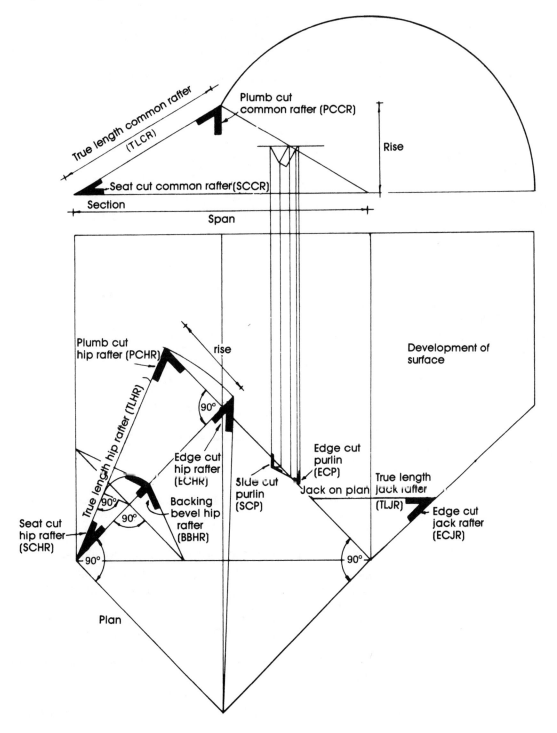

Figure 2.68 *Roofing angles and true lengths*

Join B[1] to C and indicate the following:
(a) the true length for the hip rafter (TLHR)
(b) the plumb cut for the hip rafter (PCHR)
(c) the seat cut for the hip rafter (SCHR)

Diahedral angle or backing bevel for the hip rafter – shown in Figure 2.70. The diahedral angle is the angle of intersection between the two sloping roof surfaces. It provides a level surface for the tile battens or boards on closeboarded roofs to lie flat over the jacks and hips. However, it is rarely used in roofing work today for economic reasons, the edge usually being left square.

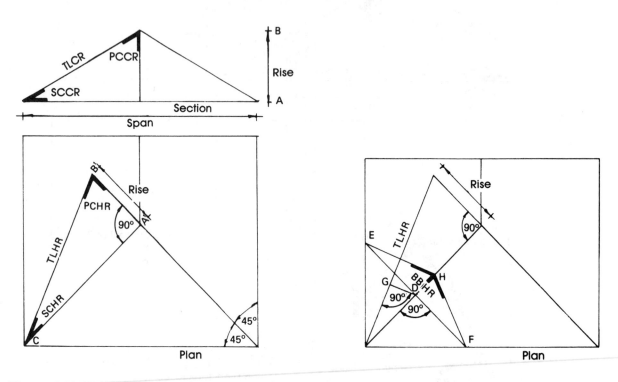

Figure 2.69 *Common and hip rafters, angles and true lengths*   **Figure 2.70** *Hip rafter backing bevel*

The method used to find the backing bevel is as follows:

- Draw a plan of the roof and mark on TLHR as before.
- Draw a line at right angles to the hip on the plan at D to touch wall plates at E and F.
- Draw a line at right angles to TLHR at G to touch point D.
- With centre D and radius DG, draw an arc to touch the hip on the plan at H.
- Join point E to H and H to F. This gives the required backing bevel (BBHR).

Edge cut to hip rafter – shown in Figure 2.71. This is applied to both sides to allow the hip to fit up to the ridge board between the crown and common rafters.

The method used to find the edge cut is as follows:

- Draw a plan of the roof and mark on TLHR as before.
- With centre I and radius IB, swing TLHR down to J. (This makes IJ, TLHR.)
- Draw lines at right angles from the ends of the hips and extend the ridge line. All three lines will intersect at K.
- Join K to J. Angle IJK is the required edge cut (ECHR).

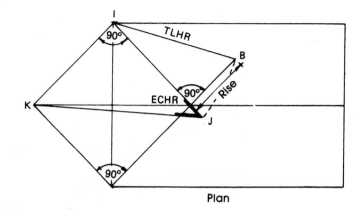

Plan

Figure 2.71 *Hip rafter edge cut*

Jack rafter true lengths and edge cut – shown in Figure 2.72. The edge cut allows the jack rafters to sit up against the hip. The plumb and seat cuts for the jacks are those used for the common rafters.

The method used to find the true lengths and edge cut is as follows:

- Draw the plan and section of roof. Mark on the plan the jack rafters.
- Develop roof surfaces by swinging TLCR down to L and project down to M^1.
- With centre N and radius NM^1, draw arc M^1O. Join points M^1 and O to ends of hips as shown.
- Continue jack rafters on to development.
- Mark the true length of jack rafter (TLJR) and edge cut for jack rafter (ECJR).

Purlin side and edge cut – shown in Figure 2.73. These allow the purlin to sit up against the hip.

The method used is as follows:

- Draw a section of the common rafter with purlin and plan of hip.
- With centre B and radii BA and BC draw arcs onto a horizontal line to give points D and E.
- Project D and E down on to plan.
- Draw horizontal lines from A^1 and C^1 to give points D^1 and E^1.
- Angle DD^1B^1 is the side cut purlin (SCP) and angle B^1E^1E is the edge cut purlin (ECP).

Purlin lip cut – this is required where deep purlins run under the bottom edge of the hip. In practice, this is rarely developed and simply cut in situ on the job.

Valley lengths and bevels – Where two sloping roof surfaces meet at an internal angle, a valley is formed. The true lengths and bevels shown in Figures 2.75 to 2.77 can be determined using the same procedure as those used for the hip and jack rafters.

Pitch line – A single line is used in roof geometry to represent the pitch line. This is a line marked up from the underside of the common rafter, one third of its depth.

As the hip and valley rafters are usually of deeper section, the pitch line on these is marked down from the top edge at a distance equal to two thirds the depth of the common rafter.

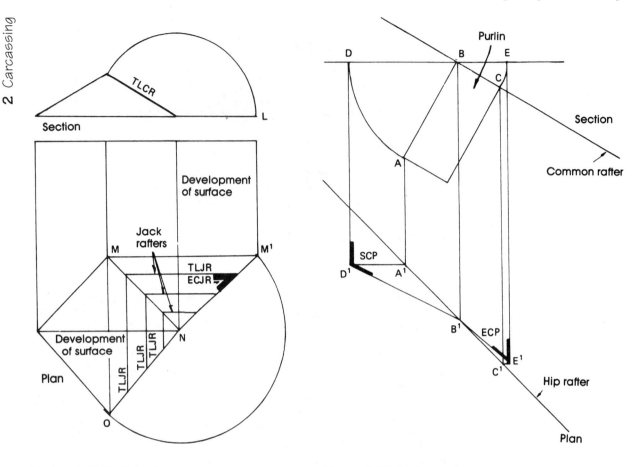

Figure 2.72 *Roof development*

Figure 2.73 *Purlin angles*

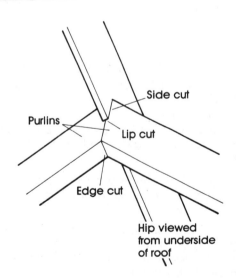

Figure 2.74 *Purlin lip cut*

Allowances – The true length of the common and hip rafters is measured on the pitch line from the centre line of the ridge to the outside edge of the wall plate. For jack rafters, it is from the centre line of the hip to the outside edge of the wall plate; for the cripple rafter it is from the centre line of the ridge to the centre line of the valley. Therefore when marking out the true lengths of the roofing components from the single line drawing, an allowance in measurement must be made. This allowance should be an addition for the eaves overhang and a reduction to allow for the thickness of the components. If this reduction is not apparent, it may be found by drawing the relevant intersecting components.

Figure 2.79 shows the intersection between the ridge, common, crown and hip rafters. The reduction of the hip rafters is shown. The reduction for the common rafters is always half the ridge thickness and for the crown rafter half the common rafter thickness. These reductions should be marked out at right angles to the plumb cut.

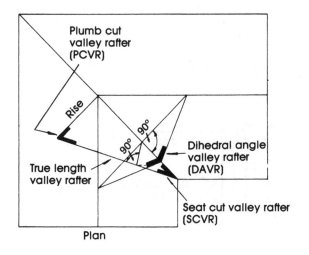

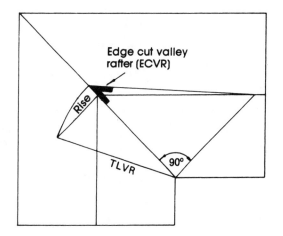

Figure 2.75 *Valley rafter, true length and angles*

Figure 2.76 *Valley rafter edge cut*

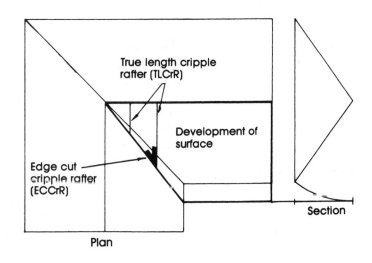

Figure 2.77 *Cripple rafter, true lengths and edge cut*

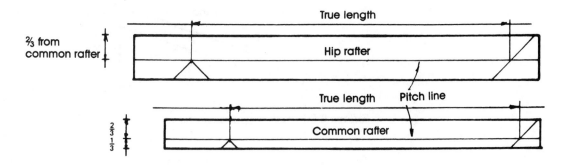

Figure 2.78 *Setting out rafters*

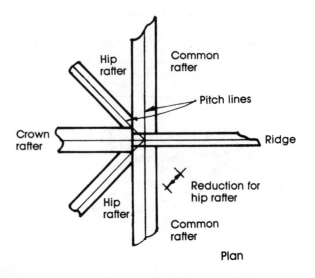

Figure 2.79 *Reduction for thickness of materials*

Roofing square

Setting out rafters – After having covered geometrically the lengths and angles required for hipped, double and valley roofs, the use of the steel square to find the same lengths and angles should be fairly straightforward, as it is merely the application of the geometric principles.

Most roofing squares contain sets of tables on them, which give rafter lengths per metre run for standard pitches, although in practice these tables are rarely used.

The wide part of a roofing square is the blade and the narrow part, the tongue (see Figure 2.80). Both the blade and the tongue are marked out in millimetres. Most carpenters will make a fence for themselves using two battens and four small bolts and wing nuts.

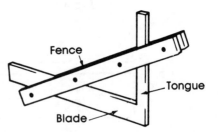

Figure 2.80 *Roofing square and fence*

To set out a roof using the roofing square, the rise of the roof is set on the tongue and the run of the rafter is set on the blade (run of rafter = half of the span). In order to set the rise and run on the roofing square, these measurements must be scaled down and it is usual to divide them by ten.

Example

For a roof with a rise of 2.5 m and a rafter run of 3.5 m, the scale lengths to set on the roofing square would be:

Rise 2.5 m ÷ 10 = 250 mm
Run 3.5 m ÷ 10 = 350 mm

Figure 2.81 shows how to set up the roofing square and fence to obtain the required lengths and angles. The lengths will, however, be scale lengths.

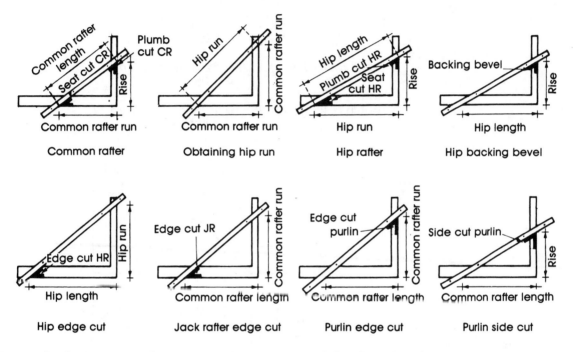

Figure 2.81 *Setting up a roofing square to obtain various scale lengths and angles*

Figure 2.82 shows how the roofing square may be stepped down the rafter ten times to obtain its actual length. Alternatively, the scale length can be measured off the roofing square and multiplied by ten to give its actual length.

Figure 2.82 *Using a roofing square*

Allowances – the roofing square like the geometrical method gives the true lengths of members on the pitch line. Therefore the same allowances in measurement as stated before must be made. The length for the shortest jack rafter can be found by dividing the length of the common rafter by one more than the number of jack rafters on each side of the hip. This measurement is then added to each successive jack rafter to obtain its length.

Example

For the roof shown in Figure 2.83 with three jack rafters on each side of the hip and a common rafter length of say 2.1 m:

Length of short jack (1) = 2.1 m ÷ 4
= 525 mm

Length of middle jack (2) = 525 mm + 525 mm
= 1.05 m

Length of long jack (3) = 1.05 m + 525 mm
= 1.575 m

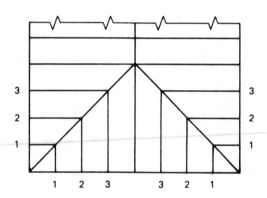

Figure 2.83 *Calculating jack rafter lengths*

The true lengths and angles for valley and cripple rafters can be found by using the same methods as used for the hip and jack rafters.

Trussed rafters

Trussed rafters (Figure 2.84) are prefabricated by a number of specialist manufacturers in a wide range of shapes and sizes. They consist of prepared timber laid out in one plane, with their butt joints fastened with nail plates.

In use the trusses are spaced along the roof at between 400 mm and 600 mm centres and fixed to the wall plate, preferably using truss clips (Figure 2.85).

In order to provide lateral stability the roof requires binders at both ceiling and apex level and diagonal rafter bracing fixed to the underside of the rafters (see Figure 2.86). These must be fixed in accordance with the individual manufacturer's instructions.

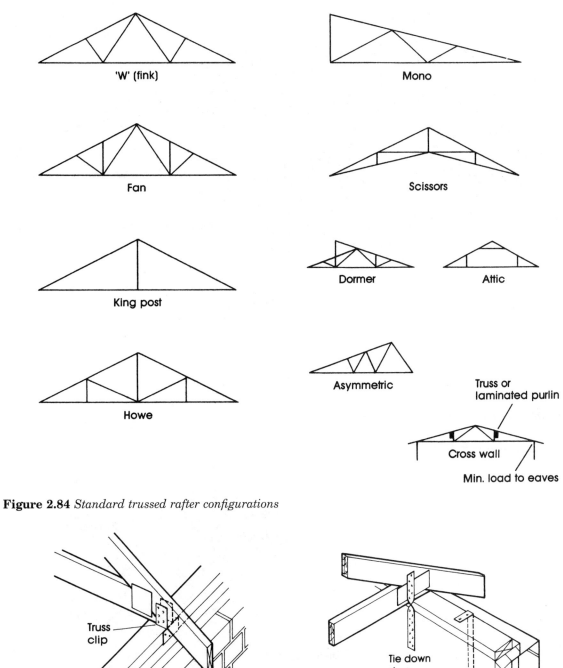

Figure 2.84 *Standard trussed rafter configurations*

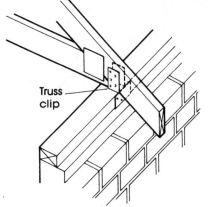

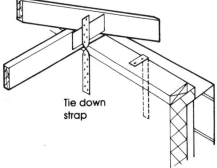

Figure 2.85 *Fixing trussed rafters to wall plate*

Figures 2.87 and 2.88 show how the gable wall must be tied back to the roof for support. This is done using lateral restraint straps at 2 m maximum centres both up the rafter slope and along the ceiling tie.

Prefabricated gable ladders (Figure 2.89) are fixed to the last truss when an overhanging verge is required.

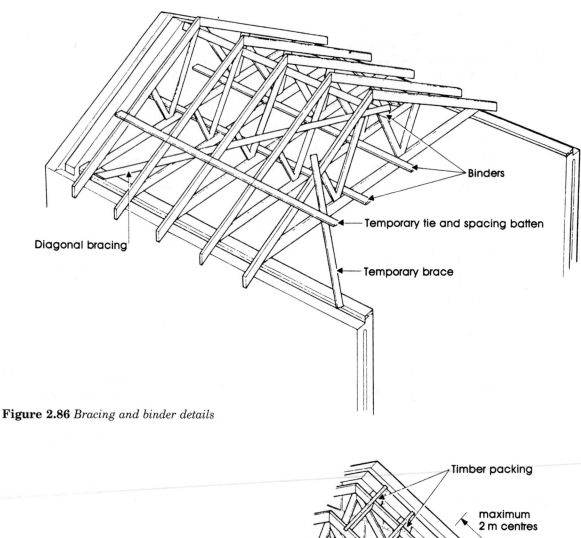

Figure 2.86 *Bracing and binder details*

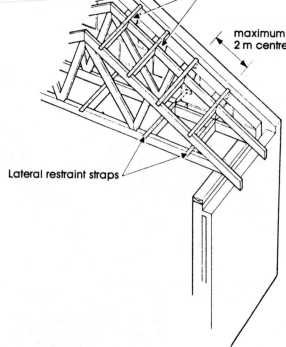

Figure 2.87 *Gable-end restraint*

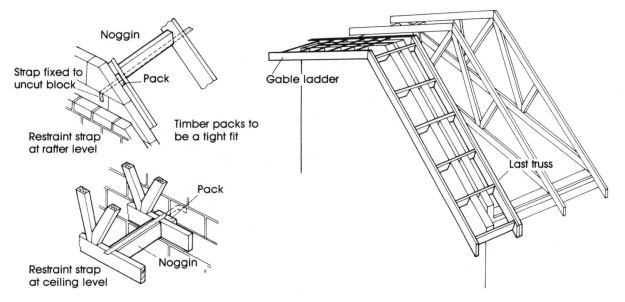

Figure 2.88 *Gable tied back to roof for support*   **Figure 2.89** *Prefabricated gable ladder*

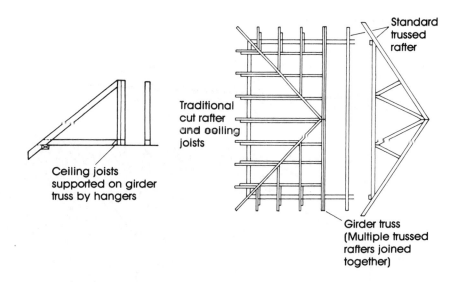

Figure 2.90 *Traditional cut rafter hip end to trussed rafter roof*

Where hip ends and valleys occur in trussed rafter roofs, these may be formed either by using loose timber and cutting normal hip and valley rafters, etc., in the traditional manner (see Figure 2.90), or by using specially manufactured components.

Figure 2.91 shows how a hip end may be formed using a compound hip girder truss to support hip mono trusses. Loose hip rafters, infill jack rafters and ceiling joists must still be cut and fixed in the normal way.

Figure 2.92 shows how a valley may be formed where two roofs intersect at a tee junction, using diminishing jack rafter frames nailed on to lay boards. The ends of the rafters on the main roof are carried across the opening by suspending them from the compound girder truss using suitable joist hangers.

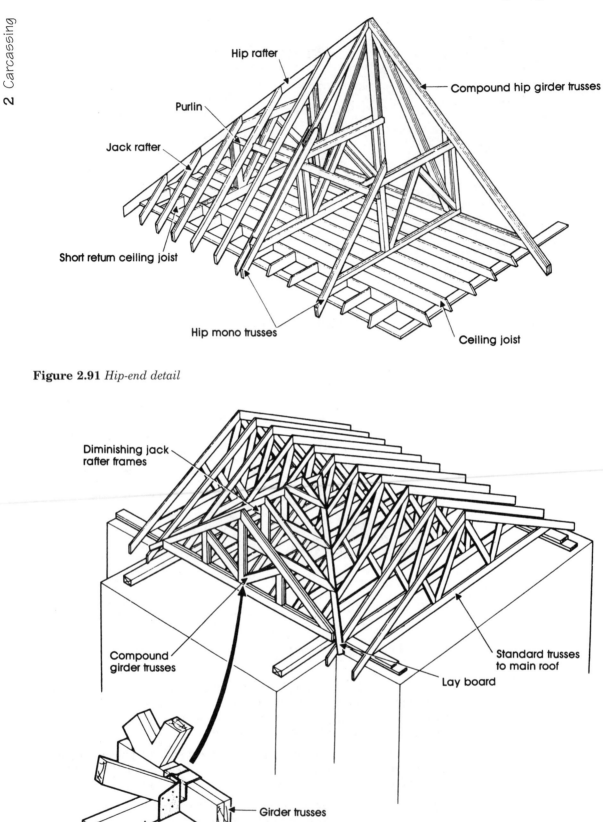

Hip rafter

Compound hip girder trusses

Purlin

Jack rafter

Short return ceiling joist

Hip mono trusses

Ceiling joist

Figure 2.91 *Hip-end detail*

Diminishing jack
rafter frames

Compound
girder trusses

Standard trusses
to main roof

Lay board

Girder trusses

Main trussed rafter

Support detail

Figure 2.92 *Valley detail*

Trimming – Wherever possible, openings in roofs for chimney stacks and loft hatches should be accommodated within the trussed rafter spacing. If larger openings are required the method shown in Figure 2.93 can be used. This entails positioning a trussed rafter on either side of the opening and infilling the space between with normal rafters, purlins and ceiling joists. For safety reasons, on no account should trussed rafters be trimmed or otherwise modified without the structural designer's approval.

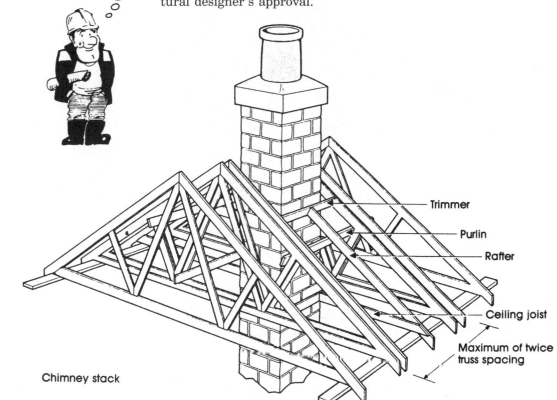

Chimney stack

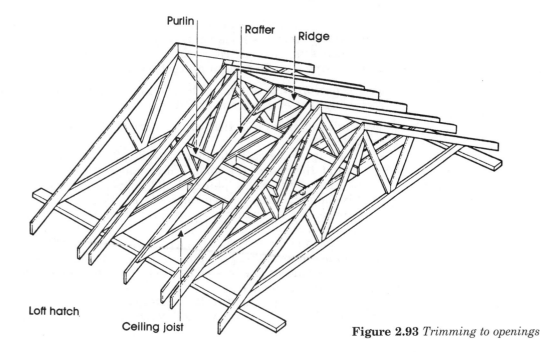

Loft hatch

Figure 2.93 *Trimming to openings*

Water tank platforms – these should be placed centrally in the roof with the load spread over at least three trussed rafters. The lower bearers of the platform should be positioned so that the load is transferred as near as possible to the mid-third points of the span (see Figure 2.94).

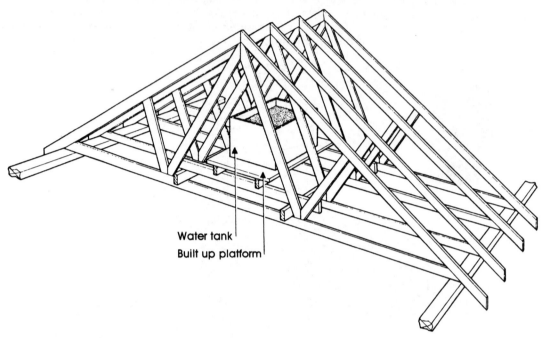

Water tank
Built up platform

Figure 2.94 *Water tank platform*

Erection of trussed rafters

The main problem encountered with the erection of trussed rafters is handling. In order not to strain the joints of the trussed rafters they should be lifted from the eaves, keeping the rafter in a vertical plane with its apex uppermost. Inadequate labour or care will lead to truss damage (Figure 2.95).

Trussed rafters may be lifted into position with the aid of a crane, either singly from the node joints using a spreader bar and slings or in banded sets. In both cases these should be controlled from the ground using a guide rope to prevent swinging.

The erection procedure – The erection procedure for a gable end roof using trussed rafters is as follows:

1) Mark the position of the trusses along the wall plates (see Figure 2.96).
2) Once up on the roof, the first trussed rafter can be placed in position at the end of the under-rafter diagonal bracing. It can then be fixed at the eaves, plumbed and temporarily braced.
3) Fix the remaining trussed rafters in position one at a time to the gable end, temporarily tying each rafter to the preceding one with a batten.
4) Fix diagonal bracing and binders.
5) Repeat the previous procedure at the other end of the roof.
6) Position and fit the trusses between the two braced ends one at a time, and fix binders.
7) Fix ladder frames and restraint straps.
8) Finish the roof at the eaves and verge with fascia, barge board and soffit as required.

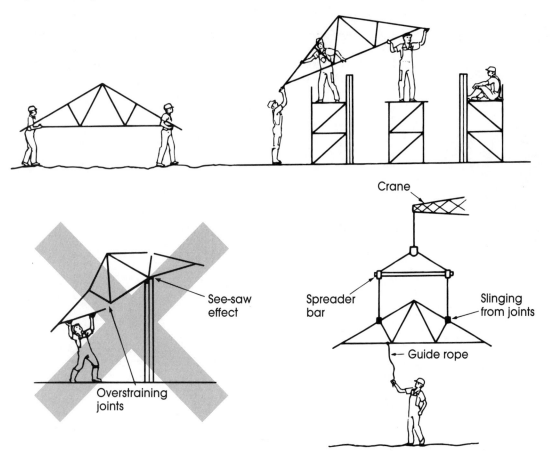

Figure 2.95 *Trussed rafter handling*

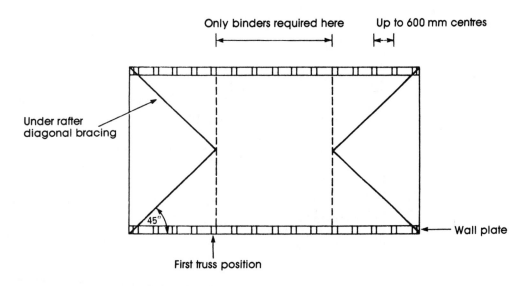

Figure 2.96 *Positioning trusses along wall plates*

TRY TO ANSWER THESE

Questions for you

51. Produce a sketch to show the difference between a single and double roof.

52. Define a flat roof.

_____

_____

53. State the purpose of the following:
(a) lay board

_____

(b) wall plate

_____

c) ridge

_____

54. Explain why a backing bevel is applied to the hip rafters of a close boarded traditional roof.

_____

_____

55. The joint used at the intersection of a rafter and wall plates is:
(a) birdsmouth
(b) splayed dovetail
(c) half lapped joint
(d) butt joint

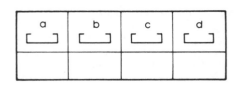

a	b	c	d

56. Explain the difference between:
(a) hip and valley rafters

_____

_____

(b) jack and cripple rafters

_____

_____

57. Explain the reason why a purlin is incorporated into a roof.

_____

_____

58. Produce a sketch to show and state the purpose of lateral restraint straps used in roofing structures.

WELL, HOW DID YOU DO?

WORK THROUGH THE SECTION AGAIN IF YOU HAD ANY PROBLEMS

2 Carcassing

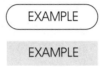

WORD-SQUARE SEARCH

Hidden in the word square are the following 20 words associated with *'Timber pitched roofs'*. You may find the words written forwards, backwards, up, down or diagonally.

Trussed	Hipped
Rafter	Flat
Roofs	Horizontal
Valleys	Diagonal
Gables	Framed
Hip	Prefabricated
Binders	Nail plates
Bracing	Lateral
Chevron	Stability
Pitched	Noggins

Draw a ring around the words, or line in using a highlight pen thus:

(EXAMPLE)

EXAMPLE

```
C N I D R S Y E L L A V A C S H D H
H E F G H J I L K A O M P F Q I I S
E R G N S N I G G O N U O E W P X P
V Z D B D C H E M K X O T O S P S O
R A E G A B L E S M R S G P T E E M
O C S L O M P R Y X A M R A B D Y E
N K S B A D I V X B R V K C I E K G
T D U P R E F A B R I C A T E D O N
I F R N D M F E S P R W T O A M T H
O J T K J A I P A E X D Z E L S O O
N J L O P R B E T C E K Z O T T C R
I S T A L F H F G H Z A P L C A B I
N R N Q R S A K C X Y Z B A D B Q Z
G E O N Z R G T E K D E O R F I Z O
I D T E P L I X P S D C K E T L X N
O N A I L P L A T E S V L T P I S T
H I B K S D P R O C K F G A B T Z A
D B R A C I N G V G Y A S L L Y U L
```

Verge and eaves finishings

Verge, pitched roof

To finish the verge of a gable end roof the ridge and wall plate are extended past the gable end wall, and an additional rafter is pitched to give the required gable overhang. Noggins are fixed between the last two rafters to form a gable ladder. This provides a fixing for the barge board, soffit and tile battens.

Barge board – the continuation of a fascia board around the verge or sloping edge of the roof (typically from 25 mm × 150 mm planed-all-round PAR softwood). It provides a finish to the verge. The lower end of the barge board is usually built up to box in the wall plate and eaves. A template may be cut for the barge board eaves shaping in order to speed up the marking out where a number of roofs are to be cut and also to ensure that each is the same shape (especially where more elaborate designs are concerned).

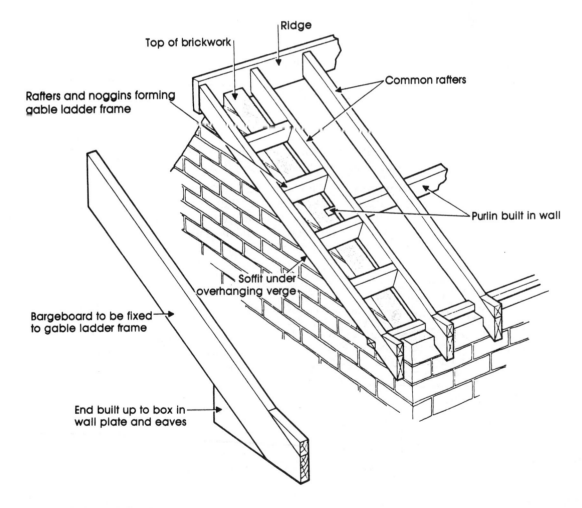

Figure 2.97 *Gable-end detail*

Two methods may be used for determining the bevels at the apex (top) and foot (bottom) of the barge board:

Marking in position – The board is temporarily fixed in position, so a spirit level can then be used to mark the plumb cut (vertical) and seat cut (horizontal) in the required positions (see Figure 2.98).

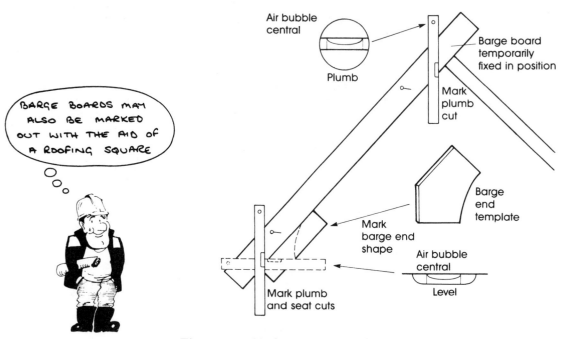

Figure 2.98 *Marking out a barge board*

Determining bevels – Adjustable bevel squares may be set to the required angles for the plumb and seat cuts, using a protractor. These angles will be related to the pitch of the roof.

Remember – The sum of all three angles in a triangle will always be 180 degrees. Therefore in a 30 degree pitched roof, the apex angle will be 120 degrees (180 – twice pitch), making the plumb cut for each barge board 60 degrees (half of apex angle). The seat cut is at right angles to the plumb cut and is at the same angle as the roof pitch.

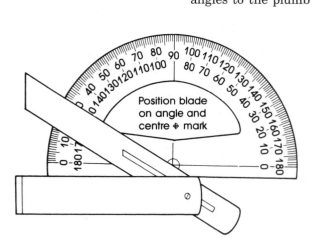

Figure 2.99 *Setting an adjustable bevel to a known angle*

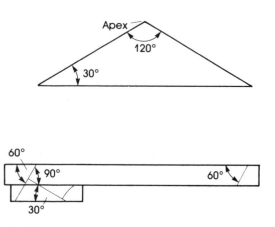

Figure 2.100 *Determining angles for a barge board*

Verge and eaves finishings

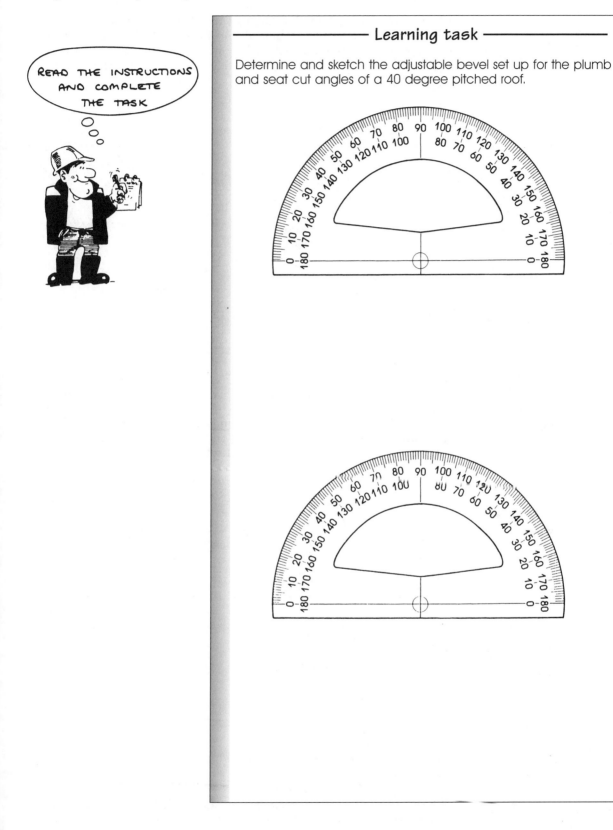

READ THE INSTRUCTIONS AND COMPLETE THE TASK

─────── **Learning task** ───────

Determine and sketch the adjustable bevel set up for the plumb and seat cut angles of a 40 degree pitched roof.

Fixing the barge board – The foot of a barge board may be either mitred to the fascia board, butted and finished flush with the fascia board or butted and extended slightly in front of the fascia board (see Figure 2.101). The actual method used will depend on the specification and/or supervisor's instructions.

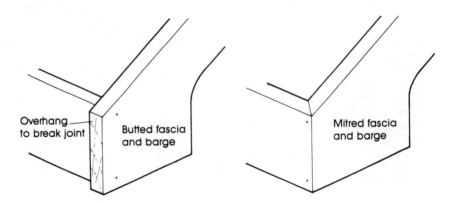

Figure 2.101 *Jointing barge to fascia board*

The mitred joint is preferred for high quality work. The angle of the mitre for the barge board and fascia is best marked in position. Temporarily fix each in position, one at a time. Use a piece of timber of the same thickness to mark two lines across the edge of the board and join the opposite corners to form the mitre. The face angle will be 90 degrees for the fascia board and a plumb cut for the barge board.

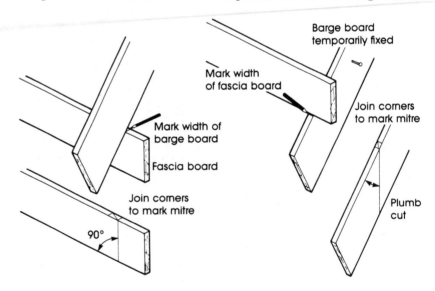

Figure 2.102 *Marking barge to fascia board mitre*

Where timber of sufficient length is not available for a continuous barge, splayed heading joints may be used as shown in Figure 2.103.

After marking, cutting to shape, mitring and fitting, the barge board can be fixed to its gable ladder by double nailing at approximately 400 mm centres. Use either oval nails, wire nails, lost-head nails or cut nails.

These should be at least two and a half times the thickness of the barge board in length in order to provide a sufficiently strong fixing. For example, an 18 mm thick barge board would require nails of at least 45 mm long (50 mm being the nearest standard length). All nails should be punched below the surface ready for subsequent filling by the painter.

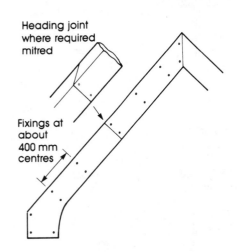

Heading joint where required mitred

Fixings at about 400 mm centres

Figure 2.103 *Barge board lengthening/fixings*

TREAT ALL CUT ENDS WITH PRESERVATIVE

Preservative treatment – It is recommended that all timber used for verge and eaves finishes is preservative treated before use. Any preservative-treated timber cut to size on site will require re-treatment on the freshly cut edges/ends. This can be carried out by applying two brush flood coats of preservative.

Eaves, pitched roof

These may be finished as (see Figure 2.104) either:

● flush
● overhanging, open or closed
● sprocketed

Flush eaves – In this method the ends of the rafters are cut off 10–15 mm past the face of the brickwork and the fascia board is nailed directly to them to provide a fixing point for the gutter. The small gap between the back of the fascia board and the brickwork allows for roof space ventilation.

VENTILATION TO THE ROOF SPACE IS A REQUIREMENT OF THE BUILDING REGULATIONS

Open eaves – These project well past the face of the wall to provide additional weather protection. The ends of the rafters should be prepared as they are exposed to view from the ground. In cheaper quality work the fascia boards are often omitted and the gutter brackets fixed directly to the side of the rafter.

Closed eaves – These overhang the face of the wall the same as open eaves except that the ends of the rafters are closed with a soffit. Cradling brackets are nailed to the sides of the rafters to support the soffit at the wall edge.

Sprocket piece – Flush, open and closed eaves often use sprocket pieces nailed to the top of each rafter to reduce the pitch of the roof at the eaves. This has the effect of easing the fast flowing rainwater under storm conditions into the gutter.

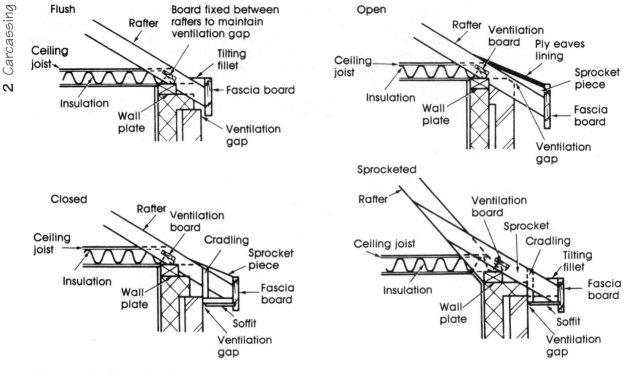

Figure 2.104 *Eaves details*

Sprocketed eaves – On steeply pitched roofs the flow of rainwater off the roof surface has a tendency to overshoot the gutter. Sprockets can be nailed to the side of each rafter to lower the pitch and slow down the rainwater before it reaches the eaves. This reduces the likelihood of rainwater overshooting the eaves and/or hitting the front of the gutter and splashing back soaking the eaves timbers, with the subsequent risk of rot. In addition the use of sprockets also enhances the appearance of a roof giving it a distinctive 'bell-cast' appearance.

Fascia board – the horizontal board (typically ex 25 mm × 150 mm PAR softwood) which is fixed to the ends of the rafters, to provide a finish to the eaves and a fixing for the guttering.

Before fixing the fascia board the rafter feet will require marking and cutting to plumb and line as shown in Figure 2.105; a seat cut may also be required depending on the assembly detail.

- Measure out from brickwork the required soffit width and mark on the last rafter at either end of the roof.
- Mark the plumb cut and the seat cut if required using a spirit level.
- Stretch a string line between the end two rafters and over the tops of the other rafters, use a spirit level to mark each individual plumb cut.
- Cut the plumb cuts using either a hand saw or portable circular saw.
- Where a seat cut is required, move the line down to the seat cut position on the end rafters, use a spirit level to mark each individual seat cut.
- Cut the seat cuts using either a hand or portable circular saw.

Where timber of sufficient length is not available for a continuous fascia board, splayed heading joints may be used. Figure 2.106 shows how these should be positioned centrally over a rafter end.

Where level fascia boards are returned around corners it is standard practice to use a mitre at the external and butt at the internal corners. Both of these joints should be secured by nailing (50 mm ovals).

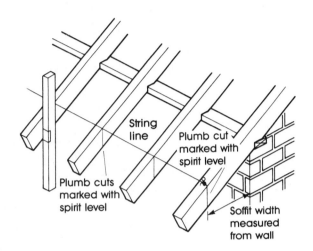
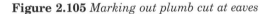

Figure 2.105 *Marking out plumb cut at eaves*

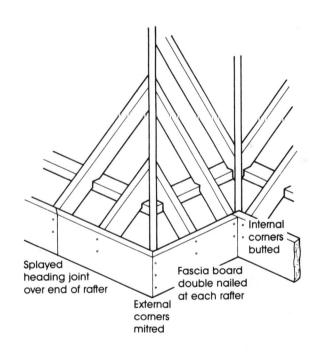

Figure 2.106 *Jointing of fascia board*

Fascia boards are fixed to the end of each rafter using two nails. These are normally either oval nails, wire nails, lost-head nails or cut nails, at least two and a half times the thickness of the fascia board in length. Typically 50 mm or 62 mm nails provide a sufficiently secure fixing. All nails should be punched below the surface ready for subsequent filling by the painter.

Prior to final fixing the fascia should be checked for line as shown in Figure 2.107.

- Drive nails on the face of the fascia at each end of the roof. Strain a line between them.
- Cut three identical pieces of packing, place one at each end under the line and use the third to check the distance between the fascia and the line at each rafter position.
- Pack out or use a saw to ease ends of rafters as appropriate, so that the packing piece just fits between the fascia and the line.

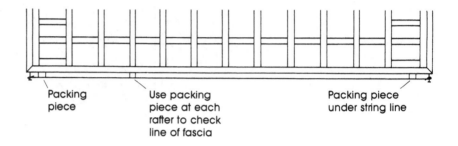

Packing   Use packing   Packing piece
piece   piece at each   under string line
                  rafter to check
                  line of fascia

Figure 2.107 *Checking fascia board for line*

Soffit board – used to close the gap between the fascia and the wall of the building, normally either strips of a non-combustible sheet material, hardboard or formed from tongued and grooved matching (T & G). Soffits normally tongue into the fascia board and are fixed to the underside of cleats or L-shaped brackets (cradling) which are themselves fixed to the sides of each rafter at the seat cut line or required soffit line.

Sheet material soffits are typically fixed using two 25 mm galvanised wire nails at each cleat or cradle position. Matchboarded soffits may be either surface nailed or secret nailed through the tongue using 38 mm oval nails at each cleat or cradle position.

Roof ventilation – To reduce the likelihood of condensation within the roof space ventilation is required by the Building Regulations 2000. All roofs must be cross ventilated at eaves level by permanent vents. These must have an equivalent area equal to a continuous gap along both sides of the roof of 10 mm or 25 mm where the pitch of the roof is less than 15 degrees. This ventilation requirement can be achieved:

- leaving a gap between the wall and soffit (this may be covered with a wire mesh to prevent access by birds, rodents and insects, etc.)
- using a proprietary ventilation strip fixed to the back of the fascia
- using proprietary circular soffit ventilators let into the soffit at about 400 mm centres.

Verge and eaves, flat roofs

The finishing of verge and eaves to flat roofs is a similar process to that of pitched roofs. Both can be finished as either flush or over-hanging details as shown in Figures 2.109 and 2.110.

A drip batten is fixed at the lower eaves, to the top of the fascia to extend the roof edge into the gutter (see Figure 2.111). This extension

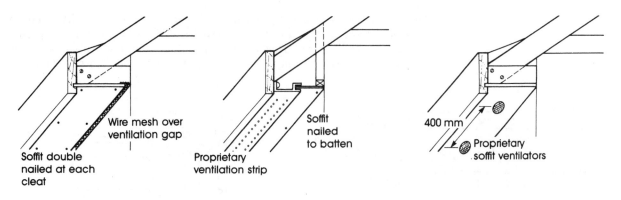

Figure 2.108 *Eaves ventilation*

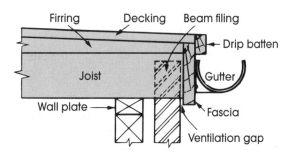

Figure 2.109 *Flush eaves*

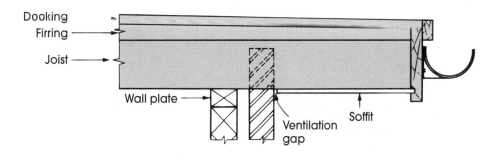

Figure 2.110 *Overhanging eaves*

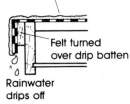

Figure 2.111 *Use of drip batten to eaves of flat roof*

enables the roofing felt to be turned around it. Rainwater flows off the drip batten into the centre of the gutter, thus ensuring efficient discharge and reducing the risk of rot damage to timber. A drip batten is also fixed at higher eaves and verge edges, again to enable roofing felt to be turned around it. Any moisture is then allowed to drip clear of the fascia and not creep back under the felt by capillary attraction, with the subsequent likelihood of rot.

Capillary attraction, or capillarity, is the phenomenon whereby a liquid can travel against the force of gravity, even vertically in fine spaces or between surfaces placed closely together. This is due to the liquid's own surface tension: the smaller the space the greater the attraction. Measures taken to prevent capillarity, such as forming a drip or groove, are known as anti-capillary measures.

Due to the depth of joists deep fascia boards are often required. These may be formed from solid timber, plywood (WBP, weather and boil proof) or matchboarding. An alternative is to reduce the depth of the joists at the ends by either a splay or square cut as shown in Figure 2.112.

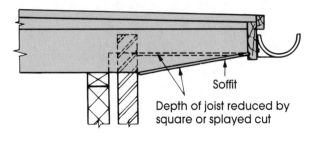

Figure 2.112 *Reducing the depth of the joist*

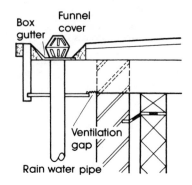

Figure 2.113 *Boxed gutter to a flat roof*

Figure 2.113 shows how a boxed or internal gutter can be formed at the eaves as an alternative to external gutters. The gutter fall (1:60) can be achieved by progressively increasing the depth of cut-out in the joist ends towards the outlet.

Angle fillets, as shown in Figures 2.114 and 2.115, are fixed around the upper eaves, verge and edges of the roof which abut brickwork. They enable the roofing felt to be gently turned at the junction; sharp turns on felt lead to cracking, subsequent leaking and risk of rot. In addition the use of angle fillets also prevents rainwater from dripping or being blown over the edges of the roof.

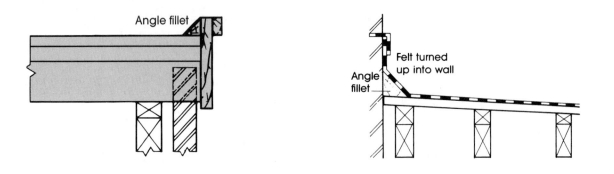

Figure 2.114 *Angle fillet at eaves*

Figure 2.115 *Use of an angle fillet to abutments on flat roofs*

Overhanging details for the verge and eaves positioned at right angles to the main joist run can be formed using two alternative methods:

Returned eaves – short joists are fixed at right angles to the last main joist using joist hangers (see Figure 2.116).

Ladder frame eaves – a ladder frame made from two joists and noggins is made up and fixed to the last joist (see Figure 2.117).

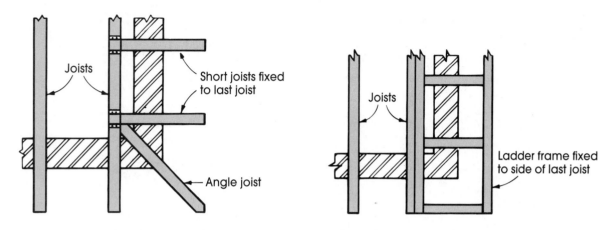

Figure 2.116 *Returned eaves*

Figure 2.117 *Ladder frame eaves*

Determining materials

Calculating the lengths of materials required for fascia boards, barge boards and soffits is often a simple matter of measuring, allowing a certain amount extra for jointing, and adding lengths together to determine total metres run.

Example

A hipped-end roof requires two 4.4 m lengths and two 7.2 m lengths of ex 25 mm × 150 mm PAR softwood for its fascia boards.

Metres run required = (4.4 × 2) + (7.2 × 2)
 = 8.8 + 14.4
 = 23.2 m

It is standard practice to allow a certain amount extra for cutting and jointing. This is often 10%. 10% of any number can be found by moving its decimal point one place forward.

10% of 23.2 = 2.32

The total metres run of timber is determined by adding the percentage increase to the original number.

Total metres run required = 23.2 + 2.32
 = 25.52 m

The length of timber required for barge boards may require calculation using Pythagoras' Theorem of right-angled triangles. This states that in any right-angled triangle the square of the hypotenuse (longest side) is equal to the sum of the square of the other two sides. Thus the length of the hypotenuse in a triangle having sides A, B, C is:

$$C = \sqrt{(B^2 + A^2)}$$

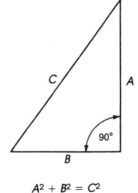

$$A^2 + B^2 = C^2$$

Figure 2.118 *Pythagoras' theorem*

Example

Determine the length of barge board required for one gable having a rise of 3 m and a span of 7 m.

A = Half span = 3.5 m

B = Rise = 3 m

C = Length of barge required for one slope

$= \sqrt{B^2 + A^2}$

$= \sqrt{(3 \times 3) + (3.5 \times 3.5)} = \sqrt{9 + 12.25}$

$= \sqrt{21.25}$

$= 4.610$ m

∴ Total length of barge board required for one gable end is 9.220 m.

Where sheet material is used for fascias and soffits the amount which can be cut from a full sheet often needs calculating. This entails dividing the width of the sheet by the width of the fascia or soffit, then using the resulting whole number to multiply by the sheet's length, to give the total metres run.

Example

Determine the total metres run of 150 mm wide soffit board that may be cut from a 1220 mm × 2440 mm sheet.

Number of lengths = 1220 ÷ 150
= 8.133 say = 8
Total metres run   = 8 × 2.440 = 19.520 m

———————— Learning task ————————

A 6.5 m × 2.8 m plan gable-end roof has a rise of 1.4 m and an eaves and verge overhang of 175 mm. Determine the total amount of ex 25 mm × 225 mm PAR softwood required for the fascia and barge boards and the number of whole 1220 mm × 2440 mm sheets required to cut the 150 mm wide eaves and verge soffit boards. Allow 10% to the total amount as a cutting allowance.

READ THE INSTRUCTIONS AND COMPLETE THE TASK

If you are unfamiliar with calculations or simply want to 'brush up' before attempting this learning task, refer to *A Building Craft Foundation*/'Numerical Skills'.

TRY TO ANSWER THESE

Questions for you

59. Name the regulations that apply to the provision of ventilation in roof spaces.

_____

_____

60. State the purpose of soffit ventilators.

_____

_____

61. Produce sketches to identify the following:
(a) flush eaves

(b) open eaves

(c) closed eaves.

62. State the purpose of a heading joint and produce a sketch of its use in a fascia board.

_____

_____

63. State the purpose of sprockets used in pitched roofs.

_____

_____

64. Produce a sketch to illustrate a sprocket.

65. State the purpose of angle fillets and drip battens used in flat roofs.

_____

_____

_____

_____

66. Produce a sketch to illustrate angle fillets and drip battens.

67. State the reason why the ends of timber sawn on site should be treated with a preservative.

_____

_____

68. Describe the application of preservative on site to a freshly-cut end.

_____

_____

_____

_____

69. Describe each of the following:
(a) fascia board

_____

_____

_____

(b) barge board

_____

_____

(c) soffit board

_____

_____

70. Name a nail suitable for fixing a 6 mm non-combustible sheet material soffit to softwood cradling.

_____

71. Name two nails suitable for fixing an ex 25 mm × 150 mm softwood fascia board to the rafter ends.

_____

_____

72. Name the joint used to return a level fascia board around the external corners of a hipped-end roof.

_____

_____

73. A hipped-end rectangular roof is 14 m long and 7 m wide. Determine:
(a) total length of fascias required

_____

_____

(b) number of 1220 mm × 2440 mm sheets required for the 200 mm wide soffits.

_____

_____

_____

74. Produce a sketch to illustrate a method of determining the plumb cut required for the upper end of a barge board.

WORD-SQUARE SEARCH

Hidden in the word square are the following 21 words associated with *'Verge and eaves finishings'*. You may find the words written forwards, backwards, up, down or diagonally.

Verge	Preservative
Eaves	Plumb cut
Soffit	Seat cut
Gable	Mitre
Hip	Ladder
Roof	Angle fillet
Rafter	Batten drip
Wallplate	Sprocket
Fascia	Ventilation
Barge board	Condensation

Draw a ring around the words, or line in using a highlight pen thus:

(EXAMPLE)

EXAMPLE

COMPLETE THE
WORD SQUARE

P	R	E	S	E	R	V	A	T	I	V	E	O	R	F	A	C	V
R	E	S	P	L	I	T	H	E	A	D	S	R	A	A	W	O	E
A	R	L	S	L	L	M	F	D	N	D	H	O	F	S	P	P	N
N	I	C	B	A	S	O	F	F	I	T	P	M	T	C	E	O	T
G	A	D	D	A	Y	A	N	E	T	T	C	O	E	I	H	R	I
L	U	V	E	R	G	E	T	G	G	U	C	R	R	A	E	T	L
E	A	N	O	E	P	A	K	U	O	C	D	E	O	I	L	T	A
F	L	W	N	P	E	S	S	L	G	T	S	D	H	O	M	N	T
I	I	T	E	A	V	E	S	A	I	A	O	D	T	A	F	E	I
L	A	C	T	C	C	P	R	T	R	E	S	A	L	E	E	D	O
L	R	O	T	E	K	C	O	R	P	S	H	L	C	I	T	N	N
E	D	N	A	L	E	G	T	O	S	O	A	E	A	O	A	E	W
T	R	S	B	A	R	G	E	B	O	A	R	D	N	N	L	P	A
O	A	T	V	I	U	S	T	S	M	E	R	O	I	C	P	E	E
L	U	R	P	L	U	M	B	C	U	T	I	A	T	I	L	D	R
K	G	A	I	I	E	L	E	T	T	E	R	R	P	D	L	N	T
F	R	C	R	A	S	B	M	L	A	D	E	D	I	R	A	I	I
C	O	N	D	E	N	S	A	T	I	O	N	R	H	G	W	E	M

99

3 First fixings

READ THIS CHAPTER, WORKING THROUGH THE QUESTIONS AND LEARNING TASKS

In undertaking this chapter you will be required to demonstrate your skill and knowledge of the following first fixing components:

- Timber stud partitions
- Straight flight stairs
- Frames and linings
- Encasing services.

You will be required practically to:

- Construct a studwork partition
- Position and fix a straight flight of stairs
- Scribe, position and fix a vertical soil pipe casing
- Position and fix a door lining.

Timber studwork partitions

Partition terminology

Partition – an internal wall used to divide space into a number of individual areas or rooms. Partitions are normally of a non-structural/non-load-bearing nature. Figure 3.1 shows how they are commonly formed from timber studwork framing, proprietary systems or lightweight blockwork.

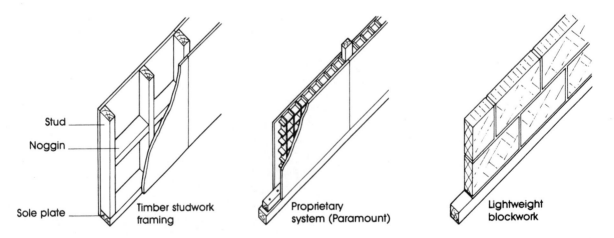

Stud

Noggin

Sole plate

Timber studwork framing

Proprietary system (Paramount)

Lightweight blockwork

Figure 3.1 *Partitions*

Studwork framing/partition – commonly known as stud partitioning. This is a partition wall built of timber or metal studs, fixed between a sole and head plate, often incorporating noggins for stiffening and fixing (see Figure 3.2).

Stud – a vertical timber or metal member of a partition wall fixed between the sole plate and head plate. The main member of a partition, it provides a fixing for the covering material.

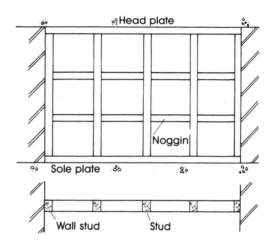

Figure 3.2 *Stud partition components*

REGULARISED TIMBER HAS A CONSISTENT-SIZED SECTION TO GIVE A FLAT FIXING SURFACE

Sole plate/head plate – a horizontal timber fixed above or below studs to provide a fixing point for the studs and ensure an even distribution of loads.

Noggin – a short horizontal piece of timber fixed between vertical studs of a partition. Its use stiffens the studs, provides an intermediate fixing point for the covering material and in addition a fixing point for heavy items which may be hung on the partition (WC cistern, hand basin, etc.).

Timber stud partitions

Traditionally, timber is used for making studwork framing. PAR (planed all round) timber is preferred not only because of its uniform cross section but also it is better to handle. Alternatively, regularised timber (timber machined to a consistent width by re-sawing or planing one or both edges) may be specified. Consistent sized sections aids plumbing of a partition and provides a flat fixing surface of the partition covering materials (Figure 3.3). A reduction from the basic sawn size has to be allowed for dimensions up to 100 mm; this is 3 mm, e.g.

Sawn size	PAR size	Regularised size
50 mm × 50 mm	47 mm × 47 mm	50 mm × 47 mm
50 mm × 75 mm	47 mm × 72 mm	50 mm × 72 mm
50 mm × 100 mm	47 mm × 97 mm	50 mm × 97 mm

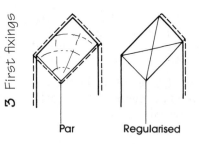

Par   Regularised

Figure 3.3 *Par and regularised sections have a constant width*

The standard covering material for partition walls is plasterboard. This is available in 9.5 mm and 12.5 mm thicknesses and in sheet sizes of 900 mm × 1800 mm and 1200 mm × 2400 mm.

Partitions may be constructed in-situ or be pre-made and later erected.

In-situ *partition* – Components are cut, assembled and fixed in situation on site.

Pre-made partition – a ready-assembled partition (either on site or in a factory) for later site erection.

Jointing partition members

Traditionally, timber partitions were framed using basic joints, to locate members and provide strength as shown in Figures 3.4 and 3.5. Studs were often housed into the head plate, slotted over a batten at the sole plate and mortised or tenoned at openings. However, present day techniques, calling for speed of erection and economy result in the majority of partitions being simply butt jointed and skew nailed (Figure 3.6). An alternative to both methods, would be the use of metal framing anchors. These provide a quick yet strong fixing, although they are rarely specified.

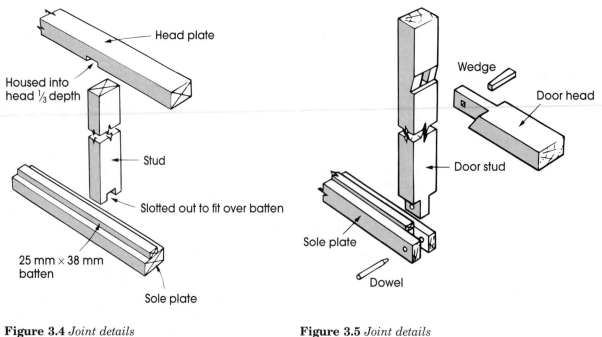

Figure 3.4 *Joint details*   **Figure 3.5** *Joint details*

Constructing *in-situ* stud partitions

Mark the intended position of the partition on the ceiling. Ideally this should either be at right angles to the joists or positioned under a joist or double joist. Where the joists run in the same direction as the partition and it is not directly under a joist, noggins will have to be fixed between joists, to provide a fixing point (see Figure 3.7).

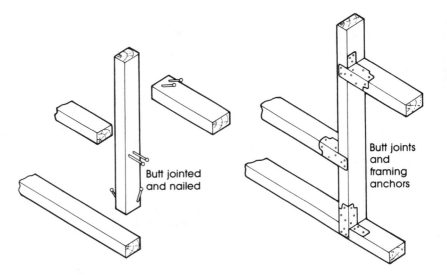

Figure 3.6 *Stud partition joints*

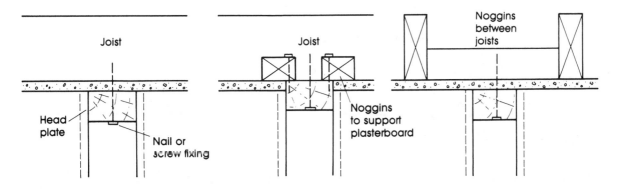

Figure 3.7 *Fixing of head plate*

Fix the head plate to ceiling, using 100 mm wire nails or oval nails at each joist position or 400 mm centres as appropriate. In older buildings, where ceilings might be in a poor position or easily damaged by nailing, 100 mm screws can be used as an alternative.

Plumb down from the head plate on one side at each end, to the floor, using either a straight edge and level or a plumb bob and line as shown in Figure 3.8. This establishes the position of the sole plate.

Fix the sole plate in position with 100 mm wire nails, oval nails or screws as appropriate. Ideally, as with head plates, this should be either at right angles to the joists or over a joist or double joist. Where the joists run in the same direction as the partition but not directly under it, noggins will have to be fixed between joists to provide a fixing point. Where the sole plate is fixed to a concrete floor this should be plugged and screwed.

It may be possible to 'shot fix' both head and sole plates to concrete surfaces. However, this is not within the scope of this package. Please refer to your supervisor for permission/instruction.

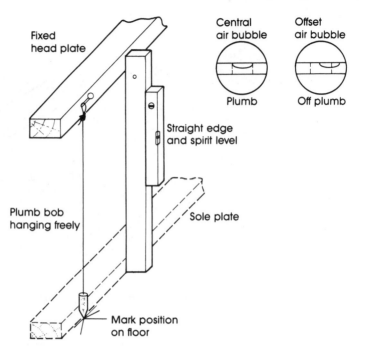

Figure 3.8 *Plumbing partition*

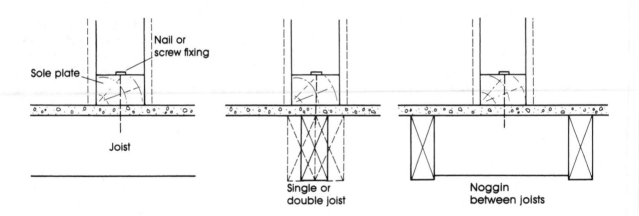

Figure 3.9 *Fixing of sole plate*

REFER BACK TO THE INDICATED SOURCES IF YOU HAVE ANY PROBLEMS

Cut, position and fix the end wall studs. These may be either:

- plugged and screwed to brickwork and blockwork using 100 mm screws into proprietary plugs or twisted timber pallets
- nailed to blockwork or into brickwork mortar joints using 100 mm cut nails
- nailed directly to brickwork using 75 mm hardened steel masonry nails. (It is essential that eye protection is used when driving masonry nails as they are liable to shatter.)

Mark the positions of vertical studs on the sole and head plates. Studs will be required at each joint in the covering material and using 1200 mm wide sheets at 400 mm centres for 9.5 mm plasterboard or at 600 mm centres for 12.5 mm plasterboard; using 900 mm wide sheets, all studs should be at 450 mm centres (see Figure 3.11).

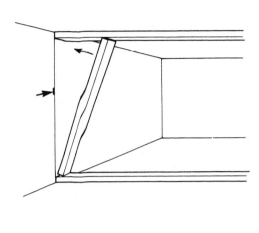

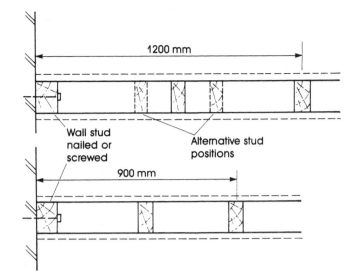

Figure 3.10 *Positioning wall stud*

Figure 3.11 *Stud spacings*

Similar centres may be employed for other covering material/cladding. Assuming 12.5 mm × 1200 mm covering, the second stud is fixed with its centre 600 mm from the wall, the third with its centre 1200 mm from the wall and the remaining studs at 600 mm centres thereafter.

Measure, cut and fix each stud to head and sole plates, using 100 mm wire or oval nails, driven at an angle (skew nailed, see Figure 3.12). Each stud should be measured and cut individually as the distance between the plates may vary along their length. Studs should be a tight fit: position one end, angle the stud and drive the other end until plumb. The length of each stud may be measured using either a tape or pinch rods as shown in Figure 3.13.

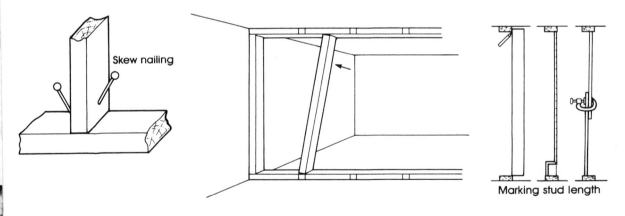

Figure 3.12 *Skew nailing*

Figure 3.13 *Marking and positioning studs*

Mark noggin centre line positions; these will vary depending on the specification. Typically they are fixed at vulnerable positions where extra strength is required: at knee height 600 mm up from floor, at waist height 1200 mm up from floor and at shoulder height 1800 mm up from floor. Where deep section skirting is to be fixed a noggin may be specified near its top edge for fixing purposes as shown in Figure 3.14. Additional noggins will also be required where heavy items are to be hung on the wall and where the covering sheet material is jointed in the height of the partition.

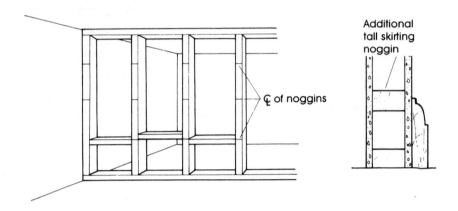

Figure 3.14 *Noggin positions*

Figure 3.15 shows how to fix the noggins, either by skew nailing using 100 mm wire or oval nails or staggering either side of the centre line and through nailing using 100 mm wire or oval nails.

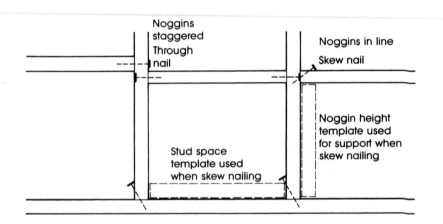

Figure 3.15 *Fixing noggins*

Timber studwork partitions

TRY TO ANSWER THESE

─────────── Questions for you ───────────

1. State the purpose of a partition wall and name **TWO** methods of construction

_____

_____

_____

_____

2. List **FIVE** component members of timber studwork framing.

_____

_____

_____

_____

_____

3. State the difference between in-situ and pre-made timber stud partitions.

_____

_____

_____

4. State the purpose of noggins used in timber studwork.

_____

_____

5. State the purpose of noggins used between floor joists either above or below timber studwork.

_____

_____

6. Name a nail suitable for fixing a head plate to a timber floor joist.

_____

_____

7. State suitable centres for studs when using 9.5 mm thick × 1200 mm wide plasterboard covering.

_____

_____

8. Name a nail suitable for securing the butt joint between a stud and noggin.

_____

_____

9. Name a nail suitable for securing wall studs directly to brickwork and state any precautions that should be observed in its use.

_____

_____

_____

_____

10. Produce a sketch to illustrate skew nailing.

WELL, HOW DID YOU DO?

WORK THROUGH THE SECTION AGAIN IF YOU HAD ANY PROBLEMS

Estimating materials

To determine the number of studs required for a particular partition the following procedure, shown in Figure 3.16, can be used:

- Measure the distance between the adjacent walls of the room or area which the partition is to divide, say 3400 mm.
- Divide the distance between the walls by the specified stud spacing, say 600 mm. This gives the number of spaces between the studs. Where a whole number is not achieved round up to the whole number above. There will always be one more stud than the number of spaces so add one to this figure to determine the number of studs. Stud centres must be maintained to suit sheet material sizes leaving an undersized space between the last two studs.
- The lengths of head and sole plates are simply the distance between the two walls. Each line of noggins will require a length of timber equal to the distance between the walls.

Example

The total length of timber required for a partition, can be determined by the following method:

7 studs at 2.4 m, 7 × 2.4	=	16.8 m
Head and sole plates at 3.4 m, 2 × 3.4	=	6.8 m
3 lines of noggins at 3.4 m, 3 × 3.4	=	10.2 m
Total metres run required, 16.8 + 6.8 + 10.2	=	33.8 m

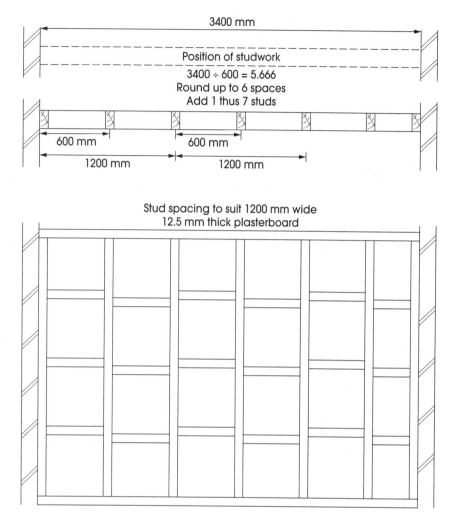

Figure 3.16 *Estimating materials for a stud partition*

Openings

Where door, serving hatch or borrowed light (internal glazing) openings are required in a studwork framing, studs and noggins should be positioned on each side to form the opening (Figures 3.17 to 3.20). The sole plate will require cutting out between the door studs. Linings are fixed around the framed opening to provide a finish and provision for hanging doors or glazing.

Returns

Should a return partition forming internal or external angles be required, stud positions must be arranged to suit. Consideration must be given to providing a support and fixing for the covering material around the return intersection. Two alternative methods, shown in Figures 3.21 and 3.22, are commonly employed. The particular method adopted will depend on whether the carpenter is fixing the covering material as the work proceeds or the plasterer is fixing it after the carpentry work is complete.

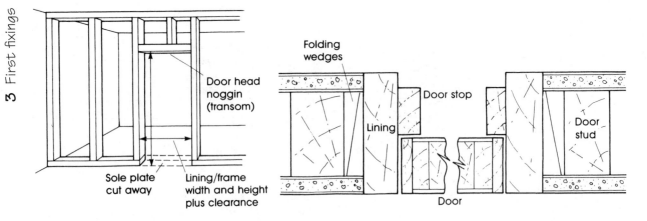

Figure 3.17 *Door opening in a stud partition*

Figure 3.18 *Typical horizontal section of door opening*

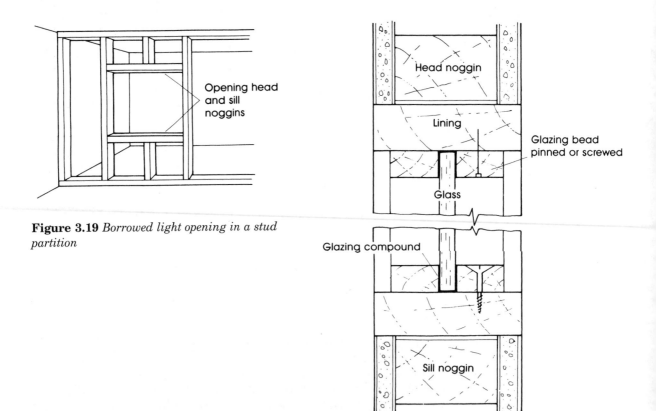

Figure 3.19 *Borrowed light opening in a stud partition*

Figure 3.20 *Typical vertical section of borrowed light*

Note: Plasterboard is normally marked up to indicate which face is suitable for plastering and dry lining. Typically the following is marked on the rear face: 'use other face for plastering and decoration'. In general the ivory face is fixed to the outside.

Plasterboard sheets are secured to the studs using plasterboard nails or plasterboard screws at approximately 150 mm centres around the sheet edges and intermediate studs. To avoid distortion, nailing should commence from the centre of the sheet working outwards. Nails should

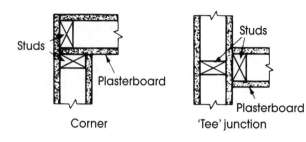

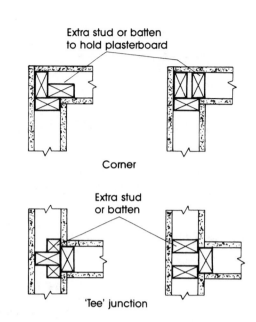

Figure 3.21 *Corner details*

Figure 3.22 *Stud treatment to provide support for coverings at returns*

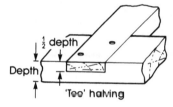

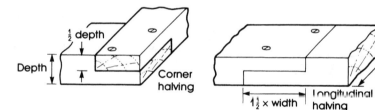

Figure 3.23 *Sole and head plate joints*

be driven just below the surface, but taking care not to break or damage the paper face of the sheet.

Wall plates in long partitions and those containing return intersections will require joining preferably using halving joints secured with screws (see Figure 3.23).

Pre-made partitions

These may be made either by the joiner in a workshop or by the carpenter on site. The method of jointing will normally be either: studs housed into plates with noggins butt-jointed and nailed, or all joints butted and nailed. In addition, occasionally pre-made partitions may be jointed using framing anchors.

This type of partition must be made under-size in both height and width, in order for it to be placed in position. Once in position folding wedges are used to take up the positioning tolerance prior to fixing (see Figures 3.24 and 3.25). Plates and wall studs are fixed using the same methods and centres as are applicable to in-situ partitions.

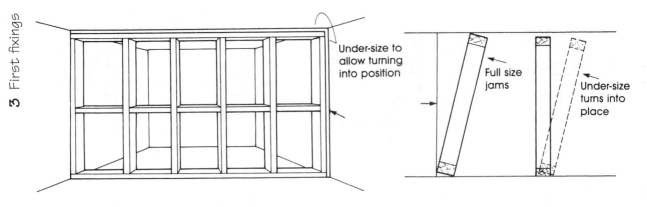

Figure 3.24 *Pre-made partitions must be constructed undersize to allow for positioning tolerances*

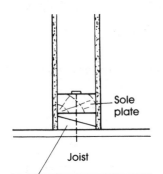

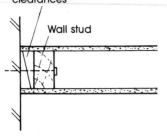

Figure 3.25 *Use of folding wedges to take up positioning tolerances*

Drilling and notching partitions

Service cables and pipes for water, gas and electricity are often concealed within stud partitions. In common with floor joists the positioning of holes and notches in studs has an effect on strength. It is recommended that holes and notches in studs should be kept to a minimum and conform to the following (Figures 3.26 and 3.27).

Holes – of up to 0.25 of the stud's width, drilled on the centre line (neutral stress line) and located between 0.25 and 0.4 of the stud's height from either end are permissible. Adjacent holes should be separated by at least three times their diameter measured centre to centre.

Notches – on either edge of the stud up to 0.15 of the stud's width and located up to 0.2 of the stud's height from either end are permissible.

Example

The position and sizes for holes and notches in 100 mm width studs, 2400 mm in length are:

Holes – between 600 mm and 960 mm in from either end of the stud and up to 25 mm in diameter.

Notches – up to 480 mm in from each end and up to 15 mm deep.

Excessive drilling and notching outside these permissible limits will weaken the stud and may lead to failure. In addition, holes and notches should be kept clear of areas where the services routed through them are likely to get punctured by nails and screws, e.g. behind skirtings, dado rails and kitchen units etc., or metal plates can be fitted for protection (Figure 3.26).

Fire resistance, thermal insulation and sound insulation

Depending on the partition's location it may be required to form a fire resisting and/or a thermal insulating and/or a sound insulating function. Specific requirements and methods of achieving them are controlled by the Building Regulations 2000 that should be referred to for information as may be required. However, the general principles for achieving these functions are:

Timber studwork partitions

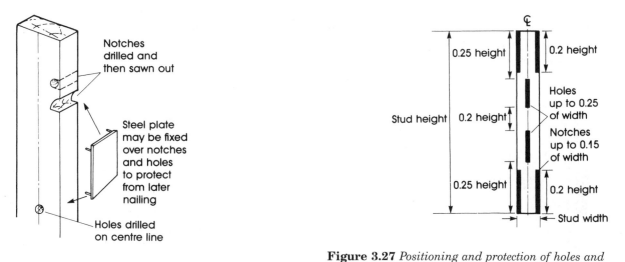

Figure 3.26 *Hole and notch details*

Figure 3.27 *Positioning and protection of holes and notches to accommodate services*

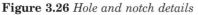

- *Fire resistance* can be increased by a double covering of plasterboard, the second outer layer being fixed so that the joints overlap those in the lower layer.

- *Thermal insulation* can be increased by filling the space between studs with either mineral wool or glass fibre quilt.

- *Sound insulation* can be increased by a discontinuous construction to avoid impact and vibration and the use of lightweight infilling material such as mineral or glass fibre quilt to absorb sound energy.

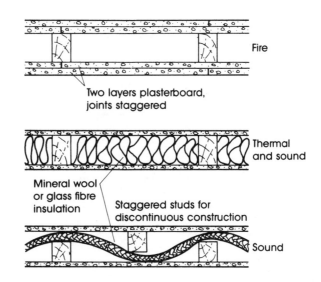

Figure 3.28 *Insulation of stud partitions*

3 First fixings

READ THE INSTRUCTIONS AND COMPLETE THE TASK

─────── **Learning task** ───────

Determine the number of 2400 mm long studs required to be spaced at 600 mm centres, for a partition between two walls 4500 mm apart.

_____

_____

_____

_____

Determine the total amount of timber required in metres run for the partition. Include head plate, sole plate, studs and three lines of noggins.

_____

_____

_____

_____

_____

_____

─────── **Questions for you** ───────

11. State the reason why pre-made partitions are constructed shorter than the height of the room where they are to be fixed.

_____

_____

12. Produce a sketch to show a suitable means of jointing a sole plate at a return.

TRY TO ANSWER THESE

13. A stud partition wall is to be dry lined. Which face should be fixed outwards?

_____

_____

14. State the purpose of drilling or notching studs.

_____

_____

_____

15. State the maximum size hole that should be drilled in a 100 mm wide stud.

_____

16. Name the regulations which govern fire resistance, thermal insulation and sound insulation of partitions.

_____

_____

_____

17. Name **TWO** methods of securing glazing beads to the lining of a borrowed light.

_____

_____

_____

18. Determine the total length of timber in metres run required for the following partition:

Eleven 50 mm × 75 mm studs 2400 mm long
Head and sole plate 4100 mm long
Three lines of noggins

_____

_____

_____

_____

WELL, HOW DID YOU DO?

WORK THROUGH THE SECTION AGAIN IF YOU HAD ANY PROBLEMS

COMPLETE THE WORD SQUARE

WORD-SQUARE SEARCH

Hidden in the word square are the following 20 words associated with *'Constructing Studwork Framing'*. You may find the words written forwards, backwards, up, down or diagonally.

Notches	Sound
Wall stud	Insulation
Stud	Intermediate
Partition	Door
Noggin	Lining
Head plate	In situ
Sole plate	Pre-made
Framing	Skew nail
Plasterboard	Wire nail
Thermal	Paramount

Draw a ring around the words, or line in using a highlight pen thus:

EXAMPLE

EXAMPLE

P	L	A	S	T	E	R	B	O	A	R	D	O	F	F	A	C	I
R	U	S	P	L	I	T	H	E	A	D	S	E	H	C	T	O	N
O	R	T	L	I	N	I	N	G	N	D	H	O	M	N	P	P	T
P	I	C	L	A	D	D	E	R	L	C	P	M	B	I	E	O	E
I	A	D	F	R	A	M	I	N	G	E	C	O	O	G	H	R	R
N	U	W	I	R	E	N	A	I	L	T	C	S	R	G	E	T	M
S	K	E	W	N	A	I	L	U	O	A	D	O	A	O	L	T	E
U	L	W	A	L	L	S	T	U	D	L	O	A	H	N	M	E	D
L	I	O	O	S	U	S	T	A	I	D	N	U	O	S	E	D	I
A	A	E	O	T	C	P	R	U	R	E	S	I	L	E	T	A	A
T	R	T	R	N	H	O	G	I	D	L	T	O	C	I	S	M	T
I	D	A	E	U	E	G	T	O	S	I	A	E	A	O	T	E	E
O	R	L	P	O	N	D	A	N	T	H	E	R	M	A	L	R	A
N	A	P	V	M	U	S	T	R	M	E	R	O	I	C	C	P	R
L	U	D	C	A	U	P	A	E	I	N	S	I	T	U	O	D	D
K	G	A	T	R	E	P	E	T	T	E	R	R	O	D	C	N	V
F	R	E	T	A	S	B	M	L	A	D	E	D	E	R	S	I	E
B	S	H	B	P	A	S	O	L	E	P	L	A	T	E	O	E	L

Stairs

A stairway can be defined as a series of steps (combination of tread and riser) giving floor-to-floor access. Each continuous set of steps is called a flight. Landings are introduced between floor levels either to break up a long flight, giving a rest point, or to change the direction of the stair.

Straight-flight stairs

These run in one direction for the entire length. Figure 3.29 shows there are three different variations.

The flight which is closed between two walls (also known as a cottage stair) is the simplest and most economical to make. Its handrail is usually a simple section fixed either directly on to the wall or on brackets.

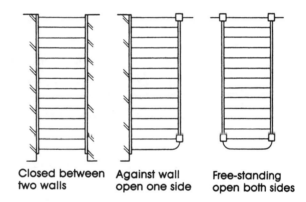

| Closed between two walls | Against wall open one side | Free-standing open both sides |

Figure 3.29 *Straight-flight stairs*

The flight fixed against one wall is said to be open on one side. This open or outer string is normally terminated and supported at either end by a newel post. A balustrade must be fixed to this side to provide protection. The infilling of this can be either open or closed and is usually capped by a handrail. Where the width of the flight exceeds one metre, a wall handrail will also be required.

Where the flight is freestanding, neither side being against a wall, it is said to be open both sides. The open sides are treated in the same way as the previous flight.

Stair terminology

Apron lining – the boards used to finish the edge of a trimmed opening in the floor.

Balustrade – the handrail and the infilling between it and the string, landing or floor. This can be called either an open or closed balustrade, depending on the infilling.

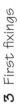

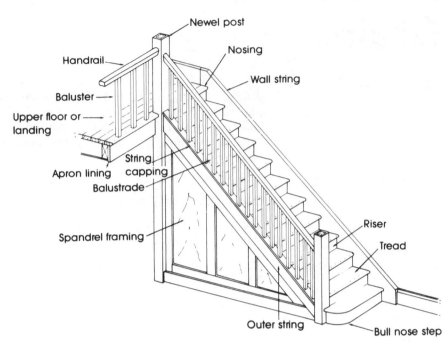

Figure 3.30 *Stairway terminology*

Baluster – the short vertical infilling members of an open balustrade.

Bull nose step – the quarter-rounded end step at the bottom of a flight of stairs.

Carriage – This is a raking timber fixed under wide stairs to support the centre of the treads and risers. Brackets are fixed to the side of the carriage to provide further support across the width of the treads.

Commode step – a step with a curved tread and riser normally occurring at the bottom of a flight.

Curtail step – the half-rounded or scroll-end step at the bottom of a flight.

Newel – the large sectioned vertical member at each end of the string. Where an upper newel does not continue down to the floor level below it is known as a pendant or drop newel.

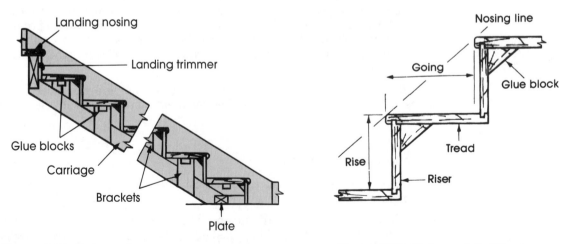

Figure 3.31 *Stair carriage*

Figure 3.32 *Stairway definitions*

Nosing – the front edge of a tread or the finish to the floorboards around a stairwell opening.

Riser – the vertical member of a step.

Spandrel – the triangular area formed under the stairs. This can be left open or closed in with spandrel framing to form a cupboard.

String – the board into which the treads and risers are housed or cut. They are also named according to their type, for example, wall string, outer string, close string, cut string, and wreathed string.

Tread – the horizontal member of a step. It can be called a parallel tread or a tapered tread, etc., depending on its shape.

Stair installation

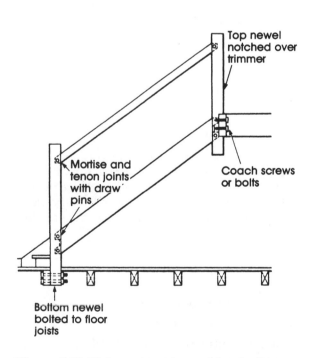

Stairs are normally delivered to site assembled as far as possible, but for ease of handling each flight will be separate. Its newels, handrail and balustrade are supplied loose, ready for on-site completion.

For maximum strength and rigidity the stairs should be fixed as shown in Figures 3.33 to 3.37. The top newel is notched over the landing or floor trimmer and either bolted or coach screwed to it. The lower newel should be carried through the landing or floor and bolted to the joists. The lower newel on a solid ground floor can be fixed by inserting a steel dowel partly into the newel and grouting this into the concrete.

The outer string and handrail are mortised into the newels at either end. With the flight in position, these joints are glued and then closed up and fixed using hardwood draw pins. The wall string is cut over the trimmer at the top and cut-nailed or screwed to the wall from the underside. The bottom riser of a flight may be secured by screwing it to a batten fixed to the floor.

Figure 3.33 *Fixing outer string and handrail*

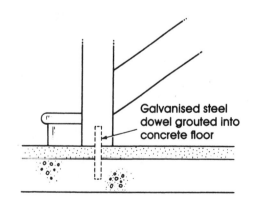

Figure 3.34 *Newel fixing*

119

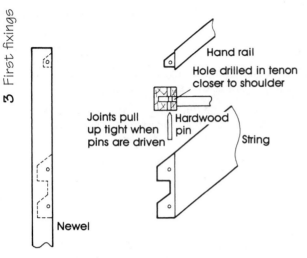

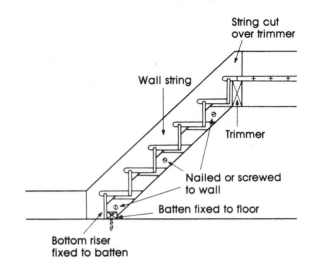

Figure 3.35 *String handrail to newel joints*

Figure 3.36 *Fixing wall string*

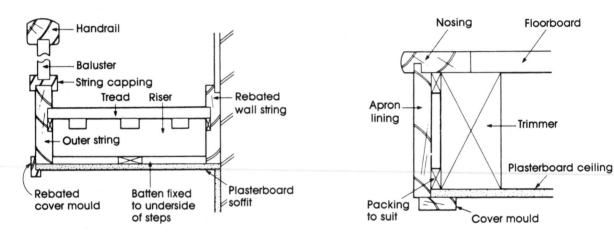

Figure 3.37 *Section across flight open one side*

Figure 3.38 *Landing detail*

Figure 3.38 shows how the trimmer around the stairwell opening is finished with an apron lining and nosing.

Where the width of the stair exceeds about one metre, a carriage may be fixed under the flight to support the centre of the treads and risers. To securely fix the carriage it is birdsmouthed at both ends, at the top over the trimmer and at the bottom over a plate fixed to the floor. Brackets are nailed to alternate sides of the carriage to provide further support across the width of the treads.

Stair handrails

Handrails to straight flights with newels as illustrated in previous examples are tenoned into the face of the newel posts.

Figure 3.39 shows how wall handrails either may be fixed by plugging, screwing and pelleting direct to the wall, or may stand clear of the wall on metal brackets fixed at about one metre centres.

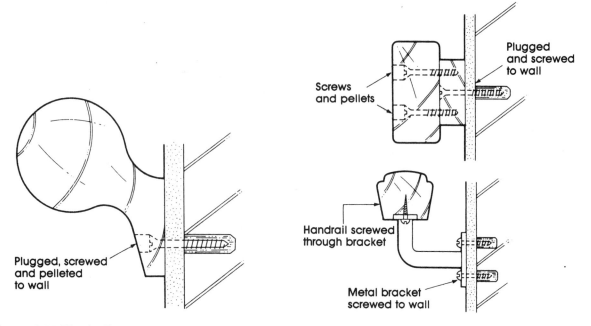

Figure 3.39 *Handrail sections*

A half newel can be used to give support to the handrail and balustrade where it meets the wall or a landing (see Figure 3.40).

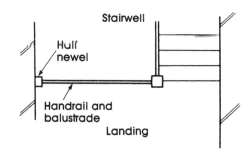

Figure 3.40 *Use of half newel*

Protection of completed work

After a new staircase has been installed, a short period spent taking measures to prevent damage during subsequent building work saves much more than it costs.

False treads made from strips of hardboard or plywood, as shown in Figure 3.41, are pinned on to the top of each step. The batten fixed to the strip ensures the nosing is well protected. On flights to be clear finished the false treads should be held in position with a strong adhesive tape, as pin holes would not be acceptable.

Strips of hardboard or plywood are also used to protect newel posts. These can be either pinned or taped in position depending on the finish (see Figure 3.42). Adequate protection of handrails and balustrades can be achieved by wrapping them in corrugated cardboard held in position with adhesive tape.

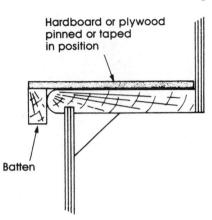

Figure 3.41 *Temporary protection of treads*

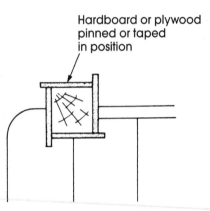

Figure 3.42 *Temporary protection of newels*

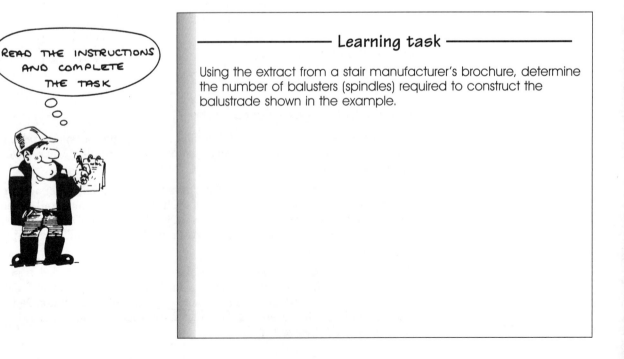

READ THE INSTRUCTIONS AND COMPLETE THE TASK

―――――――― Learning task ――――――――

Using the extract from a stair manufacturer's brochure, determine the number of balusters (spindles) required to construct the balustrade shown in the example.

S T A I R P A R T S

HELPFUL HINTS

When calculating the number of 32mm spindles needed on the staircase itself, allow 2 spindles per tread and 1 per tread where there is a newel.

On the landing, to calculate the number of spindles required, (X) simply use the following formula:

$$X = \frac{\text{Horizontal distance (in mm) on landing between newels}}{112}$$

Example

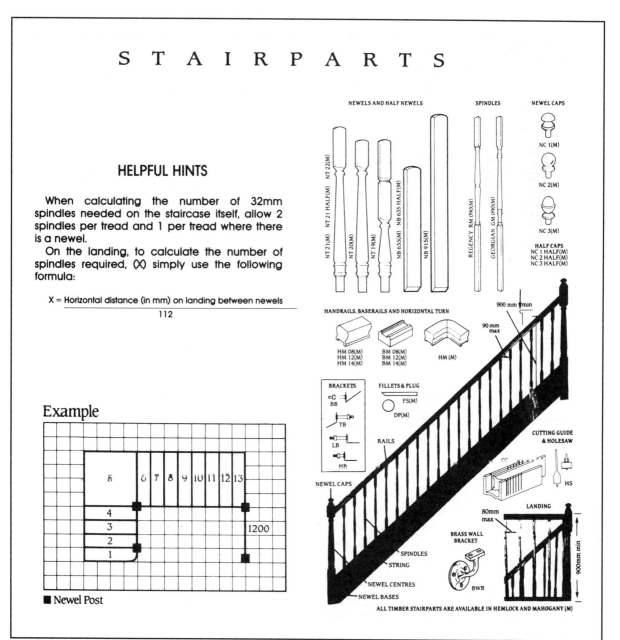

■ Newel Post

ALL TIMBER STAIRPARTS ARE AVAILABLE IN HEMLOCK AND MAHOGANY (M)

Reproduced with the permission of Richard Burbidge Ltd, Whittington Road, Oswestry, Shropshire SY11 1HZ. For further information please telephone 01691 655131.

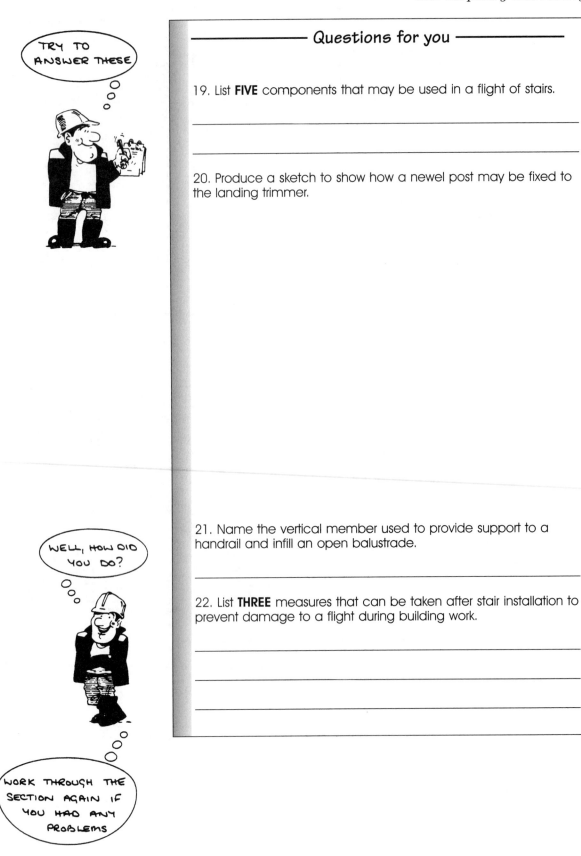

TRY TO ANSWER THESE

————————— Questions for you —————————

19. List **FIVE** components that may be used in a flight of stairs.

_____

_____

20. Produce a sketch to show how a newel post may be fixed to the landing trimmer.

21. Name the vertical member used to provide support to a handrail and infill an open balustrade.

_____

22. List **THREE** measures that can be taken after stair installation to prevent damage to a flight during building work.

_____

_____

_____

WELL, HOW DID YOU DO?

WORK THROUGH THE SECTION AGAIN IF YOU HAD ANY PROBLEMS

Frames and linings

Terminology

Frame – an assembly of components to form an item of joinery, such as a door or window; a structural framework of columns and beams or panels in steel reinforced concrete or timber.

Lining – the thin covering to door or window reveals; sheet material used to cover wall surfaces.

Door frame – the surround on which an external door or internal door is hung consisting of two jambs, a head and sometimes a threshold and transom; normally with stuck-on solid stops and of a bigger section than door linings. (See Figures 3.43 to 3.45.)

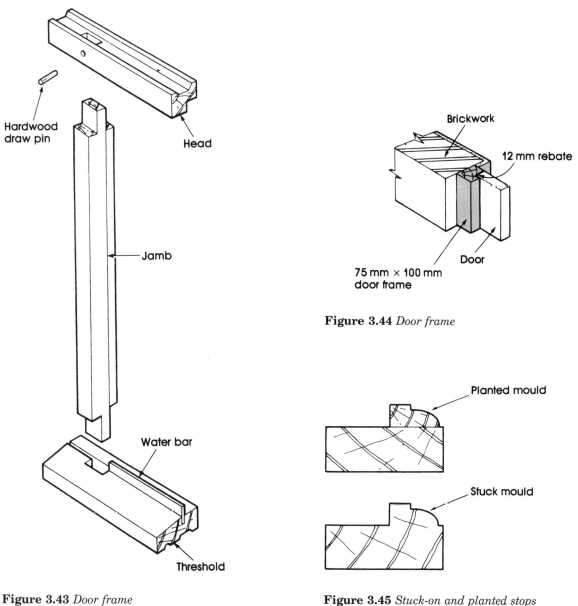

Figure 3.43 *Door frame*

Figure 3.44 *Door frame*

Figure 3.45 *Stuck-on and planted stops*

Door lining – the surround on which mainly internal doors are hung, normally of a thinner section than door frames and often have planted stops. The main difference between door frames and door linings is that linings cover the full width of the reveal in which they are fixed from wall surface to wall surface whereas frames do not (Figure 3.46).

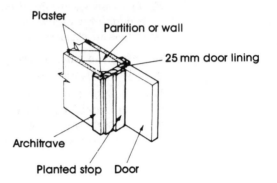

Figure 3.46 *Door lining*

Window frame – the part of a window that is fixed into the wall opening and receives the casements or sashes.

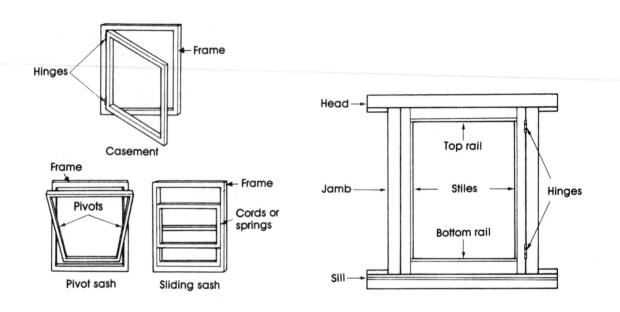
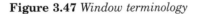

Figure 3.47 *Window terminology*

Frames

Frames can be either 'built in' or 'fixed in'.

'*Built-in*' *frames* are fixed into a wall or other element by bedding in mortar and surrounded with the walling components.

'*Fixed-in*' *frames* are inserted into a ready formed opening after the main building process.

'Built-in' frames – the majority of frames are 'built-in' by the brick-layer as the brickwork proceeds. Prior to this the frame has to be accurately positioned, plumbed, levelled and temporary strutted by the carpenter. Door frames are normally built into the brickwork as the work proceeds. Temporary struts are used to hold the frame upright. The foot of the door frame jambs, in the absence of a threshold, are held in position by galvanised metal dowels which are drilled into the end of the jambs and are grouted into the concrete. This is shown in Figure 3.48. Temporary braces and distance pieces are fixed to the frame, in order to keep it square and the jambs parallel during the 'building-in' process. The vertical positioning of external door and window frames can be achieved with the use of a storey rod shown in Figure 2.26.

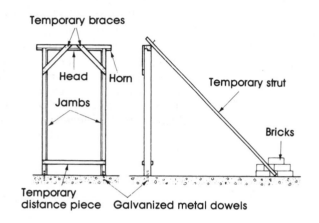

Figure 3.48 *'Building in' a frame*

A frame's head should be checked for level, and packed up as required; frames with thresholds are normally bedded level using bricklayer's mortar (see Figure 3.49).

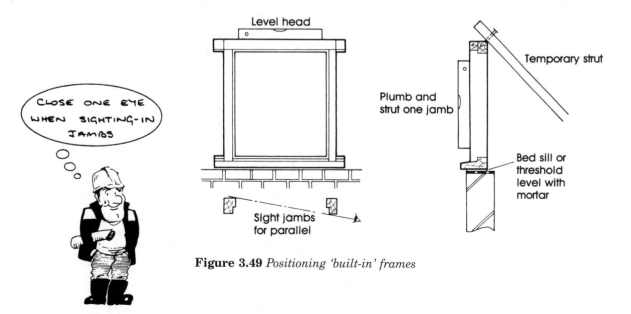

Figure 3.49 *Positioning 'built-in' frames*

Figure 3.50 *Attaching frame cramps*

Jambs should be plumbed from the face. It is standard practice to plumb and fix the first using a spirit level. The other is then sighted parallel: stand to the side of the frame, close one eye, sight the edge of the plumbed jamb with the edge of the other and adjust if required until both jambs are parallel.

As the brickwork proceeds galvanised metal frame cramps, as shown in Figure 3.50, should be screwed to the back of the jambs and built into the brickwork. Three or four cramps should be evenly spaced up each jamb.

The horns of the frame should be cut back as shown before 'building in', rather than cut off flush (see Figure 3.51). The horns will then help to fix the frame in position. After trimming the horns it is essential that the cut ends are treated with preservative in order to reduce the possibility of timber rot. This can be carried out by applying two brush flood coats of preservative.

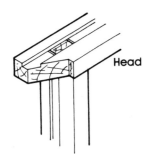

Figure 3.51 *Horn cut back ready for 'building in'*

Storey height frames may be used for internal door openings in thin blockwork partitions (Figure 3.52). The jambs and head which make up the frame are grooved out on their back face to receive the building blocks. The storey frame should be fixed in position, at the bottom to the wall plate and at the top of the joists, before the blocks are built up (see Figure 3.53). The jambs above the head are cut back to finish flush with the blockwork. As with other frames one jamb should be fixed plumb and the other sighted to it.

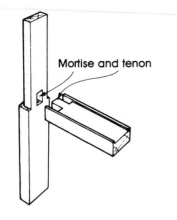

Figure 3.52 *Joint detail (storey height frame)*

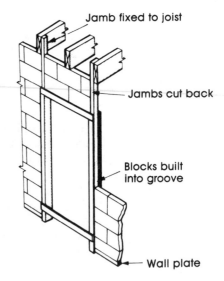

Figure 3.53 *'Building in' a storey height frame*

'Fixed-in' frames – are sometimes fixed to prepared openings. This applies mainly to expensive hardwood frames and is to protect them from possible damage or discoloration during the building process. In addition, frames that were not available during the building process or replacement frames will have to be 'fixed in'.

Horns on 'fixed-in' frames are not required as a fixing and should be sawn off flush with the back of the jambs. Remember to preservative treat the cut ends.

Place the frame in the prepared opening, temporarily holding it in position with the aid of folding wedges (Figure 3.54). Check the head or sill for level and adjust the wedges as required.

Plumb one jamb and 'sight in' the other; adjust the wedges if required.

Figure 3.55 shows how to fix the frame to the wall either by:

Nailing using cut nails into the blockwork or brickwork mortar joints or masonry nails into the actual brick.

Screwing plastic plugs and screws through the jamb. Screwheads in softwood frames may be countersunk below the surface and filled. Screwheads in hardwood frames should be concealed by counter boring and pelleting.

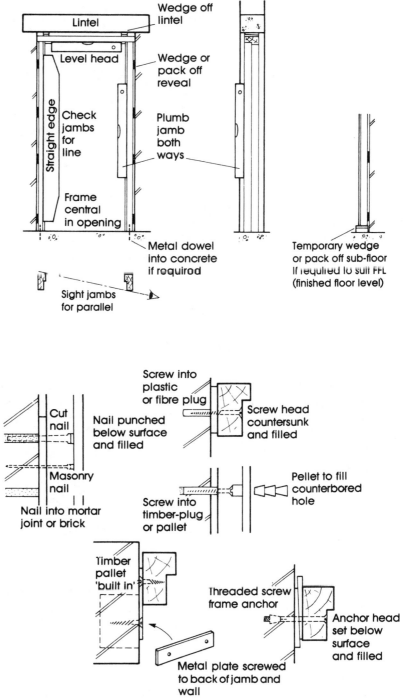

Figure 3.54 *Positioning 'fixed-in' frames*

Figure 3.55 *Methods of fixing*

Metal plates used as fixing lugs screwed at intervals to the back of jamb before the frame is put in the opening. The lugs are screwed and plugged to the brick or block reveals.

Frame anchors – proprietary fixing consisting of a metal or plastic sleeve and matching screw. The jamb and reveal are drilled out to suit the sleeve, which is inserted in position and screwed up tight.

Linings

Plain linings – (Figures 3.56 and 3.57) consist of two plain jambs and a plain head joined together using a bare-faced tongue and housing. The pinned stop is fixed around the lining after the door has been hung.

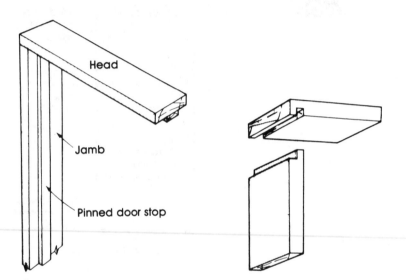

Head

Jamb

Pinned door stop

Figure 3.56 *Plain lining*   **Figure 3.57** *Joint detail (plain lining)*

Rebated linings – (Figures 3.58 and 3.59) are used for better quality work. They consist of two rebated jambs and a rebated head. The rebate must be the correct width so that when the door is hung it finishes flush with the edges of the lining.

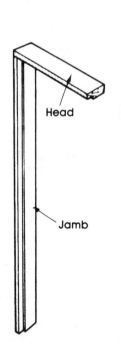

Head

Jamb

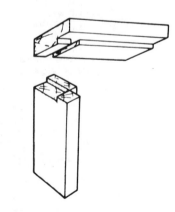

Figure 3.58 *Rebated lining*   **Figure 3.59** *Joint detail (rebated lining)*

Fixing linings

The opening in the wall to receive the lining is normally formed while the wall is being built and the lining is fixed at a later stage.

Fixings may be:

- *Nailing to twisted wooden plugs* (see sequence of operations)
- *Nailing and screwing to timber pallets* that have been built into the brick joints by the bricklayer, or into the door stud of a stud partition. Folding wedges are used as packings down the sides of the jambs.
- *Nailing directly into the blockwork reveal* or brickwork mortar joint. Folding wedges will be required as packing.
- *Using plugs and screws* or other proprietary fixing.

Sequence of operations to fix a lining (using twisted timber plugs) as shown in Figure 3.60:

1) Assemble lining. This is normally done by skew nailing through the head into the jambs.
2) Fix a distance piece near the bottom of the jambs, as in Figure 3.60, and when required, diagonal braces at the head.
3) Rake out brickwork joints and plug (see Figure 3.61). There should be at least four fixing points per jamb. Omit this stage if the bricklayer has 'built in' wooden pallets or pads into the brickwork.
4) Offer lining into opening and mark where the plugs need to be trimmed. The plugs should project equally from both reveals.
5) Cut the plugs and check the distance with a width rod. The ends of the plugs should be in vertical alignment. Check with a straight edge and spirit level.

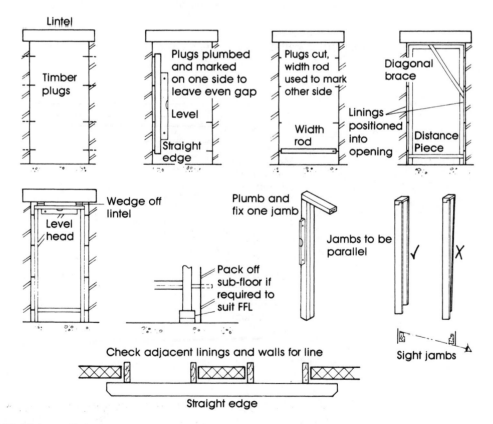

Figure 3.60 *Fixing a lining*

6) Fix lining plumb and central in the opening by nailing or screwing through the jambs into the plugs. Before finally fixing check head for level, wedge off lintel, ensure the lining is out of wind: check by sighting through the jambs. When fixing to unplastered walls, check adjacent linings and wall surfaces are lined up.

7) Ensure lining jambs are packed up off a concrete sub floor if required to suit the finished floor level (FFL).

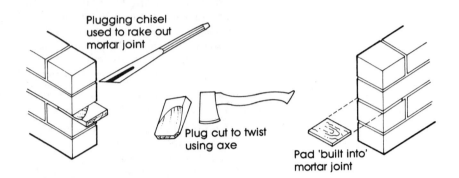

Figure 3.61 *Plugs or pads used for fixing lining*

Datums

Internal datum – datum positions or lines are often marked around the walls inside a building, particularly in large areas. They should be indicated thus ⊼. The datum line, shown in Figure 3.62, is established at a convenient height, say 1 m above finished floor level (FFL). From this level the position of other building components and finishes can be measured up or down; for example, the heights of floor screed, suspended ceilings, door heads and wall panelling, etc.

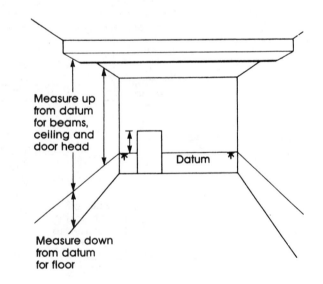

Figure 3.62 *Datum line*

To establish the datum line, transfer a level position to each corner of the room using either a water level, as shown in Figure 3.63, or a straight edge and spirit level.

Having established the corner positions, stretch a chalk line between each two marks in turn and spring it in the middle, leaving a horizontal chalk dust line on the wall.

Before using a water level it must be prepared by filling it from one end with water, taking care not to trap air bubbles. Check by holding up the two glass tubes side by side: the levels of the water should settle to the same height.

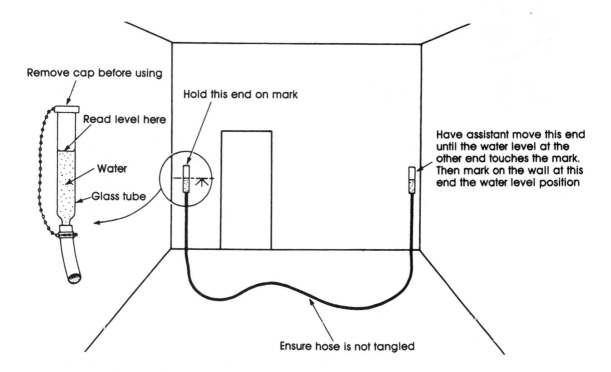

Figure 3.63 *Using a water level to establish datum line*

READ THE INSTRUCTIONS AND COMPLETE THE TASK

--- **Learning task** ---

Refer to the floor plans, range drawing and schedules shown in Figures 4.25 and 4.26.

Determine in metres run the amount of 38 mm × 125 mm and 38 mm × 100 mm required to construct the door linings. Use 10% for a cutting allowance.

_____

_____

_____

_____

_____

_____

Questions for you

23. Produce a sketch to show the difference between a door frame and a door lining.

24. Explain the difference between 'built-in' and 'fixed-in' frames and state an occasion where **EACH** might be used.

_____

_____

_____

_____

25. Explain the reason why a steel dowel may be included in the base or foot of newel post and door frame jambs.

_____

26. State the reason why the sawn ends of timber are treated with preservative.

_____

_____

27. Explain how to 'sight in' the jambs of a frame.

_____

_____

28. Explain the purpose of a datum.

_____

_____

29. List **THREE** forms of fixing that can be used to secure frames or linings.

_____

_____

_____

Encasing services

Encasing terminology

Encasing – the casing or boxing in of services. The term casing or boxing, refers to the framework, cladding and trim used to form an enclosure in which service pipes are housed.

Service pipes – the system of pipes for either gas, water or drainage. These are normally fixed within, or on the surface of floors and walls.

Service pipework is cased or boxed in to conceal the pipes thus providing a neat, tidy appearance, which when decorated blends with the main room decoration. In addition they must also provide access to stop valves (stop cocks), drain down valves and cleaning or rodding points.

Encasing guidelines

In many situations encasing services is a simple process of forming an L- or U-shaped box from timber battens, covered with a plywood or hard-board facing (see Figures 3.64 to 3.66). Consider the following simple rules when planning and fixing casings.

● Use standard sections of timber where possible.
● Where casing is to be tiled, ensure the dimensions are simple widths of whole or half tiles.
● Note any stop valve or other fitting which may require access. Fit a separate length of facing board over this section.
● Use WBP (weather and boil proof) plywood or an oil-tempered hard board for casings in wet areas, e.g. kitchens, bathrooms and laundries, etc.

Battens, typically 32 mm × 32 mm may be fixed to the wall using plugs and screws or nails, cut or masonry, depending on the wall hardness.

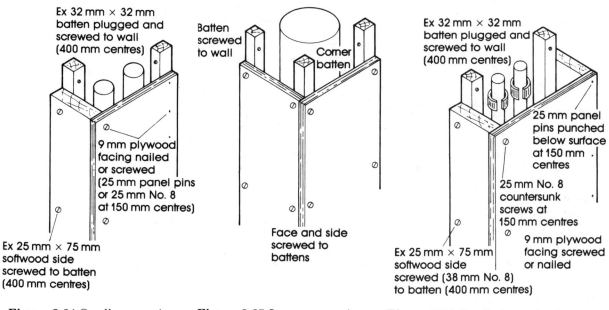

Figure 3.64 *Small corner pipe casing*

Figure 3.65 *Large corner pipe casing*

Figure 3.66 *Small pipe casing in run of wall*

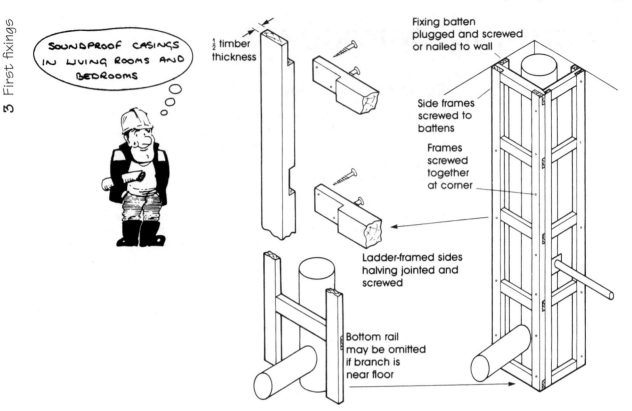

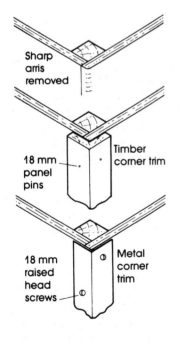

Figure 3.67 *Use of ladder frame for pipe casing*

When using 6 mm plywood or 6 mm hardboard, timber ladder frames (see Figure 5.67) are required for support. These are typically 25 mm × 50 mm softwood half lapped together. 9 mm and 12 mm plywood can be used for casing sides direct to battens without a supporting framework. Plywood facing can be nailed or screwed to battens/frames.

Access panels can be screwed in position using brass cups and screws typically 25 mm No. 8. Alternatively they may be hinged as a small door.

Casings have to be scribed to wall surfaces and finished more neatly if they are to be painted or papered rather than tiled. All nails and screws should be punched or sunk below the surface ready for subsequent filling by the painter. The sharp corner arris needs to be removed with glass paper or, as an alternative, may be covered with a timber, metal or plastic trim, as shown in Figure 3.68.

Where casings are located in living rooms or bedrooms they can be packed out with fibreglass, mineral wool or polystyrene in order to quieten the noise of water passing through.

L-shaped casings – are used for pipes in a corner.

● Mark plumb lines on walls. (Use a spirit level and straight-edge, as shown in Figure 3.69.)
● Fix battens to the marked lines.
● Fix the side to the batten.
● Fix the front facing to the side and batten.

or

● Make up and fix a ladder frame and fix the facings.

Figure 3.68 *Alternative corner treatments*

U-shaped casings – are used for pipes in the middle of a wall.

- Mark plumb lines on the wall.
- Fix battens to the marked lines.
- Fix the sides to the battens.
- Fix the front to the sides.

Where pipes branch off the main one, the side will require notching or scribing over them.

For small pipes simply mark the side, drill a hole and saw the side to form a notch as shown in Figure 3.70.

Larger branch pipes are best scribed around with the face split on the pipe's centre line as shown in Figure 3.71.

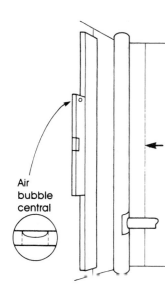

Air bubble central

Figure 3.69 *Marking plumb line on wall*

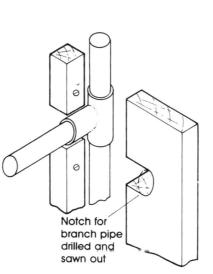

Notch for branch pipe drilled and sawn out

Figure 3.70 *Cutting around small branch pipe*

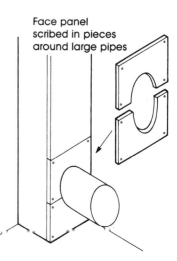

Face panel scribed in pieces around large pipes

Figure 3.71 *Cutting around large branch pipe*

Uneven wall surfaces – Sides and faces that fit to an uneven wall surface will require scribing as shown in Figures 3.72 to 3.74.

- Position the side against the wall, place a pencil on the wall surface and move it down to mark a parallel line on the side. Plane to the line, slightly undercutting to ensure a tight fit.
- Cut the ply face oversize (say, 15 mm over required width).
- Position the face against the wall.
- Temporarily nail the face in position, keeping the overhang on the side the same distance from top to bottom.
- Set a compass or gauge slip to the width of overhang. Mark a parallel line on the face.
- Plane or saw to this line, slightly undercutting to ensure a tight fit.

Access panels – the edges of access panels are often chamfered as shown in Figure 3.75. This breaks the straight joint and permits a better paint finish. In addition, removal of the panel is eased without risk of damage. Simply remove screws, run a trimming knife along chamfered joints to cut paint film and lift off panel. Alternatively, access panels may be hinged into a lining and finished with an architrave trim as shown in Figure 3.76.

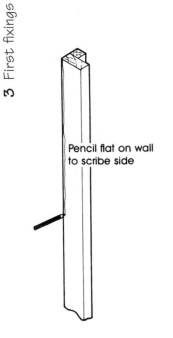

Pencil flat on wall to scribe side

Figure 3.72 *Scribing to wall with pencil*

Undercut scribed edge to ensure a tight fit

Figure 3.73 *Undercutting scribes*

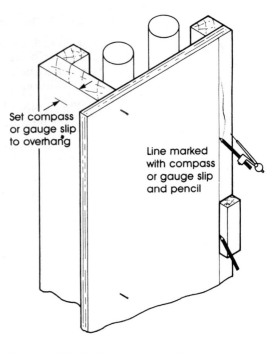

Set compass or gauge slip to overhang

Line marked with compass or gauge slip and pencil

Figure 3.74 *Scribing to wall using compass or gauge slip*

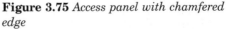
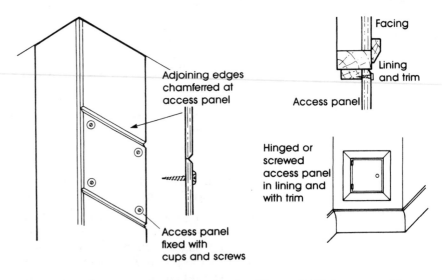

Adjoining edges chamferred at access panel

Facing

Lining and trim

Access panel

Access panel fixed with cups and screws

Hinged or screwed access panel in lining and with trim

Figure 3.75 *Access panel with chamfered edge*

Figure 3.76 *Access panel in lining*

Horizontal pipe casings – are mainly at skirting level. They can be formed using the same construction as vertical casings (Figure 3.77). Alternatively, they can be formed using a skirting board fixed to a timber top as shown in Figure 3.78.

Taller horizontal casings may have their top extended over the front facing in order to form a useful shelf (Figure 3.79).

● Mark a level line on the wall. (Use a spirit level and straight edge.)
● Mark a straight line on the floor.
● Fix battens to the marked lines.
● Fix the top and front facing.

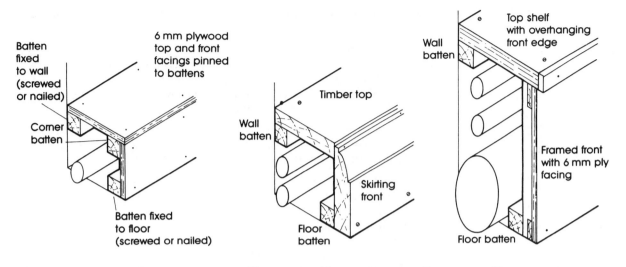

Figure 3.77 *Horizontal pipe casing*

Figure 3.78 *Skirting pipe casing*

Figure 3.79 *Shelf top to horizontal pipe casing*

Bath front casings

These are termed bath panels. They can be either a standard, normally plastic, set or purpose made.

Standard panels – normally simply fit up under the bath rim and are fixed along their bottom edge to a floor batten as shown in Figure 3.80. Read the specific instructions supplied with the panel for details.

Purpose-made panels – have to be fixed (nailed or screwed) to a batten framework as shown in Figure 3.81. This is typically made from ex 25 mm × 50 mm PAR softwood, halved and screwed together.

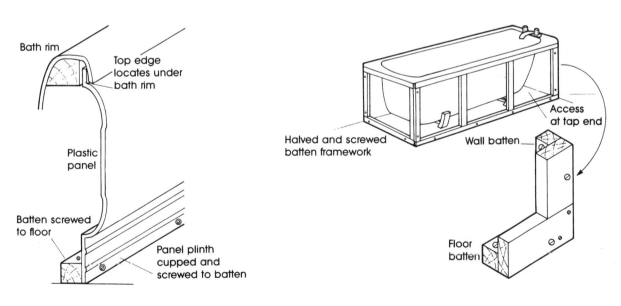

Figure 3.80 *Fixing standard bath panel*

Figure 3.81 *Batten framework for a bath panel*

The panels can be formed from a variety of materials. For example,

- 9 mm plywood covered with tiles
- 9 mm plywood covered with carpet
- 9 mm veneered plywood with applied mouldings to create a traditional panelled effect
- Matchboarding, TG & V (tongued, grooved and vee jointed)
- 3 mm melamine-faced hardboard

An access panel is often formed at the tap end of the bath for maintenance purposes, rather than removing the whole panel. Figure 3.82 shows how this may be screwed in position or hinged on.

- Ensure the batten framework is set back far enough under the bath rim to allow for the panel thickness (see Figure 3.83).
- Mark plumb lines on the walls.
- Mark a straight line on the floor.
- Fix wall and floor battens to the marked lines.
- Make and fix the battened framework.
- Fix the panel to the framework.

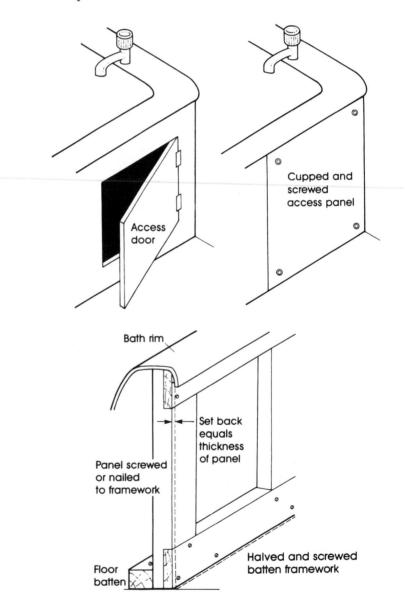

Figure 3.82 *Bath access panels*

Figure 3.83 *Positioning batten framework*

TRY TO ANSWER THESE

Questions for you

30. State the reason why WBP plywood is used for casings in wet areas.

_____

_____

31. State the reason why pipe casings located in living rooms or bedrooms may be packed out with fibre glass or mineral wool.

_____

_____

32. State why a removable access trap may be included in pipe casings.

_____

33. State the purpose of encasing services.

_____

_____

34. Explain why a supporting framework is required when using thin sheet material for pipework casings.

_____

_____

WELL, HOW DID YOU DO?

WORK THROUGH THE SECTION AGAIN IF YOU HAD ANY PROBLEMS

WORD-SQUARE SEARCH

Hidden in the word square are the following 20 words associated with *'Encasing Services'*. You may find the words written forwards, backwards, up, down or diagonally.

Bath	Plywood
Panel	Access
Services	Skirting
Pipe	Softwood
Batten	Halving
Insulation	Plumb
Boxing	Level
Casing	Gauge slip
Scribe	Compass
Notching	Branch pipe

Draw a ring around the words, or line in using a highlight pen thus:

(EXAMPLE)

EXAMPLE

B	R	A	N	C	H	P	I	P	E	D	L	B	F	B	A	C	S
R	U	C	P	L	I	T	H	E	A	D	S	A	R	O	W	O	E
O	R	C	S	L	L	M	F	D	N	D	H	T	M	X	P	P	R
P	I	E	L	L	E	V	E	L	L	E	P	T	B	I	E	O	V
R	A	S	D	O	Y	A	N	E	T	P	C	E	O	N	H	R	I
I	U	S	L	P	L	U	M	B	G	I	C	N	L	G	E	T	C
E	A	N	O	E	P	A	K	U	O	P	D	N	A	I	L	T	E
T	L	W	V	P	A	N	E	L	G	L	S	E	B	I	R	C	S
F	I	T	O	S	U	S	Y	A	I	P	O	R	T	A	E	E	S
P	A	C	O	H	C	P	R	T	R	E	S	T	S	E	D	D	G
I	R	G	R	T	H	O	G	I	D	L	G	O	S	I	O	N	N
L	D	N	E	A	E	G	T	O	S	N	A	E	A	O	O	E	I
S	R	I	P	B	N	D	O	N	I	S	D	B	P	N	W	P	V
E	A	T	V	I	U	W	T	H	M	E	R	O	M	C	Y	E	L
G	U	R	C	O	T	P	C	E	R	S	I	A	O	I	L	D	A
U	G	I	T	F	E	T	E	G	N	I	S	A	C	D	P	N	H
A	R	K	O	A	O	B	M	L	A	D	E	D	E	R	S	I	E
G	S	S	B	N	A	R	I	N	S	U	L	A	T	I	O	N	L

WORD PUZZLE

Solve the clues to complete the word puzzle. All the answers are associated with 'First Fixings'. The number of letters in each word is shown in brackets e.g. (6) indicates a six-letter word and (4, 3) indicates two words having four and three letters each.

Across

2. Regularised studs have a ———— width (10)
5. Timber-framed internal wall (4, 9)
6. Lining around stairwell (5)
8. Horizontal measurement of a stair (5)
10. Vertical member fixed at end of string (5)
11. Member cut to fit (7)
12. Used to fill a gap (8)

Down

1. Can be used to help fix a frame (5)
2. Trim to length (3)
3. Stair member that is cut over trimmer (6)
4. Cut to length (4)
5. Provides floor to floor access (6)
7. Not a frame (6)
9. Vertical (5)

4 Second fixings and finishings

In undertaking this chapter you will be required to demonstrate your skill and knowledge of the following second fixing components:

- Doors and ironmongery
- Finishing trim (horizontal and vertical mouldings)
- Kitchen units
- Panelling and cladding.

You will be required practically to:

- Hang an external door
- Position and fix mortise lock and letter plate
- Position and fix architraves, skirting and dado rail
- Position and fix floor units, wall units and pre-laminated work top
- Position and fix grounds and vertical matchboard panelling.

Doors

Doors may be classified by their method of construction: panelled, glazed, matchboarded, flush, fire resistant, etc. (Figure 4.1), and by their method of operation: swinging, sliding and folding.

Methods of construction

Panelled doors – have a frame made from solid timber rails and stiles, which are jointed using either dowels or mortise and tenon joints. The frame is either grooved or rebated to receive two or more thin plywood or timber panels. Interior doors are thinner than exterior doors.

Glazed doors – are used where more light is required. They are made similar to panelled doors except glass replaces one or more of the plywood or timber panels. Glazing bead is used to secure the glass into its glazing rebates. Glazing bars may be used to divide large glazed areas.

Matchboarded doors – are used mainly externally for gates, sheds and industrial buildings. They are simply constructed from matchboarding, ledges and braces clench nailed together. The bottom end of the braces must always point towards the hanging edge of the door to provide the required support. Framed matchboarded doors constructed with the addition of stiles and rails are used where extra strength is required.

Flush doors – are made with outer faces of plywood or hardboard. Internal doors are normally lightweight having a hollow core, solid timber edges and blocks which are used to reinforce hinge and lock positions. New flush doors will have one edge marked 'LOCK' and the other 'HINGE'; these must be followed. External and fire resistant flush doors are much heavier, as normally they have a solid core of either timber strips or chipboard.

READ THIS CHAPTER, WORKING THROUGH THE QUESTIONS AND LEARNING TASKS

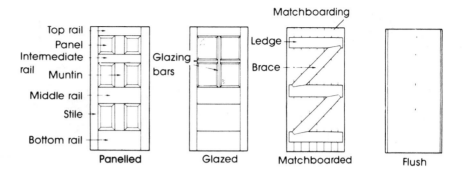

Figure 4.1 *Doors*

Fire resisting doors – The main function of this type of door is to act as a barrier to a possible fire by providing the same degree of protection as the element in which it is located. They should prevent the passage of smoke, hot gases and flames for a specified period of time. This period of time will vary depending on the relevant statutory regulations and the location of the door.

The fire resistance of a building element and thus the performance of a fire resisting door can be defined by reference to the following criteria:

- Stability: resistance to the collapse of the door
- Integrity: resistance to the passage of flames or hot gases to the unexposed face
- Insulation: resistance to the excessive rise in temperature of the unexposed face

All fire doors can be called 'fire resisting doors', although they should be prefixed by their stability and integrity rating respectively. Thus a 60/45 fire resisting door has a minimum 60 minutes stability rating and a 45 minutes integrity rating.

The more commonly used terms for fire doors are 'fire check' and 'fire resisting'. 'Fire check' is used to signify doors with a reduced integrity.

Table 4.1 *Requirements of fire doors*

Door type	Stability (mins)	Integrity (mins)
Half hour fire check	30	20
Half hour fire resisting	30	30
One hour fire check	60	45
One hour fire resisting	60	60

The weak point in fire door construction is the joint between the door and frame. This is where the fire and smoke will penetrate first. Intumescent strips, shown in Figure 4.2, may be fitted around the door opening: when activated by heat in the early stages of a fire these strips expand, sealing the joint and prolonging the door's integrity.

REFER TO THE BUILDING REGULATIONS FOR FIRE DOOR REQUIREMENTS

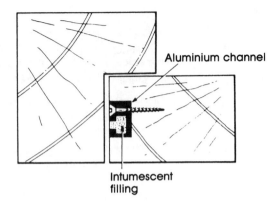

Figure 4.2 *Intumescent seal*

Door sizes

All mass produced doors may be purchased from a supplier in a range of standard sizes as shown in Figures 4.3 and 4.4. Special sizes or purpose-made designs are normally available to order from suppliers with joinery shop contacts.

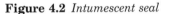

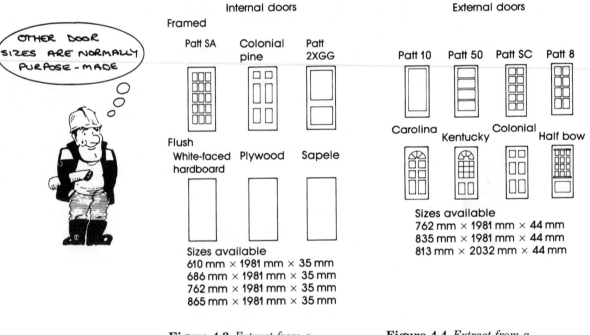

Figure 4.3 *Extract from a manufacturer's door list showing range of stock size internal doors*

Figure 4.4 *Extract from a manufacturer's door list showing range of stock size external doors*

Methods of operation

Swinging doors – Side hung on hinges is the most common means of door operation. It is also the most suitable for pedestrian use and the most effective for weather protection, fire resistance, sound and thermal insulation. See Figure 4.5.

Sliding doors – are mainly used either to economise on space where it is not possible to swing a door, or for large openings which would be difficult to close off with swinging doors.

Folding doors – are a combination of swinging and sliding doors. They can be used as either movable internal partitions to divide up large rooms, or alternatively as doors for large warehouses and show-room entrances.

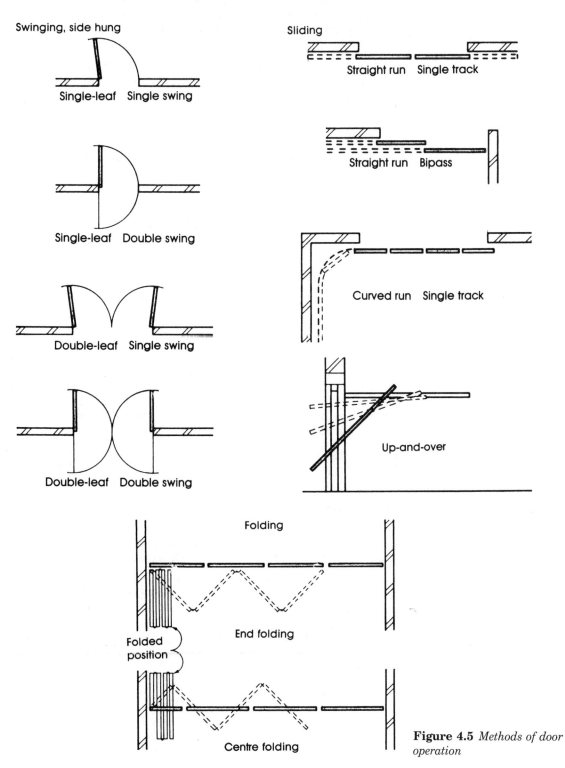

Figure 4.5 *Methods of door operation*

Door ironmongery

Door ironmongery is also termed door furniture and includes hinges, locks, latches, bolts, other security devices, handles and letter or postal plates. The hand of a door is required in order to select the correct items of ironmongery. Some locks and latches have reversible bolts, enabling either hand to be adapted to suit the situation.

View the door from the hinge knuckle side; if the knuckles are on the left the door is left handed, whereas if the knuckles are on the right, the door is right handed. Figure 4.6 shows how doors may also be defined as either clockwise or anticlockwise closing.

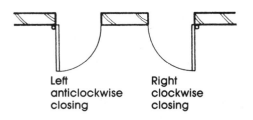

Figure 4.6 *Typical handing diagram*

Hinges

Hinges are available in a variety of materials: pressed steel is commonly used for internal doors and brass for hardwood and external doors. Do not use steel hinges on hardwood or external doors because of rusting and subsequent staining problems. Do not use nylon, plastic or aluminium hinges on fire-resistant doors because they melt at fairly low temperatures.

Butt hinge – is a general purpose hinge suitable for most applications. As a general rule the leaf with the greatest number of knuckles is fixed to the door frame.

Washered butt hinges – are used for heavier doors, to reduce knuckle wear and prevent squeaking.

Parliament hinges – have wide leaves to extend knuckles and enable doors to fold back against the wall clearing deep architraves, etc.

Rising butts – are designed to lift the door as it opens to clear obstructions such as mats and rugs. They also give a door some degree of self-closing action. In order to prevent the top edge of the door fouling in the frame as it opens and closes, the top edge must be eased as shown in Figure 4.7. The hand of the door must be stated when ordering this item, as they cannot be reversed (i.e. they cannot be altered to suit either hand of door).

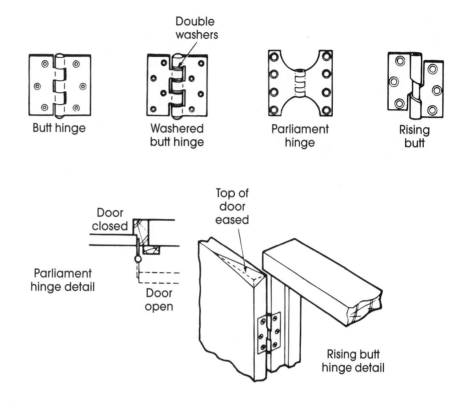

Figure 4.7 *Range of hinges*

Locks and latches

Cylinder rim latches – are mainly used for entrance doors to domestic property but, as they are only a latch, provide little security on their own (Figure 4.8). When fitted, the door can be opened from the outside with the use of a key and from the inside by turning the handle. Some types have a double locking facility that improves their security.

Mortise deadlock – provides a straightforward key-operated locking action and is often used to provide additional security on entrance doors where cylinder rim latches are fitted (Figure 4.9). They are also used on doors where simple security is required, e.g. storerooms.

Mortise latch – is used mainly for internal doors that do not require locking (Figure 4.10). The latch that holds the door in the closed position can be operated from either side of the door by turning the handle.

Mortise lock/latch – is available in the two types shown in Figure 4.11. The horizontal one is little used nowadays because of its length, which means that it can only be fitted to substantial doors. The vertical type is more modern and can be fitted to most types of doors. It is often known as a narrow-stile lock/latch. Both types can be used for a wide range of general purpose doors in various locations. They are, in essence, a combination of the mortise deadlock and the mortise latch.

Rebated mortise lock/latch – should be used when fixing a lock/latch in double doors that have rebated stiles. The front end of this lock is cranked to fit the rebate on the stiles (see Figure 4.12).

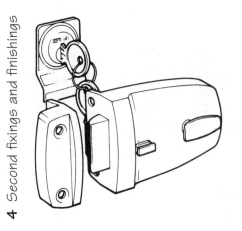

Figure 4.8 *Cylinder rim latch*

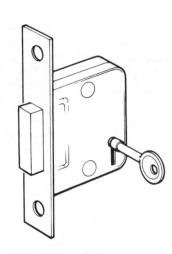

Figure 4.9 *Mortise deadlock*

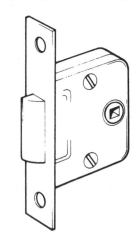

Figure 4.10 *Mortise latch*

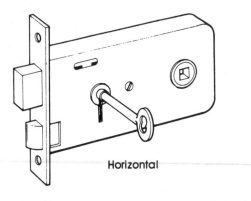

Horizontal

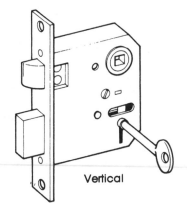

Vertical

Figure 4.11 *Mortise lock/latches*

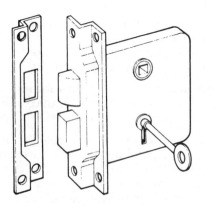

Figure 4.12 *Rebated mortise lock/latch*

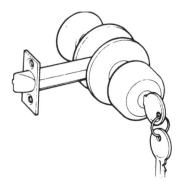

Figure 4.13 *Knobset*

Knobset – consists of a small mortise latch and a pair of knob handles that can be locked with a key, so that it can be used as a lock/latch in most situations both internally and externally (Figure 4.13). Knobsets can also be obtained without the lock in the knob for use as a latch only.

Knob furniture – is for use with the horizontal mortise lock/latch (Figure 4.14). It should not be used with the vertical type as hand injuries will result.

Keyhole escutcheon plates – are used to provide a neat finish to the keyhole of both deadlocks and horizontal mortise lock/latches (Figure 4.15).

Lever furniture – is available in a wide range of patterns, for use with the mortise latches and mortise lock/latches (Figure 4.16).

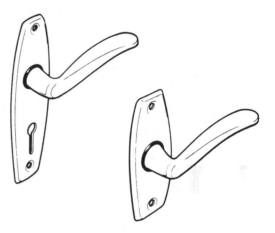

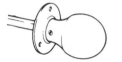

Figure 4.14 *Knob furniture*   **Figure 4.15** *Escutcheon plate*   **Figure 4.16** *Lever furniture*

Barrel bolts – are used on external doors and gates to lock them from the inside (Figure 4.17). Two bolts are normally used, one at the top of the door and the other at the bottom.

Flush bolt – is flush fitting and therefore requires recessing into the timber (see Figure 4.18). It is used for better quality work on the inside of external doors to provide additional security and also on double doors and French windows to bolt one door in the closed position. Two bolts are normally used, one at the top of the door and the other at the bottom.

Security chains – can be fixed on front entrance doors, the slide to the door and the chain to the frame (Figure 4.19). When the chain is inserted into the slide, the door will only open a limited amount until the identity of the caller is checked.

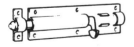

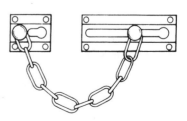

Figure 4.17 *Barrel bolt*   **Figure 4.18** *Flush bolt*   **Figure 4.19** *Security chain*

Ironmongery positioning

Hinge positions – are shown in Figures 4.20 and 4.21. Lightweight internal doors are normally hung on one pair of 75 mm hinges; glazed, half-hour fire resistant and other heavy doors need one pair of 100 mm hinges. All external doors and one-hour fire resistant doors need one and a half pairs of 100 mm hinges. The standard hinge positions for flush doors are 150 mm down from the top, 225 mm up from the bottom and the third hinge where required, positioned centrally. On panelled and glazed doors the hinges are often fixed in line with the rails to produce a more balanced look.

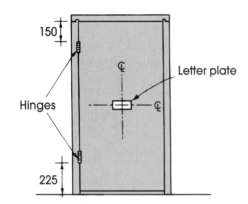

Figure 4.20 *Position of hinges and letter plate*

Figure 4.21 *Position of hinges on glazed doors*

Other furniture positions – will depend on the type of door construction, the specification and the door manufacturer's instructions.

The standard position for mortise locks and latches, shown in Figure 4.22, is 990 mm from the bottom of the door to the centre line of the lever or knob furniture spindle. However, on a panelled door with a middle rail, locks/latches may be positioned centrally in the rail's width. Cylinder rim latches are positioned in the door's style between 1200 mm and 1500 mm from the bottom of the door and the centre line of the cylinder. Before fitting any locks/latches the width of the door stile should be measured to ensure the lock/latch length is shorter than the stile's width, otherwise a narrow stile lock may be required. Letter plates

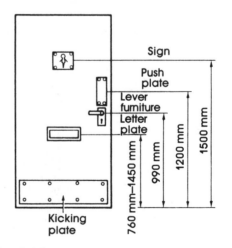

Figure 4.22 *Fixing heights*

are normally positioned centrally in a door's width and between 760 mm and 1450 mm from the bottom of the door to the centre line of the plate. Again on panelled doors letter plates may be positioned centrally in a rail and sometimes even vertically in a stile.

Always read the job specification as exact furniture positions may be stated.

Always read both the door manufacturer's instructions and the ironmongery manufacturer's instructions to ensure the intended position is suitable to receive the item, e.g. the positioning of the lock block on a flush door, and the item is fixed correctly. See Figure 4.23.

READ AND FOLLOW MANUFACTURER'S INSTRUCTIONS TO ENSURE IRONMONGERY IS FIXED CORRECTLY

Fixing Instructions

1. At the desired height drill a 15mm ($^{19}/_{32}$″) diameter spindle hole at a distance of 44mm (1$^3/_4$″) from the edge of the door. 57mm (2$^1/_4$″) for 3″.
2. At the position of the key hole cut away a section to suit, in line with the spindle hole.
3. Mortice door for lock case and forend.
4. Remove upper forend by removing small lug screws.
5. Fit mortice lock and secure with screws provided.
6. Replace upper forend. Align striking plate with lock and mortice frame to suit.
7. Fix striking plate with two wood screws.

NOTE:
The bolt is reversible. Simply remove lock case, remove latch mechanism, reverse and replace.

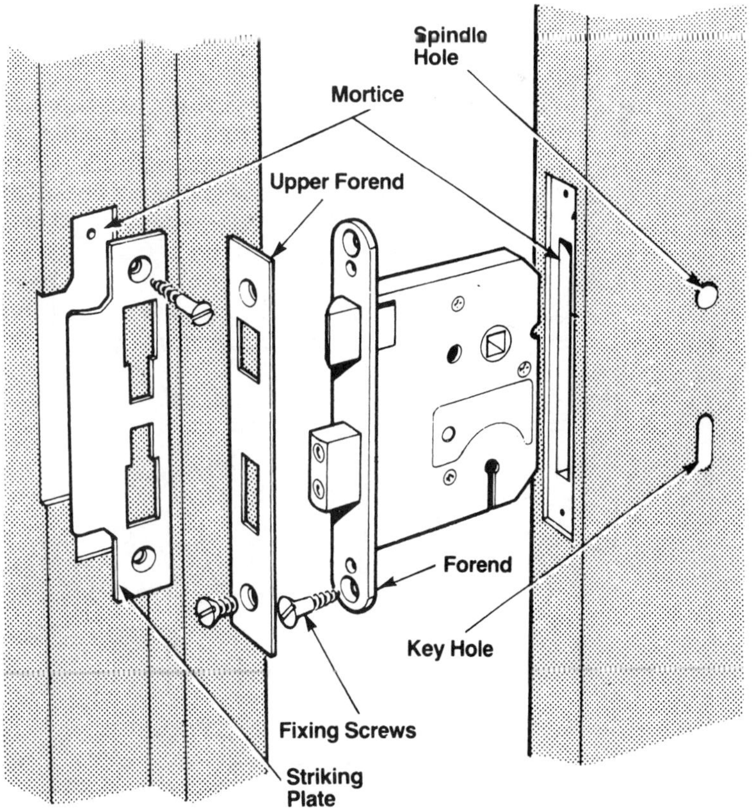

Figure 4.23 *Typical manufacturer's fixing instructions*

153

Door and ironmongery schedules

Schedules are used to record repetitive design information. Read with a range drawing and floor plans, they may be used to identify a type of door, its size, the number required, the door opening in which it fits, the hinges it will swing on and details of other furniture to be fitted to it. See Figures 4.24 to 4.26.

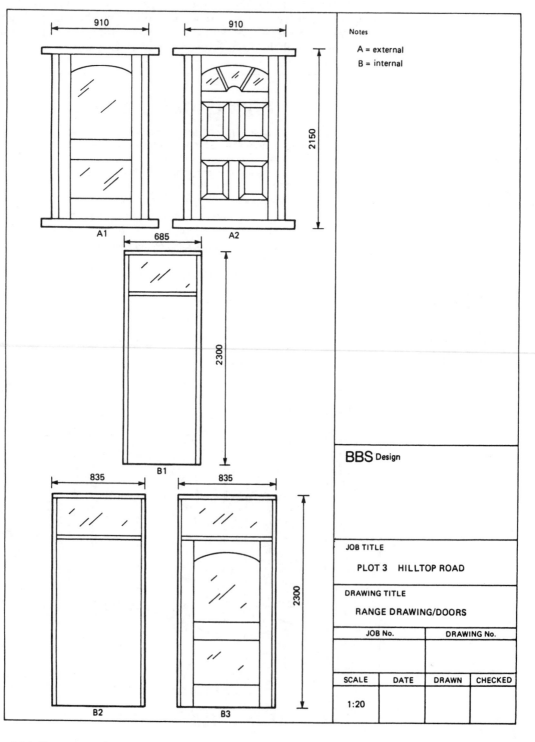

Figure 4.24 *Door range drawing*

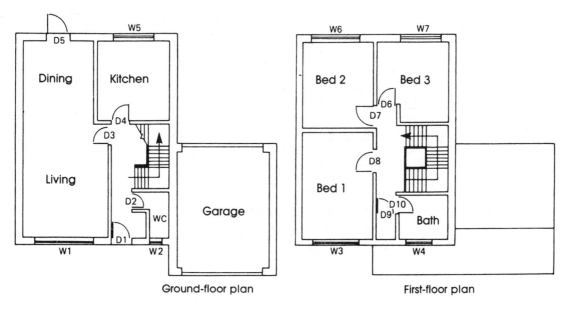

Figure 4.25 *Floor plans*

Description	D1	D2	D3	D4	D5	D6	D7	D8	D9	D10			NOTES
<u>Type (see range)</u>													
External glazed A1					●								
External panelled A2	●												
Internal flush B1									●				
Internal flush B2		●				●	●	●		●			
Internal glazed B3			●	●									
<u>Size</u>													
813 mm × 2032 mm × 44 mm	●				●								
762 mm × 1981 mm × 35 mm		●	●	●		●	●	●		●			
610 mm × 1981 mm × 35 mm									●				
<u>Material</u>													**BBS** DESIGN
Hardwood	●												
Softwood			●	●	●								
Plywood/polished		●											JOB TITLE PLOT 3 Hilltop Road
plywood/painted						●	●	●	●	●			DRAWING TITLE Door Schedule/doors
<u>Infill</u>													
6 mm tempered safety glass													JOB NO. / DRAWING NO.
clear			●	●	●								
obscured	●												SCALE / DATE / DRAWN / CHECKED

Figure 4.26a *Door schedules*

4 Second fixings and finishings

Description	D1	D2	D3	D4	D5	D6	D7	D8	D9	D10			NOTES
Frames													
75 mm × 100 mm (outward opening)					●								
75 mm × 100 mm (inward opening)	●												
Linings													
38 mm × 125 mm		●	●	●									
38 mm × 100 mm						●	●	●	●	●			
Shape													
Rebated stop	●				●								
Planted stop		●	●	●		●	●	●	●	●			
Transom		●	●	●		●	●	●	●				
Sill	●				●								BBS DESIGN
Material													
Hardwood	●												
Softwood		●	●	●	●	●	●	●	●	●			JOB TITLE PLOT 3 Hilltop Road
Fanlight infill													DRAWING TITLE Door Schedule/frames/lining
6 mm tempered safety glass													JOB NO. DRAWING NO.
clear													
obscured		●							●				
6 mm plywood								●					SCALE DATE DRAWN CHECKED

Description	D1	D2	D3	D4	D5	D6	D7	D8	D9	D10			NOTES
Hanging													
Pair 100 mm pressed steel butt hinges			●	●	●¹·⁵								
Pair 100 mm brass butt hinges	●¹·⁵												
Pair 75 mm pressed steel butt hinges						●	●	●	●¹·⁵	●			
Pair 75 mm brass butt hinges		●											
Fastening													
Rim night latch	●												
Mortise deadlock	●												
Mortise lock/latch		●		●					●				
Mortise latch			●	●		●	●	●	●				
100 mm brass bolts	●²				●²								BBS DESIGN
Miscellaneous													
Brass lock/latch furniture		●		●					●				
Brass latch furniture			●	●		●	●	●	●				JOB TITLE PLOT 3 Hilltop Road
Brass letterplate	●												DRAWING TITLE Ironmongery schedule/doors
Brass knocker	●												
Brass coat hook		●²								●²			JOB NO. DRAWING NO.
Brass escutcheon	●²												
													SCALE DATE DRAWN CHECKED

Figure 4.26b and c *Door schedules – continued*

Details relevant to a particular door opening are indicated in the schedules by a dot or cross, a figure is also included where more than one item is required. Extracting details from a schedule is called 'taking off'. The following information concerning the WC door D2 has been taken off the schedules:

> One polished plywood internal flush door type B2 762 mm × 1981 mm × 35 mm, hung on one pair of 75 mm brass butts and fitted with one mortise lock/latch, one brass mortise lock/latch furniture and two brass coat hooks.

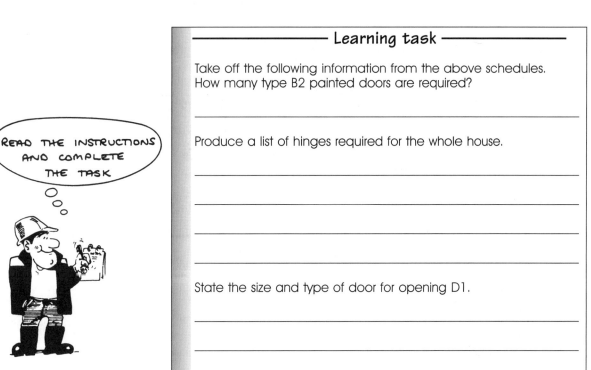

─────────────────── **Learning task** ───────────────────

Take off the following information from the above schedules. How many type B2 painted doors are required?

_____

Produce a list of hinges required for the whole house.

_____

_____

_____

_____

State the size and type of door for opening D1.

_____

_____

Door hanging

Door hanging is normally carried out before skirtings and architraves are fixed. Speed and confidence in door hanging can be achieved by following the procedure illustrated in Figure 4.27 and outlined below:

1) Measure height and width of door opening.
2) Locate and mark the top and hanging side of the opening and door.

Note: On flush and fire-check doors these should have been marked by the manufacturer. When the hanging side is not shown on the drawing, the door should open into the room to provide maximum privacy, but not onto a light switch.

3) Cut off the horns (protective extensions on the top and bottom of each stile) on panelled doors. Flush doors will probably have protective pieces of timber or plastic on each corner; these need to be prised off.
4) 'Shoot' (plane to fit) in the hanging stile of door to fit the hanging side of the opening. A leading edge will be required to prevent binding.
5) 'Shoot' the door to width. Allow a 2 mm joint all around between door and frame or lining. Many carpenters use a two penny coin to check. The closing side will require planing to a slight angle to allow it to close.

6) 'Shoot' the top of the door to fit the head of the opening. Saw or shoot the bottom of the door to give a 6 mm gap at floor level or to fit the threshold.

7) Mark out and cut in the hinges. Screw one leaf of each hinge to the door.

8) Offer up the door to the opening and screw the other leaf of each hinge to the frame.

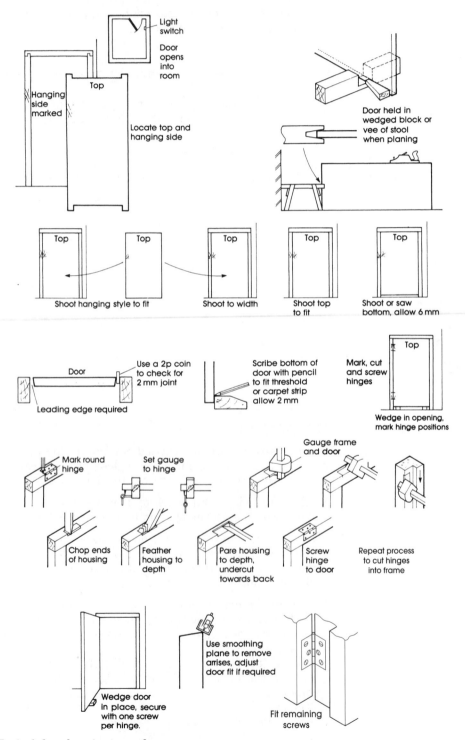

Figure 4.27 *Typical door hanging procedure*

9) Adjust fit as required. Remove all arrises (sharp edges) to soften the corners and provide a better surface for the subsequent paint finish. If the closing edge rubs the frame, the hinges may be proud and require the recesses being cut deeper. If the recesses are too deep, the door will not close fully and tend to spring open, which is known as 'hinge bound'. In this case a thin cardboard strip can be placed in the recess to pack out the hinge.
10) Fit and fix the lock.
11) Fit any other ironmongery, e.g. bolts, letter plates, handles, etc.

It is usual practice to only fit and not to fix the other ironmongery, e.g. handles and bolts, etc., at this stage. They should be fixed later during the finishing stage after all painting works are completed.

Mortise dead lock – fitting procedure is shown in Figure 4.28.

Cylinder rim – fitting procedure is shown in Figure 4.29.

Mortice deadlock, latch or lock/latch

Mark position on door edge

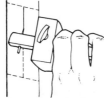
Gauge centre line on door edge

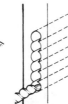
Drill out to width and depth of lock

Pare sides to form mortice

Mark lock face plate

Let-in face plate

Mark spindle and keyhole centres as required

Drill holes, cut keyhole to guide key

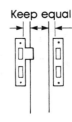
Mark bolt position on frame/lining

Keep equal

Mark position of striking plate

Let–in striking plate, cut mortice for bolts

Figure 4.28 *Fitting procedure for locks and latches*

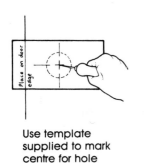
Use template supplied to mark centre for hole

Drill hole, insert cylinder, let-in rimlock if required

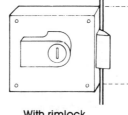
With rimlock screwed in place mark striking plate position

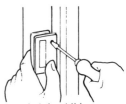
Let–in striking plate, screw in place

Figure 4.29 *Fitting procedure for a cylinder rim night latch*

Letter plate – fitting procedure is shown in Figure 4.30.

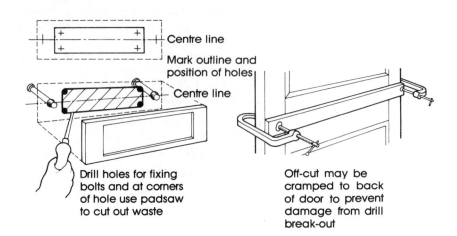

Figure 4.30 *Fitting procedure for a letter plate*

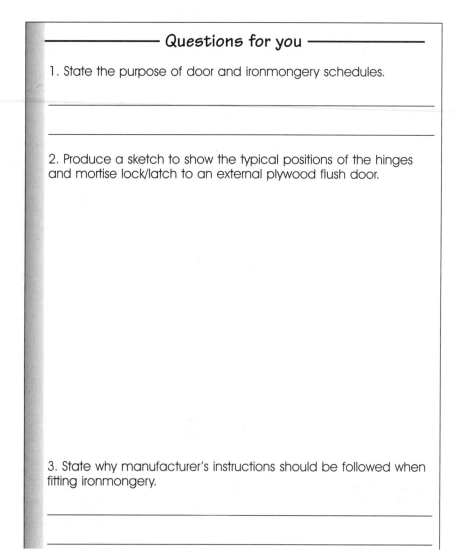

—————————— Questions for you ——————————

1. State the purpose of door and ironmongery schedules.

2. Produce a sketch to show the typical positions of the hinges and mortise lock/latch to an external plywood flush door.

3. State why manufacturer's instructions should be followed when fitting ironmongery.

4. State the purpose of a leading edge to door stiles.

_____

_____

5. Define 'arris' and state why they should be removed from door edges.

_____

_____

_____

6. Explain the treatment required to the top edge of a door head when hung using rising butts.

_____

_____

7. State why the stile of a door should be measured before ordering any ironmongery.

_____

_____

8. List the sequence of operations for hanging an external front door to a domestic property.

_____

_____

_____

_____

_____

_____

_____

_____

_____

_____

_____

_____

_____

WELL, HOW DID YOU DO?

WORK THROUGH THE SECTION AGAIN IF YOU HAD ANY PROBLEMS

WORD-SQUARE SEARCH

Hidden in the word square are the following 20 words associated with *'Doors and door ironmongery'*. You may find the words written forwards, backwards, up, down or diagonally.

Door	Mortise
External	Cylinder
Panelled	Knobset
Flush	Lever
Folding	Security
Knuckle	Bolt
Hinge	Letter
Lock	Schedule
Latch	Hanging
Hand	Shoot

Draw a ring around the words, or line in using a highlight pen thus:

EXAMPLE

EXAMPLE

E	X	T	E	R	N	A	L	F	K	D	E	L	L	E	N	A	P
E	G	H	F	F	G	H	J	M	N	O	Q	S	U	W	Y	A	B
H	S	U	L	F	E	I	K	M	H	P	R	T	V	X	Z	C	T
C	A	C	E	O	F	K	G	B	E	I	G	I	K	N	H	O	E
T	B	R	H	L	T	G	J	C	F	H	N	J	M	L	A	P	S
A	C	E	K	D	E	N	C	F	G	K	D	G	A	G	N	E	B
L	A	V	G	I	E	I	K	J	I	O	H	G	E	F	D	C	O
C	B	E	C	N	I	G	Z	X	O	Y	C	O	P	E	D	I	N
Y	B	L	I	G	N	N	G	R	O	S	S	L	O	W	E	D	K
T	D	O	O	K	C	A	S	E	F	I	R	O	O	D	O	G	O
I	C	I	H	E	R	H	I	A	C	O	M	C	I	C	B	E	R
R	O	E	A	M	O	R	L	A	Y	H	O	K	K	O	T	X	E
U	B	A	C	O	B	R	T	S	L	C	O	V	E	L	R	O	T
C	A	H	T	R	S	F	E	G	I	E	D	A	O	L	E	M	T
E	C	I	M	T	X	Y	Z	A	N	A	M	B	K	T	L	H	E
S	F	J	O	I	R	P	Q	S	D	G	N	C	F	U	O	Y	L
B	G	K	P	S	W	T	U	V	E	H	O	E	V	O	L	I	E
E	L	U	D	E	H	C	S	E	R	M	K	N	U	C	K	L	E

Finishing trim

Vertical and horizontal mouldings

These are often referred to as trim and include architraves, skirting, dado rail, picture rail and cornice. They are used to cover the joint between adjacent surfaces, such as wall and floor/ceiling or the joint between plaster and frames. In addition they provide a decorative feature, and may also serve to protect the wall surface from knocks.

Vertical – a line at right angles to the skyline. It is perpendicular to the horizon or horizontal.

Horizontal – a plane or line lying from side to side, parallel with the skyline as opposed to vertical which is up and down at right angles to the horizontal.

Architrave – the decorative trim that is placed internally around door and window openings to mask the joint between wall and timber and conceal any subsequent shrinkage and expansion.

Skirting – the horizontal trim, often a timber board, that is fixed around the base of a wall to mask the joint between the wall and floor (see Figure 4.32). It also protects the plaster surface from knocks at low level.

Dado rail – a moulding applied to the lower part of interior walls at about waist height approximately 1 m from the floor. It is also known as a chair rail as it designed to coincide with a tall chair back height to protect the plaster.

Picture rail – a moulding applied to the upper part of interior walls between 1.8 m and 2.1 m from the floor. Special clips are hooked over the rail in order to suspend the picture frames.

Cornice – the moulding used internally at the wall/ceiling junction. It is normally formed from plaster, only rarely from timber.

Trim – the collective term for vertical and horizontal mouldings (Figure 4.32). They are normally ready to assemble, machined to a range of standard profiles (shapes) as shown in Figure 4.33.

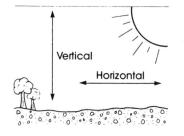

Figure 4.31 *Vertical is up and down, horizontal is side to side*

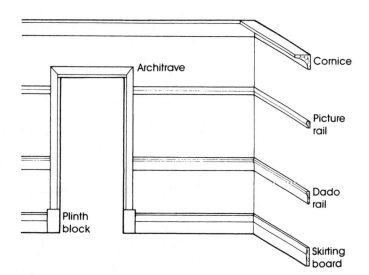

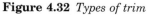

Figure 4.32 *Types of trim*

163

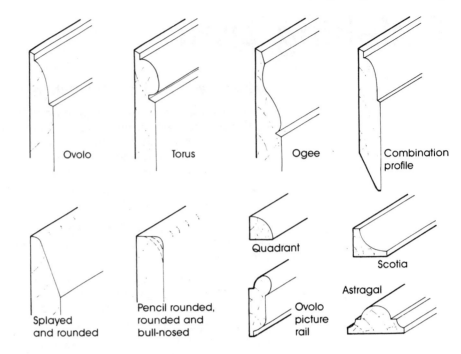

Figure 4.33 *Standard trim sections*

Skirting is often mass produced using a combination profile, e.g. with an ovolo mould on one face and edge and splayed and rounded on the other. This enables it to be used for either purpose and also reduces the timber merchant's stock range. In addition the moulding profile has the effect of an undercut edge enabling it to fit snugly to the floor surface.

Cutting and fixing trim

Solid timber either softwood or hardwood is used for the majority of mouldings. However, MDF (medium density fibreboard) and low density foamed core plastics are used to a limited extent for moulding production.

The following cutting and fixing details are generally suitable for all three of these materials. Consult manufacturer's instructions prior to starting to fix other proprietary mouldings/trim.

Architraves – Figure 4.34 shows that a set of architraves consist of a horizontal head and two vertical jambs or legs.

A 6 mm to 9 mm margin is normally left between the frame or lining edge and the architrave (Figure 4.35). This margin provides a neat appearance to an opening; an unsightly joint line would result if architraves were to be kept flush with the edge of the opening.

The return corners of a set of architraves are mitred. For right-angled returns (90 degrees) the mitre will be 45 degrees (half the total angle) and can be cut using a mitre box or block as shown in Figures 4.36 and 4.37.

Mitres for corners other than right angles will be half the angle of intersection. They can be practically found by marking the outline of the intersecting trim on the frame/lining or wall, and joining the inside and outside corners to give the mitre line (see Figure 4.38). Moulding can be marked directly from this or alternatively an adjustable bevel can be set up for use.

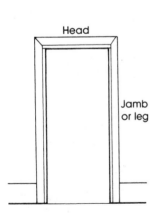

Figure 4.34 *Architraves*

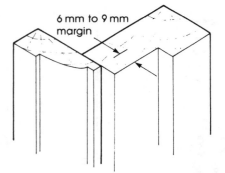

Figure 4.35 *Margin to architraves*

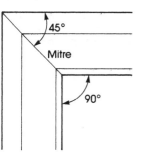

Figure 4.36 *Mitre to architraves*   **Figure 4.37** *Cutting mitre*

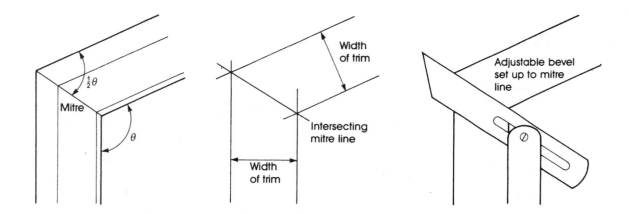

Figure 4.38 *Determining mitre for corners other than right angles*

The head is normally marked, cut and temporarily fixed in position first as shown in Figure 4.39. The jambs can then be marked, cut, eased if required and subsequently fixed.

Where the corner is not square or you have been less than accurate in cutting the mitre, it will require easing, either with a block plane or by running a tenon saw through the mitre.

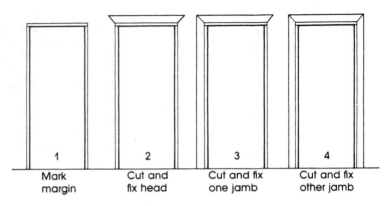

Figure 4.39 *Marking and fixing architraves*

Fixing is normally direct to the door frame/lining at between 200 mm and 300 mm centres using typically 38 mm or 50 mm long oval or lost-head nails (Figure 4.40). These should be positioned in the fillets or quirks (flat surface or groove in moulding, see Figure 4.41) and punched in.

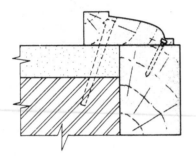

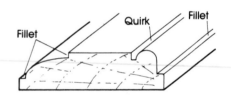

Figure 4.40 *Normal method of fixing architraves*

Figure 4.41 *Fixings best positioned in fillets or quirks for concealment*

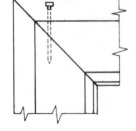

Figure 4.42a *Nailing mitre joints at corners of architraves*

Figure 4.42b

Mitres should be nailed through their top edge to reinforce the joint and ensure both faces are kept flush (see Figure 4.42a). 38 mm oval or lost-head nails are suitable for this purpose.

In addition architraves, especially very wide ones, are often fixed back to the wall surface using either cut or masonry nails. (Do not forget eye protection.)

A *plinth block* is a block of timber traditionally fixed at the base of an architrave to take the knocks and abrasions at floor level (see Figure 4.43). It is also used to ease fixing problems that occur when skirtings are thicker than the architrave.

In current practice plinth blocks will rarely be found except in restoration work, new high quality work in traditional style or where the skirting is thicker than the architrave.

Architraves may be butt jointed to the plinth block, but traditionally they were joined using bare-faced tenon and screws.

Architraves should be scribed (one member cut to fit over the contour of another) to fit the wall surface, where frames/linings abut a wall at right angles.

166

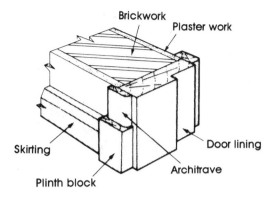

Figure 4.43 *Use of plinth blocks*

- Temporarily fix the architrave jamb in position, keeping the overhang the same all the way down. Figure 4.44 shows how to set a compass to the required margin plus the overhang, or alternatively use a piece of timber this size (gauge block).
- Mark with the compass or gauge slip the line to be cut.
- By slightly undercutting the edge (making it less than 90 degrees) it will fit snugly to the wall contour as shown in Figure 4.45.

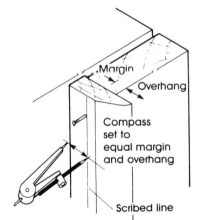

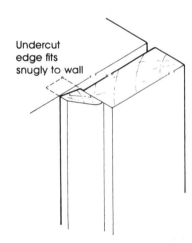

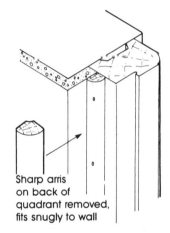

Figure 4.44 *Scribing architraves*

Figure 4.45 *Scribe should fit snugly to wall surface*

Figure 4.46 *Use of quadrants as an alternative to scribing*

A quadrant mould or scotia mould is often used to cover the joint to provide a neat finish to the reveal of external door frames. Quadrant moulds may also be used in place of an architrave jamb where the frame/lining join to a wall at right angles. The sharp arris on the quadrant mould is best pared off with a chisel, as shown in Figure 4.46, to enable the mould to sit snugly into the plaster/timber intersection.

All nails used for fixings should be punched below the surface on completion of the work. This is in preparation for subsequent filling by the painter.

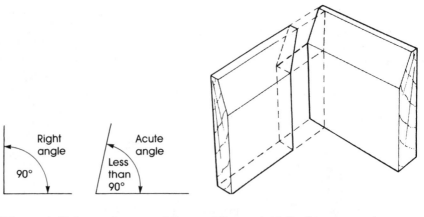

Figure 4.47 *Internal corners 90° or less*

Figure 4.48 *Scribing internal corners*

Skirting – this is normally cut and fixed directly after the architrave.

Internal corners of 90 degrees and less (right angles and acute angles) are scribed, one piece being cut to fit over the other.

Scribes can be formed in one of two ways:

Mitre and scribe – Fix one piece and cut an internal mitre on the other piece to bring out the profile as shown in Figure 4.49. Cut the profile square on mitre line to remove waste. Use a coping saw for the curve.

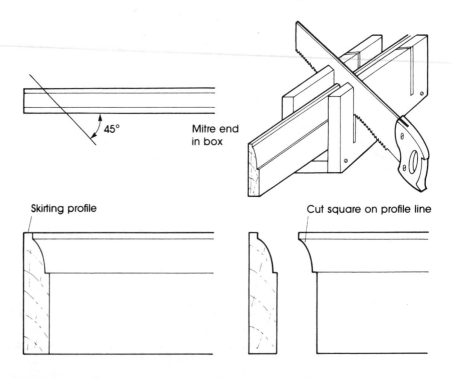

Figure 4.49 *Cutting an internal scribe (mitre and scribe)*

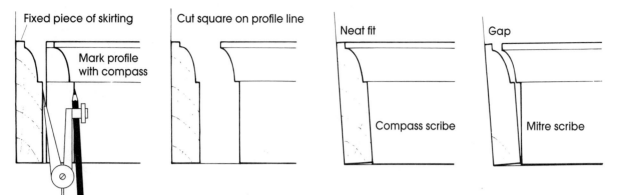

Figure 4.50 *Compass marking and cutting a scribe*

Compass scribe – Fix one piece, place other piece in position. Scribe with a compass as shown in Figure 4.50. Cut square on the scribed line to remove waste.

Scribing is the preferred method, especially where the walls are slightly out of plumb. The mitred scribe would have a gap, but the compass scribe would fit the profile neatly.

Mitres are not normally used for internal corners of skirting. Wall corners are rarely perfectly square, making the fitting difficult. In addition mitres open up as a result of shrinkage, forming a much larger gap than scribes.

However, internal corners on bullnosed or pencil rounded skirtings may be cut with a false or partial mitre on the top rounded edge and the remaining flat surface scribed to fit as shown in Figure 4.51.

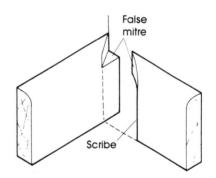

Figure 4.51 *False mitre and scribe*

Internal corners over 90 degrees, called obtuse angles (Figure 4.52), are best jointed with a mitre.

External corners should be mitred (Figure 4.53). These return the moulding profile at a corner rather than a butt joint, as seen in Figure 4.54, which would show unsightly end grain.

Mitres for 90 degree external corners may be cut in a mitre box.

Figure 4.52
Internal corner over 90°

169

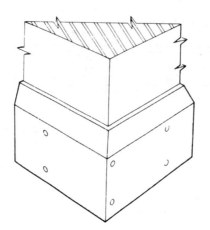

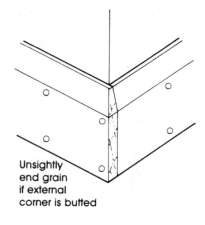

Unsightly
end grain
if external
corner is butted

Figure 4.53 *Mitring external corners*

Figure 4.54 *Butting of external corners not recommended*

Mitres for both internal and external corners over 90 degrees can be marked out using the following method, illustrated in Figures 4.55 to 4.57, and then cut freehand.

1) Use a piece of skirting to mark line and width of skirting on floor either side of the mitre (Figure 4.55).

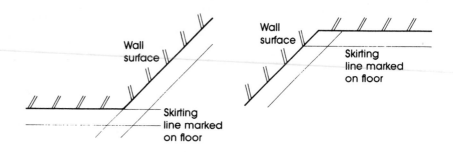

Figure 4.55 *Line of skirting for corners over 90°*

2) Place length of skirting in position.
3) Mark position of plaster arris on top edge of skirting. For internal corners this will be the actual back edge of the skirting (Figures 4.56 and 4.57).
4) Mark outer section on front face of skirting.
5) Use try square to mark line across face and back surface of skirting.
6) Cut mitre freehand.
7) Repeat marking out and cutting procedure for other piece.
8) Fix skirting to wall; external corners should be nailed through the mitre.

Long lengths are fixed first as indicated in Figure 4.58, starting with those having two trapped ends (both ends between walls). Marking and jointing internal corners is much easier when one end is free.

Where the second piece to be fixed also has two trapped ends, a piece slightly longer than the actual length required, by say 50 mm, can be

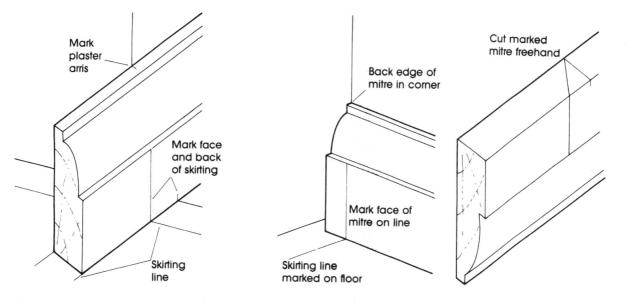

Figure 4.56 *Marking out external corners over 90°*

Figure 4.57 *Marking out internal corners over 90°*

angled across the room or allowed to run through the door opening for scribing the internal joint (Figures 4.59 and 4.60).

After scribing and cutting to length it can be fixed in position.

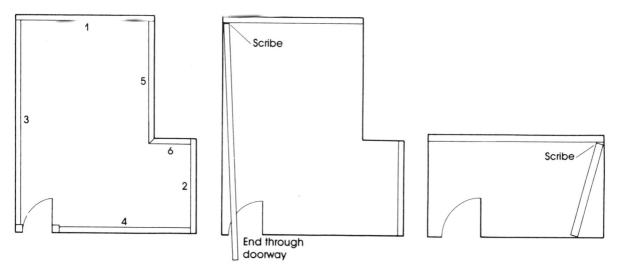

Figure 4.58 *Order of fixing (trapped ends first)*

Figure 4.59 *Extend through doorway to permit scribing of joint*

Figure 4.60 *Angle and scribe when second piece has both ends trapped*

Very short lengths of skirting returned around projections may be fixed before the main lengths. The two short returns are mitred at their external ends, cut square at their internal ends and fixed in position as shown in Figure 4.61.

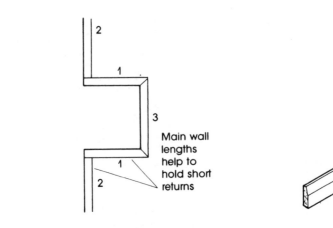

Figure 4.61 *Small pieces may be fitted first*

Main wall lengths are scribed and fixed in position. These help to hold the short returns. Finally the front piece is cut and fixed in position by nailing through the mitres.

Heading joints can be used where sufficiently long lengths of skirting are not available. Mitres are preferred to butts, because the two surfaces are held flush together by nailing through the mitre (see Figure 4.62). In addition mitres mask any gap appearing as a result of shrinkage.

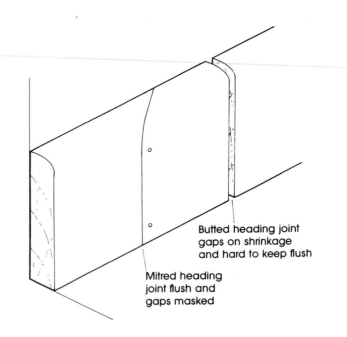

Figure 4.62 *Mitres are preferred for heading joints*

Where skirtings and other trim is to be fixed around a curved surface, the back face will almost certainly require *kerfing*. This involves putting saw cuts in the back face at regular intervals to effectively reduce the thickness of the trim. This is shown in Figures 4.63 and 4.64. The kerfs, which may be cut with a tenon saw, should be spaced between 25 mm and 50 mm apart. The tighter the curve, the closer together the kerfs should be. The depth of the kerfs must be kept the same. They should extend through the section to the maximum extent, but just keeping back from the face and top edge.

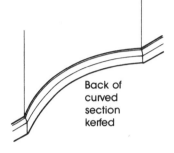

Figure 4.63 *Fixing to a curved surface*

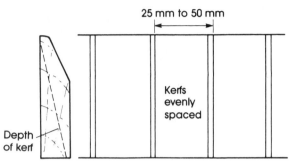

Figure 4.64 *Kerfing to the back of a skirting board*

Care is required when fixing trim back to the wall, to ensure that it is bent gradually and evenly. It is at this time that accuracy in cutting the kerfs evenly spaced to a constant depth is rewarded. Any over-cutting and the trim is likely to snap at that point.

Mitres at the ends of curved sections may be marked out and cut using the same methods as described for other obtuse angles.

Skirtings and other mouldings may occasionally be required to stop part way along a wall, rather than finish into a corner or another moulding. In these circumstances the profile should be returned to the wall or floor. This can be achieved by either mitring the end and inserting a short mitred return piece or, alternatively, the return profile can be cut across the end grain of the main piece as shown in Figure 4.65.

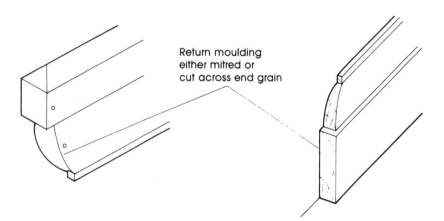

Figure 4.65 *Return the profile of moulding that stops part way along a wall*

Fixing – Skirting can be fixed back to walls with the aid of:

● grounds
● timber twisted plugs
● direct to the surface

Grounds are timber battens which are fixed to the wall surface using either cut nails in mortar joints or masonry nails (see Figure 4.66). One ground is required for skirtings up to 100 mm in depth. Deeper skirtings require either the addition of vertical soldier grounds at 400 mm to 600 mm centres or an extra horizontal ground. The top ground should be fixed about 10 mm below the top edge of the skirting.

Packing pieces may be required behind the grounds to provide a true surface on which to fix the skirting. Check the line of ground with either a straight edge or string line. Skirtings can be fixed back to grounds using, typically, 38 mm or 50 mm oval or lost-head nails.

Twisted timber plugs are rarely used. They are shaped as shown in Figure 4.67 to tighten when driven into the raked-out vertical brickwork joints at approximately 600 mm apart. When all the plugs have been fixed, they should be cut off to provide a true line. An allowance should be made for the thickness of the plaster.

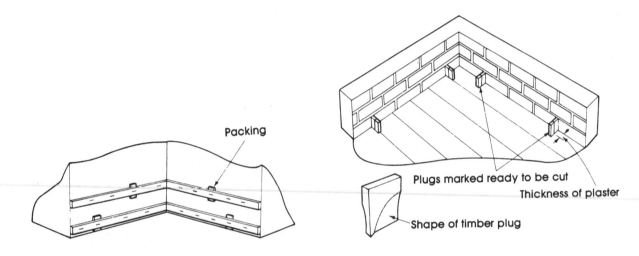

Figure 4.66 *Fixing skirting to timber grounds*   **Figure 4.67** *Fixing skirting to timber plugs*

Skirtings can be fixed back into the end grain of the plugs using, typically, 50 mm cut nails. These hold better in the end grain than would oval or lost-head nails.

Prior to fixing mouldings across any wall, a check should be made to see if any services are hidden below the wall surface. Fixing into electric cables and gas or water pipes is potentially dangerous and expensive to repair. Wires to power points normally run vertically up from the floor. Wires to light switches normally run vertically down from the ceiling. Therefore keep clear of these areas when fixing. Buried pipes in walls are harder to spot. Vertical pipes may just be seen at floor level; outlet points may also be visible (see Figure 4.68). Assume both of these run the full height of the wall, both up and down. Therefore, again keep clear of these areas when fixing. When in doubt an electronic device can be used to scan the wall surface prior to fixing. This gives off a loud noise when passing over buried pipes and electric cables.

Direct to the wall. Skirtings are fixed back to the wall after plastering, using typically either 50 mm cut nails or 50 mm masonry nails depending on the hardness of the wall. Oval or lost-head nails may be used to fix skirtings to timber studwork partitions.

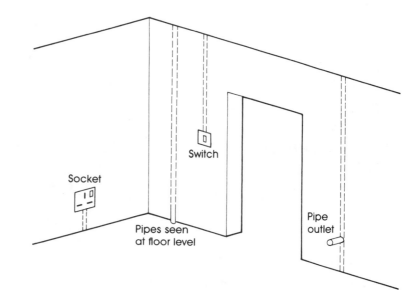

Figure 4.68 *Locating hidden services*

Figure 4.69 shows that fixings should be spaced at 400 mm to 600 mm centres. These should be double nailed near the top and bottom edge of the skirting or alternatively they may be staggered between the top and bottom edge. Remember all nails should be punched below the surface.

Hardwood skirtings for very high quality work may be screwed in position. These should either be counterbored and filled with cross-grained pellets on completion, or brass screws and cups as shown in Figure 4.70 should be used.

The Building Regulations 2000 restricts the use of combustible materials (including timber) around heat-producing appliances and their flues. In general no structural timber (joists and rafters) is to be built into a flue, or be within 200 mm of the flue lining, or nearer than 40 mm to the outer surface of a flue.

Figure 4.69 *Spacing of fixings*

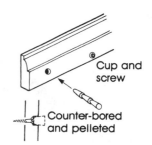

Figure 4.70 *Screws sometimes used to fix hardwood skirtings*

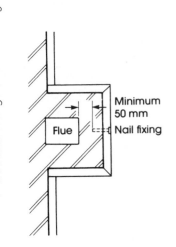

Figure 4.71 *Fixings near flues*

Figure 4.72 *Keeping skirting tight to floor surface when fixing*

Skirtings, architraves, mantel shelves and other trim are non-structural and therefore exempt from this requirement. However, any metal fixings associated with these must be at least 50 mm from the flue (see Figure 4.71). Metal rapidly conducts heat which could cause the trim to catch fire. Therefore, do not use overlong fixings in this situation.

When fixing narrow skirtings, say 75 mm to 100 mm in depth, they may be kept tight down against a fairly level floor surface with the aid of a *kneeler*. This is a short piece of board placed on the top edge of the skirting and held firmly by kneeling on it as shown in Figure 4.72.

Deeper skirtings and/or uneven floor surfaces may require scribing to close the gaps before fixing. This is carried out if required, after jointing but prior to fixing.

1) Place cut length of skirting in position.
2) Use gauge slip or compass set to widest gap to mark on the skirting a line parallel to the uneven surface as shown in Figure 4.73.
3) Trim skirting to line using either a handsaw or plane.
4) Undercut the back edge to ensure the front edge snugly fits the floor contour (see Figure 4.74).

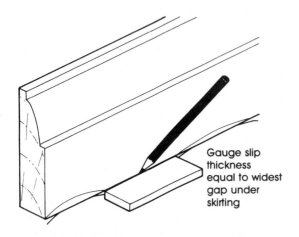

Figure 4.73 *Scribing skirting to an uneven floor surface*

Figure 4.74 *Bottom edge of skirting can be undercut (aids snug fit to floor)*

Dado and picture rails, being horizontal mouldings, may be cut and fixed using similar methods to those used for skirtings.

Start by marking a level line in the required position around the walls as shown in Figure 4.75. (Use a straight edge and spirit level or a water level and chalk line.) The required position may be related to a datum line where established.

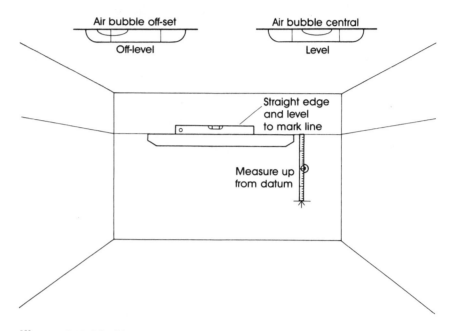

Air bubble off-set — Off-level

Air bubble central — Level

Straight edge and level to mark line

Measure up from datum

Figure 4.75 *Marking positions of dado and picture rails*

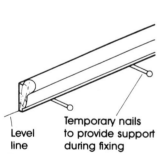

Level line

Temporary nails to provide support during fixing

Figure 4.76 *Temporary support for dado and picture rails during fixing*

When working single-handed, temporary nails can be used at intervals to provide support prior to fixing (see Figure 4.76).

Simple sections can be scribed at internal corners, as are skirtings; otherwise, use mitres. External corners should be mitred.

Fixings are normally direct to the wall surface at about 400 mm centres using typically either 50 mm cut nails or 50 mm masonry nails depending on the hardness of the wall. 50 mm oval or lost-heads can be used when fixing mouldings to timber studwork partitions.

Mitres around external corners should be secured with nails through their edge. Typically 38 mm ovals or lost heads are used for this purpose.

Remember all nails should be punched below the surface.

Estimating materials

To determine the amount of trim required for any particular task is a fairly simple process, if the following procedures are used:

Architraves – The jambs or legs in most situations can be taken to be 2100 mm long. The head can be taken to be 1000 mm. These lengths assume a standard full-size door and include an allowance for mitring the ends. Thus the length of architrave required for one face of a door lining/frame is 5200 mm or 5.2 m.

Multiply this figure by the number of architrave sets to be fixed. This will determine the total metres run required, say 8 sets, both sides of four door openings:

$$5.2 \times 8 = 41.6 \text{ m}$$

Skirtings and other horizontal trim can be estimated from the perimeter. This is found by adding up the lengths of the walls in the area. The widths of any doorways and other openings are taken away to give the actual metres run required.

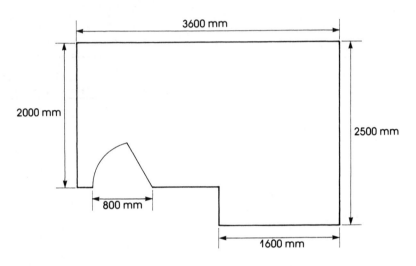

Figure 4.77 *Floor plan of room*

Example

Determine the total length of timber required for the room shown in Figure 4.77.

Perimeter $= 2 + 3.6 + 2.5 + 1.6 + 0.5 + 2$
$= 12.2$ m
Total metres run required $= 12.2 - 0.8$ (door opening)
$= 11.4$ m

An allowance of 10% for cutting and waste is normally included in any estimate for horizontal moulding.

Example

Determine the total metres run of skirting required for the run shown including an allowance of 10% for cutting and waste.

Total metres run required $= 11.4$ m

Total metres run required including a 10% cutting and waste allowance
$= 11.4 + 1.14$
$= 12.54$ m, say 12.5 m

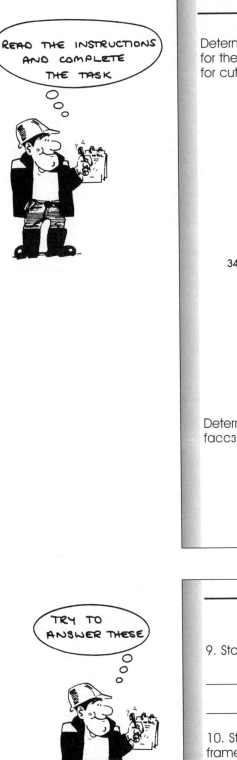

Learning task

Determine the total metres run of skirting and dado rail required for the room shown in the diagram. Include an allowance of 10% for cutting and waste.

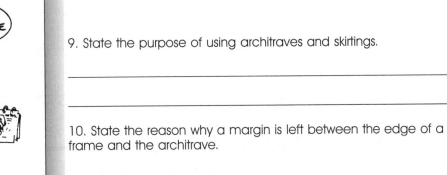

Determine the total metres run of architrave required for both faces of the doors that open into the room shown.

Questions for you

9. State the purpose of using architraves and skirtings.

_____

_____

10. State the reason why a margin is left between the edge of a frame and the architrave.

_____

_____

11. State the purpose of mitring architraves.

_____

_____

12. Describe a plinth block and state where it may be used.

_____

_____

13. Explain the reason why architraves and skirtings may be scribed.

_____

_____

_____

_____

14. Produce a sketch to show a situation where a quadrant mould has been used in the place of one architrave jamb.

15. Explain why scribes are used in preference to mitres for the internal corners of skirting.

_____

_____

16. Explain the situation where heading joints may be used in skirtings.

_____

_____

17. Describe how skirting may be prepared to be fixed around a curved surface.

_____

_____

18. Describe a situation where the profile of a moulding may be returned to the wall surface.

_____

_____

19. Produce a sketch to show a torus mould to the edge of a skirting.

WELL, HOW DID
YOU DO?

WORK THROUGH THE
SECTION AGAIN IF
YOU HAD ANY
PROBLEMS

20. Name the fixing used to secure an architrave to a door lining.

_____

_____

..

COMPLETE THE WORD SQUARE

WORD-SQUARE SEARCH

Hidden in the word square are the following 20 words associated with '*Finishing trim*'. You may find the words written forwards, backwards, up, down or diagonally.

Moulding	Ogee
Trim	Astragal
Skirting	Splayed
Architrave	Bullnosed
Dado rail	Scotia
Picture rail	Quadrant
Cornice	Kerfing
Scribe	Acute
Mitre	Obstuse
Ovolo	Right angle

Draw a ring around the words, or line in using a highlight pen thus:

EXAMPLE

EXAMPLE

```
P I C T U R E R A I L S O L F M C B
R U O P L G N I F R E K R A E O O U
O R R S L L M F D N D I O G M U P L
P I N L O D A E A L C R M A M L O L
R A I D V Y C N I T E T O R U D R N
I U C L O G U T T G T I S T N I T O
E A E O L P T K O O A N N S I N T S
T L W V O E E S C G L G A A C G N E
R I T O S U S Y S I P O R T A E E D
I A T R I M P E T R E S T L E T D O
G R O R I H S G I A Q H L C I S N E
H D N E L U G D O U O I E A M T E B
T R S P T N E A A C A D B N I P P I
A A T B I Y S D S R E O O I T C E R
N U O C A U R L O R G I A T R O D C
G G A L L A L D T E E R R O E C N S
L R P T N S A M E A D E D E B S I E
E S P T O D R D E V A R T I H C R A
```

Kitchen units and fitments

Units fall into two distinct categories:

Purpose made – a unit made in a joiner's shop for a specific job. Most will be fully assembled prior to their arrival on site.

Proprietary – a unit or range of units mass produced to standard designs by a manufacturer. Budget-priced units are often sent in knock-down form (known as flat packs) ready for on-site assembly. Better quality units are often ready assembled in the factory (known as rigid units).

The two main methods of construction for both proprietary and purpose-made units, shown in Figure 4.78, are box construction and framed construction.

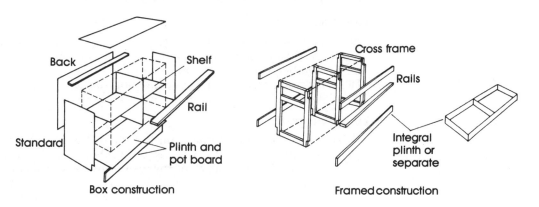

Figure 4.78 *Unit construction*

Box construction

This is also known as slab construction. This uses vertical standards and rails and horizontal shelves.

A back holds the unit square and rigid. The plinth and pot board are normally integral with the unit.

Proprietary units are almost exclusively made from 15 mm to 19 mm thick melamine-faced chipboard or medium density fibre board (MDF). Purpose-made units may be constructed using chipboard, MDF, blockboard, melamine-faced board or, more rarely, solid timber.

Flat packs use knock-down fittings or screws to join the panels. Assembly is a simple process of following the manufacturer's instructions and drawings, coupled with the ability to use a screwdriver.

Rigid and purpose-made units may be either dowelled or housed together. Glue is used on assembly to form a rigid carcass.

Framed construction

This is also known as skeleton construction. This uses frames either front and back joined by rails or standards, or cross frames joined by rails. The plinth and pot board are normally separate items.

The frames of proprietary units are normally dowelled, whereas purpose-made ones would be mortised and tenoned together.

Flat pack assembly and installation

The method of assembling and installing flat-pack units will vary from manufacturer to manufacturer. However, each unit is supplied with its own instructions. It is most important to take the time to read through these prior to commencing work. In general this is a three-stage process.

Assembly – Put carcasses together. Unpack and assemble units one at a time and check contents. Open more than one and you risk confusing the parts!

Installation – Fix base units to the wall starting with corner base unit and working outwards from either side. Finally install wall units, again working from the corner outwards.

Finishing – Fit worktops, drawers and doors. This should not be done until all units are firmly fixed to wall and connected together.

Typical assembly instructions are shown in Figure 4.79.

Fixing base units –

1) Position base units level and plumb using wedges provided if required. Ensure all top edges and fronts of units are flush. Secure units together using connecting screws.
2) Drill, plug and screw units to wall, using the brackets provided.
3) Trim floor wedges flush to unit with a knife.

Fixing wall units –

1) Draw a level horizontal line from the top of the tall unit if being used. It is normal practice to keep tall units and wall units level. Draw another line the depth of the wall units below this line. This marks the position of the underside of the wall units. Where tall units are not being used, wall units are normally fixed with a gap of 450 mm between their underside and the work surface.
2) Temporarily fix a batten on the marked level line, to act as a support while marking fixing holes and screwing.
3) Rest the unit on the batten. Ensure the tops of wall units and tall units are flush.
4) Mark the wall through the fixing holes.
5) Drill, plug and screw the unit to the wall.
6) Packing behind a fixing may be required on an uneven wall surface to ensure the units are plumb.
7) Position the remaining wall units in place one at a time.
8) Ensure the top edges and fronts are flush and secure together using connecting screws.

Fixing worktops –

1) Measure and cut the worktop to the required size. (Post formed, see 'Worktops', following, for other types.)
2) Metal filler/joint strips are used to connect worktops in corners.
3) Position worktop and screw in place through the fixing brackets.
4) Sawn bare ends of the top can be covered with a metal trim or a plastic pre-glued edge banding. Iron edge banding into place, using a sheet of paper in between banding and iron for protection.

Fixing drawers – Insert drawers, made up previously, onto drawer runners.

Fixing doors –

1) Lay the doors face down on a flat clean surface.
2) Locate the hinges over the previously fixed hinge plate and secure hinges with a mounting screw.
3) Adjust the hinges if required to ensure accurate door alignment.

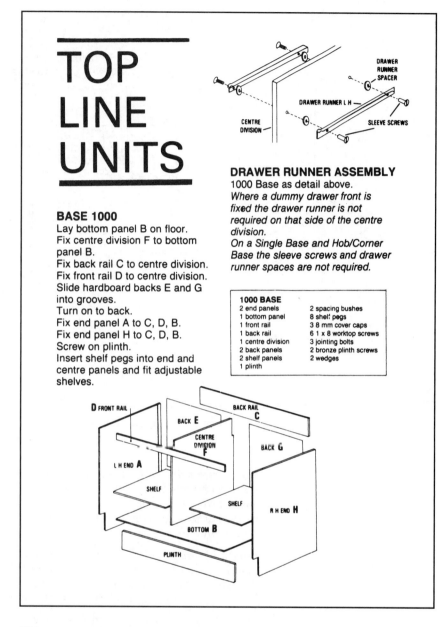

TOP LINE UNITS

DRAWER RUNNER ASSEMBLY
1000 Base as detail above.
Where a dummy drawer front is fixed the drawer runner is not required on that side of the centre division.
On a Single Base and Hob/Corner Base the sleeve screws and drawer runner spaces are not required.

BASE 1000
Lay bottom panel B on floor.
Fix centre division F to bottom panel B.
Fix back rail C to centre division.
Fix front rail D to centre division.
Slide hardboard backs E and G into grooves.
Turn on to back.
Fix end panel A to C, D, B.
Fix end panel H to C, D, B.
Screw on plinth.
Insert shelf pegs into end and centre panels and fit adjustable shelves.

1000 BASE

2 end panels	2 spacing bushes
1 bottom panel	8 shelf pegs
1 front rail	3 8 mm cover caps
1 back rail	6 1 x 8 worktop screws
1 centre division	3 jointing bolts
2 back panels	2 bronze plinth screws
2 shelf panels	2 wedges
1 plinth	

Figure 4.79 *Typical manufacturer's assembly instructions*

Rigid and purpose-made installation

The installation of rigid and purpose-made units follows the general procedures used for flat-pack units.

Good quality rigid units have adjustable legs for easier levelling on an uneven floor. In addition wall units often have adjustable wall brackets which enable fine adjustment to plumb and level.

Purpose-made units often have provision for scribing to uneven floor and wall surfaces (see Figure 4.80).

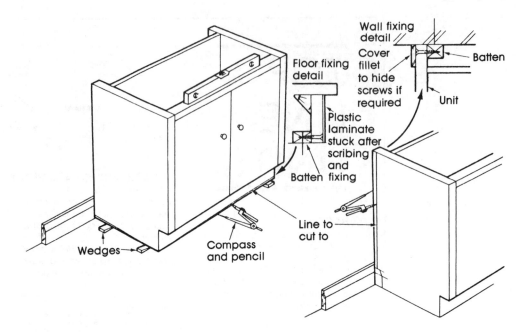

Figure 4.80 *Scribing to uneven surfaces*

Worktops

Three main types as shown in Figure 4.81 are in common use:

Post formed – a chipboard base covered with a plastic laminate which has been formed over a rolled edge. The most popular type of worktop for proprietary units, it is ready finished and simply requires fixing in place.

Wood trimmed – a chipboard base covered with either a plastic laminate or ceramic tiles. A hardwood trim is tongued and glued to the front edge, providing a neat finish. This is mainly used for higher quality work. Hardwood trim is normally supplied loose, ready for mitring and gluing on site.

Laminate topped and edged – a chipboard base edged and covered in plastic laminate, rarely used for standard jobs, as post-formed worktops are readily available at a low cost. The following procedure can be used for covering a worktop with a plastic laminate:

1) Fix units and chipboard base of worktop in position.
2) Cut edging strips. This can best be done by setting a marking or cutting gauge to the required width and running it along the edge of the laminate to score its surface. The strip is separated by applying thumb pressure along the score, at the same time lifting up the edge of the strip.

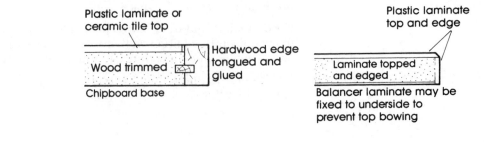

Figure 4.81 *Worktops*

3) Stick on edging strips with contact adhesive, following the manufacturer's recommendations.

Note: Two coats of adhesive should be applied to the edge of the worktop. The first acts as a primer to seal the absorbent surface.

4) File all the edges and corners to a neat finish.
5) Cut top laminate slightly over the required size. This can be done by scoring the sheet with a laminate cutter and breaking the sheet upwards along the scored line.
6) Thoroughly dust off the work surface and the back of the laminate. Apply a contact adhesive to both surfaces and allow to become touch dry.
7) Lay small prepared strips of timber on the work surface at about 150 mm intervals. Place the laminate sheet on top of the strips.
8) Ensuring that the laminate is correctly positioned, remove the strips one at a time and press the laminate down onto the top, working from the centre to the edge of the sheet each time to avoid air traps.

Note: The purpose of the timber strips is to separate the two surfaces until they are correctly located. A sheet of building paper can be used instead of strips. This is progressively pulled out as the laminate is pressed down.

9) Apply pressure to the surface by rubbing down from the centre with the palm of the hand.
10) Trim the edges, preferably using a powered router. Where this is not available a file, block plane or cabinet scraper can be used.

TRY TO ANSWER THESE

—————— Questions for you ——————

21 Describe the difference between flat-pack and rigid proprietary kitchen units.

_____

_____

_____

22. Produce a sketch to show the following **THREE** worktop edge details:
(a)   post formed
(b)   wood trimmed
(c)   laminate edged

23. Name the adhesive used for bonding plastic laminate to a work surface.

24. A kitchen is to be fitted with a range of units to form an L shape. Describe the sequence in which these units should be fixed.

_____

_____

_____

Panelling and cladding

Panelling

Wall panelling is the general term given to the covering of internal wall surfaces and sometimes ceilings, with timber or other materials to create a decorative finish (Figure 4.82). All panelling may be classified by its height and method of construction.

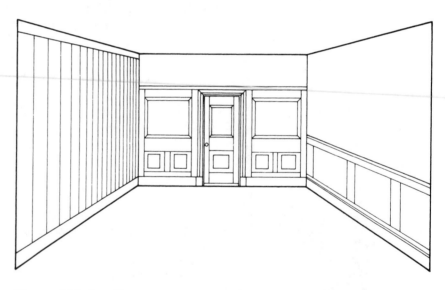

Figure 4.82 *Panelling*

Heights of panelling

Dado height panelling – extends from the floor up the walls to the window sill level or chair back height, i.e. about 1 m above the floor.

Three-quarter height panelling – also known as frieze height panelling. It extends from the floor up the walls to the top of the door, i.e. about 2 m. Traditionally a plate shelf was incorporated on top of this type of panelling to display plates and other frieze ornaments.

Full height panelling – as its name suggests, covers the whole of the wall from floor to ceiling.

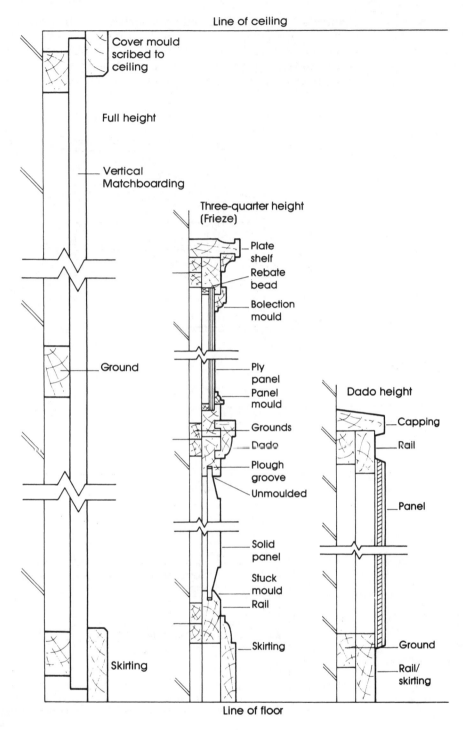

Figure 4.83 *Panelling heights*

Construction of panelling

Traditional panelling consists of stiles, rails and muntins, mortised and tenoned together, with panels infilled between the framing members, which are themselves fixed back to grounds. In modern usage the term panelling is also loosely applied to wall linings made up of sheet material, or matchboarding.

Grounds – provide a flat and level surface on which the panelling can be fixed (see Figure 4.84). They are normally preservative-treated softwood and may have been framed up using halvings or mortise and tenon joints or, alternatively, supplied in lengths for use as separate grounds or counter battening (a double layer fixed at right angles).

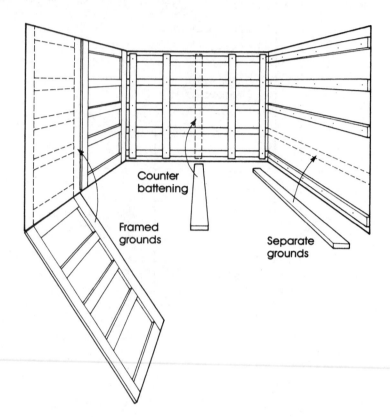

Counter battening

Framed grounds

Separate grounds

Figure 4.84 *Types of grounds*

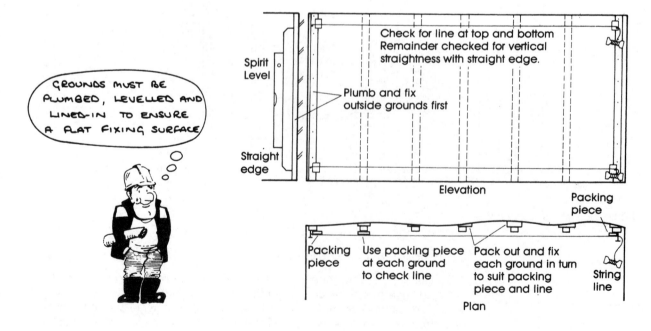

GROUNDS MUST BE PLUMBED, LEVELLED AND LINED-IN TO ENSURE A FLAT FIXING SURFACE

Spirit Level

Straight edge

Check for line at top and bottom
Remainder checked for vertical straightness with straight edge.

Plumb and fix outside grounds first

Elevation

Packing piece

Packing piece

Use packing piece at each ground to check line

Pack out and fix each ground in turn to suit packing piece and line

String line

Plan

Figure 4.85 *Plumbing and lining grounds*

190

Grounds are fixed back to the wall surface either by:

- plugging and screwing,
- cut-nailing into the mortar joint or brickwork
- cut-nailing direct into the surface of blockwork,
- nailing direct into the brickwork using hardened nails or by using cartridge fixing tools. (Goggles for eye protection should be worn.)

They must be plumbed and lined in to provide a flat surface (see Figure 4.85).

Fixing to grounds – the fixing of panelling to grounds should as far as possible be concealed.

Panelling should be lowered into position and held in place by inter-locking grounds, one fixed to the wall and the other to the panelling (see Figure 4.86).

Figure 4.86
Concealed fixings

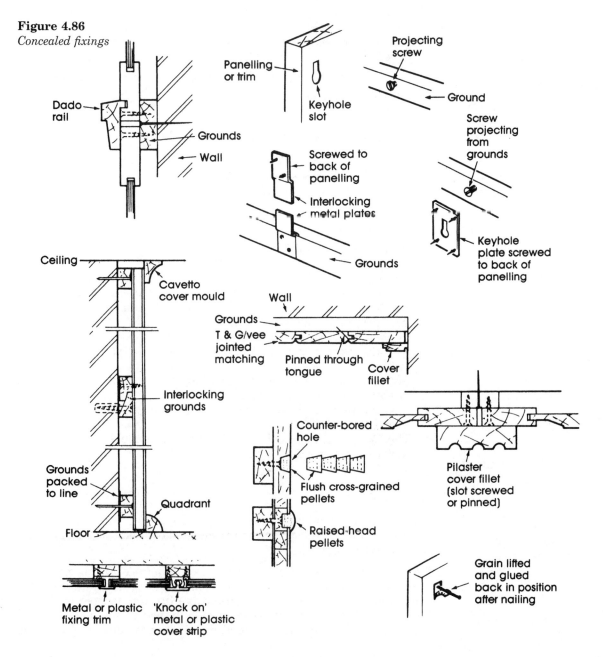

Interlocking metal plates or keyhole slots and screws also provide a fixing when the panelling is lowered into position. Cover fillets or other trim may be used to conceal panelling that has been surface screwed.

Corner details – the method of forming internal and external angles will depend on the type of panelling, but in any case they should be adequately supported by grounds fixed behind. Figure 4.87 shows various details. Tongued-and-grooved joints, loose tongues, rebates or cover fillets and trims have been used to locate the panelling members and at the same time conceal the effects of moisture movement.

Where matchboarding or similar timber strips are used for panelling, the boards at either end of a wall should be of equal width (see Figure 4.88).

A simple calculation can be carried out to determine the required width.

Example

A 3.114 m length of wall is to be panelled with 95 mm (90 mm covering width) matchboard.

Divide the length of wall in millimetres by the covering width of the board.

3114 ÷ 90 = 34.6 boards

Therefore 35 boards are required = 33 whole boards and two end boards.

Width of cut end boards = 1.6 × 90 ÷ 2
= 72 mm

General requirements of panelling

1) Before any panelling commences it is essential that the wall construction has dried sufficiently.
2) All timber should be of the moisture content required for the respective situation (equilibrium moisture content, M/C).
3) The backs of the panelling sections should be sealed prior to fixing, thus preventing moisture absorption.
4) Timber for grounds should be preservative treated.
5) A ventilated air space is desirable between the panelling and the wall.
6) Provision must be made for a slight amount of moisture movement in both the panelling sections and the trim.
7) The positioning of the grounds must be planned to suit the panelling.
8) The fixing of the panelling to the grounds should be so designed that it is concealed as far as possible.

Cladding

Cladding is the non-loadbearing skin or covering of external walls for weathering purposes, e.g. timber boarding, sheet material, tile hanging and cement rendering.

Timber cladding for either timber-framed buildings or those of brick or blockwork construction is fixed to battens or grounds spaced at a maximum of 600 mm centres. A **moisture barrier** is fixed below the cladding to battens in timber-framed buildings to provide a second line of protection to any wind-driven rain that might penetrate the

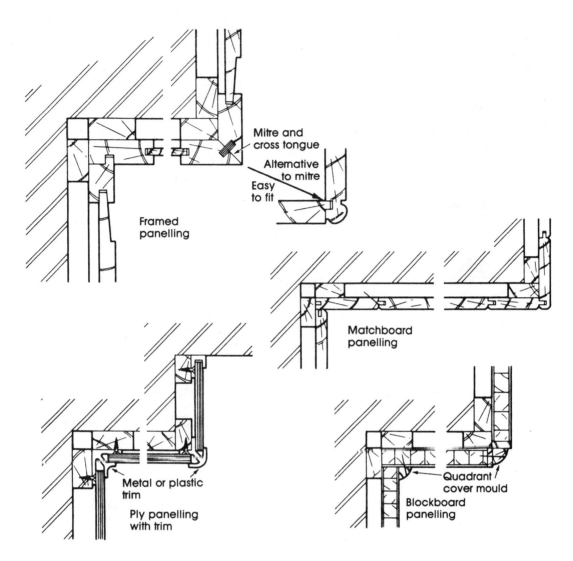

Figure 4.87 *Corner details*

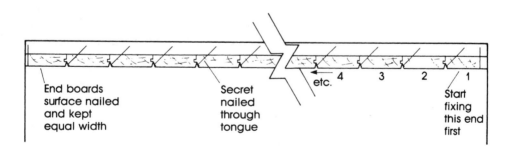

Figure 4.88 *Layout of matchboard panelling*

cladding. This is often termed a breather paper, as it must allow the warm air vapour to pass or breath through it from inside the building and not get trapped in the wall. The moisture barrier is often omitted for claddings over brick or blockwork.

The battens are fixed to the studs of the timber frame or direct to the brick or block surface. They must be lined and levelled to provide a flat surface.

Cladding is normally specified as 16 mm. Feather-edged boards will taper to about 6 mm at their thin edge. Natural durable timber cladding such as Western Red Cedar may be used without preservative treatment or any subsequent finish. Most other softwood claddings are not naturally durable and must be preservative treated.

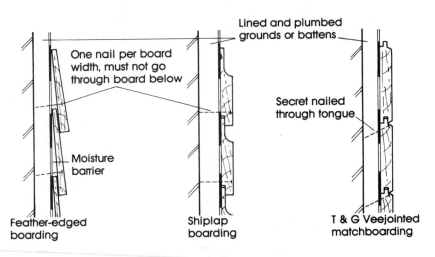

Figure 4.89 *Types of cladding*

It is recommended that all timber used for cladding, the grounds as well as the boarding, is preservative treated before use. There is little point in treating the face of cladding after it has been fixed, leaving the joints or overlapping areas, back faces and grounds untreated. Any preservative-treated timber cut to size on site will require re-treatment on the freshly cut ends and edges. This can be carried out by applying two brush flood coats of preservative.

Timber is a hygroscopic material, it readily absorbs or gives off moisture to achieve a balance with its surroundings. In doing so it expands or shrinks. Cladding sections should be designed to minimise, mask or cover any unsightly gaps resulting from moisture movement (see Figure 4.90).

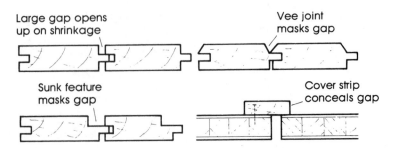

Figure 4.90 *Effects of moisture movement and the remedy*

Fixings – are normally nails at least 2½ times in length the cladding's thickness. Ferrous metal (metal that will rust) nails should be galvanised or sherardised to resist corrosion. Copper or aluminium nails must be used with Western Red Cedar as it accelerates rusting in ferrous metals and causes unsightly timber staining.

Plywood used for cladding must be WBP rated. This means that its veneer layers have been glued using a weather and boilproof adhesive to give it a very high resistance to all weather conditions.

Fibreboard or hardboard must be of the oil tempered kind for weather resistance. Before fixing, hardboard sheets will require conditioning. This involves brushing up to one litre of water into the back face (rough surface) of each sheet 24 to 48 hours before fixing. The purpose of conditioning is to expand the sheet, which ensures that it dries out and shrinks on its fixings and remains flat. If this were not done it could expand after fixing resulting in a bowing or buckling of the surface.

TRY TO ANSWER THESE

—————— Questions for you ——————

25. Produce a sketch to show the difference between dado and frieze height panelling.

26. Explain why grounds must be plumbed and lined in.

_____

_____

27. Explain why exterior plywood cladding should be specified as WBP rated.

_____

_____

28. Explain the reason for using copper nails when fixing Western Red Cedar cladding.

_____

_____

29. State the purpose of the vee joint in matchboard panelling.

_____

_____

30. State the purpose of incorporating a moisture barrier below external timber cladding.

_____

_____

31. State a reason why Western Red Cedar may be specified for external cladding.

_____

_____

32. Produce a sketch to show how wall panelling may be secret fixed using interlocking grounds.

33. Describe the conditioning of hardboard prior to fixing, and state why this process is carried out.

_____

_____

_____

WELL, HOW DID YOU DO?

WORK THROUGH THE SECTION AGAIN IF YOU HAD ANY PROBLEMS

WORD-SQUARE SEARCH

Hidden in the word square are the following 20 words associated with *'Panelling and cladding'*. You may find the words written forwards, backwards, up, down or diagonally.

Panel	Cladding
Dado	Stile
Ground	Vapour
Batten	Breather
Rebate	Preservative
Matchboarding	Feather edge
Frieze	Levelled
Tongue	Conditioning
Groove	Hygroscopic
Interlocking	Keyhole

Draw a ring round the words, or line in using a highlight pen thus:

EXAMPLE

EXAMPLE

```
G  N  I  D  R  A  O  B  H  C  T  A  M  A  C  B  D  P
B  E  F  H  G  J  I  L  K  O  M  P  N  Q  N  R  R  S
C  R  G  N  I  D  D  A  L  C  T  U  V  E  W  E  X  Y
O  Z  R  R  D  C  I  E  M  K  X  W  I  U  S  A  S  O
N  A  O  D  R  E  B  A  T  E  M  T  S  E  P  T  E  M
D  C  O  L  O  M  P  R  Y  X  A  M  R  D  B  H  Y  E
I  K  V  B  A  E  I  U  X  B  R  V  K  C  H  E  K  G
T  D  E  K  E  Z  X  O  Z  C  A  O  D  H  B  R  O  N
I  F  N  D  F  E  S  P  W  T  C  A  M  T  O  P  Q  I
O  J  E  K  J  I  D  A  I  X  Z  E  L  O  H  Y  E  K
N  L  U  M  P  R  R  V  Q  V  K  P  M  D  K  X  D  C
I  O  G  L  G  F  E  A  T  H  E  R  E  D  G  E  A  O
N  Q  N  Q  B  K  C  E  P  G  D  E  L  L  E  V  E  L
G  H  O  L  A  H  G  F  O  K  A  Z  A  P  L  C  B  R
I  R  T  E  B  E  C  D  N  U  O  R  G  B  I  K  D  E
O  D  P  N  H  E  K  A  M  D  F  H  E  D  T  C  E  T
H  E  R  A  N  D  E  D  P  R  O  K  C  F  S  B  G  N
D  C  I  P  O  C  S  O  R  G  Y  H  A  E  G  K  F  I
```

5 Woodworking machining

READ THIS CHAPTER, WORKING THROUGH THE QUESTIONS AND LEARNING TASKS

In undertaking this chapter you will be required to demonstrate your skill and knowledge of:

● Using and maintaining a hand fed circular rip saw.

You will be required practically to:

● Use a hand fed circular rip saw complying with current regulations to produce sawn components: square, rectangular, bevelled, angled, wedged and tapered.

Hand fed circular rip saw

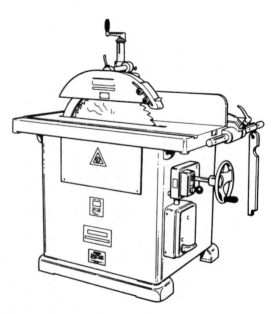

Figure 5.1 *Rip saw*

The main purpose of a rip saw (Figure 5.1) is to resaw timber from its marketable sectional size into the required section.

198

This may involve:

- cutting the timber to the required width, known as *flatting*.
- cutting the timber to the required thickness, known as *deeping*.
- cutting the timber to the appropriate angle or bevel. Machine operators will make their own bed pieces and saddles that enable them safely to carry out angle and bevel ripping.
- cutting the timber to the appropriate taper or wedge shape. Machine operators will make their own push blocks having the required taper or wedge shape on their edge which enable them safely to carry out tapered ripping or wedge cutting.

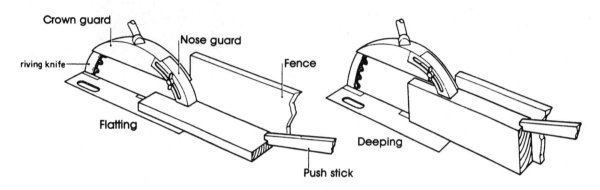

Figure 5.2 *Flatting and deeping*

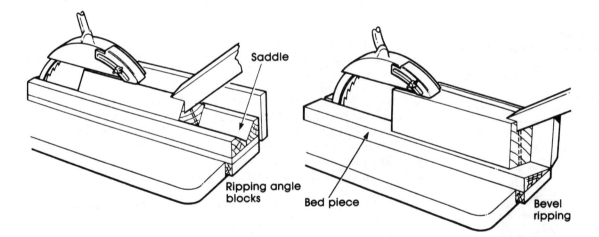

Figure 5.3 *Bed pieces and saddles*

Figure 5.5 shows the following parts of the rip saw:

- The *crown guard* (A) is vertically adjustable and when set up for sawing, it must completely cover the gullets of the top teeth.
- The *nose guard* (B) should be adjusted for each cutting operation so that the gap between the nose guard and the material being cut is as close as practicably possible. A maximum of 12 mm is permissible.
- The *pillar* (C) and adjusting handle for the crown guard.
- The *riving knife* (D) rises and falls along with the saw when the depth of cut is altered. Whenever a saw blade is changed, the riving

199

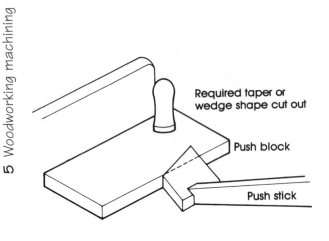

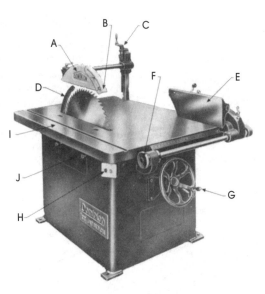

Figure 5.4 *Use of push block to cut wedges*

Figure 5.5 *Parts of the rip saw*

knife must be adjusted so that it is as close as practicably possible to the saw blade and, in any case, the distance between the riving knife and the teeth of the saw blade should not exceed 12 mm. It should be thicker than the saw blade as its purpose is to stop the material binding on the saw blade while being cut and also to guard the back edge of the saw blade.

- The *fence* (E) is adjusted by slackening the hand lever and moving the fence on its slide to give the required width of cut. The fence should be set so that the arc at the end of the fence is in line with the gullets of the saw teeth at table level. This helps to prevent the timber binding on the saw blade.
- The *knurled adjusting knob* (F), by rotation, gives a fine adjustment of the fence. The measurement between the saw blade and fence is indicated on the graduated scale above the slide.
- The *rise and fall handle* (G) raises or lowers the blade.
- *Start* and *stop* controls (H).
- The *table groove* (I) enables a cross-cut guide or mitre fence to be used.
- The *access cover* (J) is removed to give access to the spindle when changing saw blades.
- The *finger plate* (K) is removed to give access to the spindle when changing saw blades. Some saws have a recess on each side of the blade where it enters the table. These recesses are to receive felt packings, a hardwood mouthpiece and a hardwood backfilling. The packings and backfillings prevent the saw being deflected and keep it cutting in a true line (Figure 5.6). The mouthpiece protects the packing from damage by the saw teeth and prevents the underside of the timber breaking out or 'spelching'. The backfilling also prevents damage to the saw teeth should it run out of true.

Figure 5.6 *Saw packings and mouthpiece.*

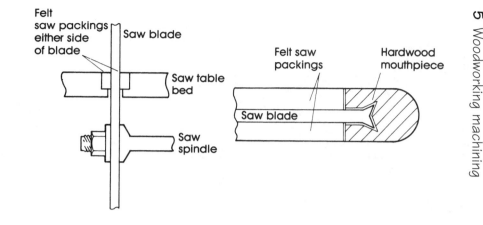

Safety in operation

The safeguarding of woodworking machines is covered by the British Standard Code of Practice BS 6854. This standard takes into account both the practical aspects of safeguarding and the legal requirements contained in the Health and Safety at Work Act, the Woodworking Machine Regulations (now revoked) and the Provision and use of Work Equipment Regulations.

The main points to be considered wherever woodworking machines are in use may be summarized as follows (Figure 5.7 refers):

1) The cutters of every machine must be enclosed by a substantial guard to the maximum possible extent.
2) In general no adjustment should be made to the guards or any other part of the machine while the cutters are in motion.
3) Every machine must have an effective starting and stopping device. This should be located so that it is easily used by the operator especially in the case of an emergency.
4) The working area around a machine must be kept free from obstruction, offcuts, shavings, etc.
5) The floor surface of the work area must be level, non-slip and maintained in good condition.
6) A reasonable temperature must be maintained in the workplace and in any case must not fall below 13°C or 10°C in a saw mill. Where this is not possible because the machine is situated in the open air, radiant heaters must be provided near or adjacent to the work area, to enable operators to warm themselves periodically.
7) No person must use any woodworking machine unless he/she has been properly trained for the work being carried out or he/she is under close supervision as part of the training.
8) Machine operators must:
   (a) Use correctly all guards and safety devices required by the regulations.
   (b) Report to the supervisor or employer any faults or contraventions of the regulations.
9) Any person who sells or hires a woodworking machine must ensure it complies with the regulations.

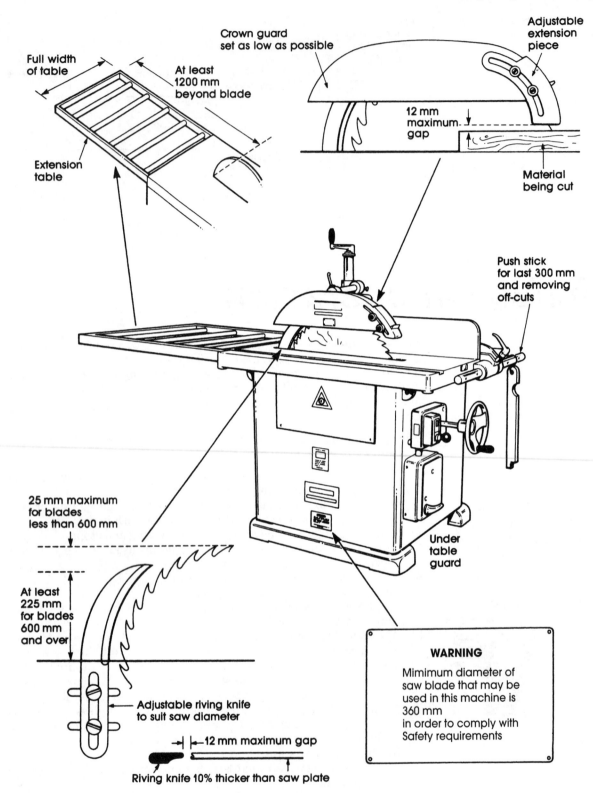

Full width of table

At least 1200 mm beyond blade

Extension table

Crown guard set as low as possible

Adjustable extension piece

12 mm maximum gap

Material being cut

Push stick for last 300 mm and removing off-cuts

Under table guard

25 mm maximum for blades less than 600 mm

At least 225 mm for blades 600 mm and over

Adjustable riving knife to suit saw diameter

12 mm maximum gap

Riving knife 10% thicker than saw plate

WARNING

Mimimum diameter of saw blade that may be used in this machine is 360 mm in order to comply with Safety requirements

Figure 5.7 *Circular saw safety requirements*

The safety requirements applicable to circular saws are:

1) The part of the saw blade which is below the saw table must be enclosed to the maximum possible extent.

2) A strong, adjustable riving knife must be fitted directly behind the saw blade. Its purpose is to part the timber as it proceeds through the saw and thus prevents it jamming on the blade and being thrown back towards the operator.

3) The upper part of the saw blade must be fitted with a strong adjustable crown guard which has flanges that cover the full depth of the saw teeth. The adjustable extension piece should be positioned to within 12 mm of the surface of the material being cut.

4) The diameter of the saw blade must never be less than ⁶⁄₁₀ (60%) of the largest saw blade for which the machine is designed. In the case of a multi-speed machine the diameter of the saw blade must never be less than 60% of the largest saw blade which can be properly used at the highest speed. A notice must always be fixed to each machine clearly stating the minimum diameter of the saw blade that may be used.

5) Circular saws must not:
   (a) Be used for cutting tenons, grooves, and rebates or moulding unless effectively guarded. These normally take the form of Shaw 'tunnel type' guards which, in addition to enclosing the blade, apply pressure to the work piece, keeping it in place.
   (b) Be used for ripping unless the saw teeth project above the timber, i.e. deeping large sectioned material in two cuts is not permissible.

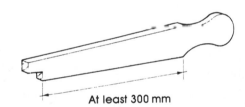

Figure 5.8 *Push stick*

At least 300 mm

6) A suitable push stick (Figure 5.8) must be provided and kept readily available at all times. It must be used for:
   (a) Feeding material where the cut is 300 mm or less.
   (b) Feeding material over the last 300 mm of the cut.
   (c) Removing cut pieces from between the saw blade and fence.

A push block may be used in conjunction with a push stick for cutting short sections.

7) Anyone working at the machine, except the operator, must stand at the delivery end. A full-width table extension must be fitted so that the distance between the nearest part of the saw blade and the end of the table is at least 1200 mm (except in the case of a portable saw bench having a saw blade of 450 mm or less in diameter). See Figure 5.9.

8) The safe working position for the operator is at the feed end offset away from the fence and out of the blade line.

9) It is recommended that operators wear personal protection (Figure 5.10): ear protection to reduce the risk of hearing loss; dust mask, particularly when cutting hardwood to reduce the risk of respiratory problems.

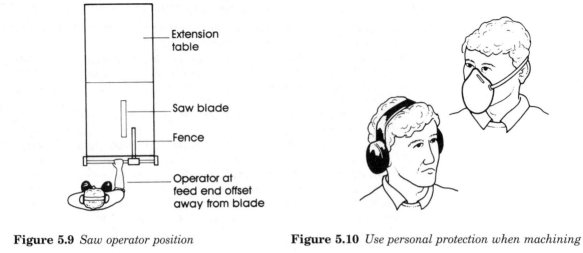

Figure 5.9 *Saw operator position*

Figure 5.10 *Use personal protection when machining*

Tooling

The teeth and their terminology for a circular saw blade used for most ripping operations is illustrated in Figure 5.11.

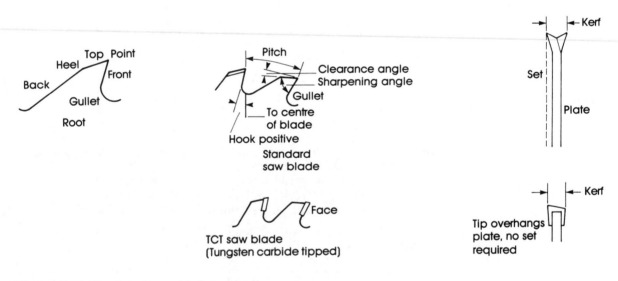

Figure 5.11 *Circular rip saw blade terminology*

Pitch – is the distance between two teeth.

Hook – is the angle of the front of the tooth. Positive hook is required for ripping. (The teeth incline towards the timber.) An angle of 20 to 25 degrees is normally used for softwoods and 10 to 15 degrees for hardwoods.

Clearance angle – ensures the heel clears the timber when cutting. An angle of 15 degrees is normally used for softwoods and 5 to 10 degrees for hardwoods.

Top bevel – is the angle across the top of the tooth. An angle of 15 degrees is normally used for softwood and 5 to 10 degrees for hardwoods.

Gullet – is the space between two teeth. It carries away the sawdust.

Kerf – is the total width of the saw cut in the timber made by the blade. It equals twice the set plus the thickness of the saw plate or twice the overhang plus the thickness of the saw plate on tungsten carbide tipped saws (TCT).

Set – is the amount each tooth is bent or sprung out to give a clearance on the sawplate. The cutting edge of sprung set blades quickly dull when ripping abrasive timbers. Many sawmills now use tungsten carbide tipped (TCT) saws. These stay sharper much longer and don't require a set as they overhang the sawplate.

Maintenance

ENSURE MACHINE IS ISOLATED FROM POWER SUPPLY BEFORE UNDERTAKING MAINTENANCE

Saw blade maintenance

After a period of use, saw blades will start to dull (lose their cutting edge). This will progressively cause a poor finish to the saw cut including burning of both the timber and the blade and possibly cause blade wobble due to overheating. In addition, it will require excessive pressure by the operator to force the timber through the saw.

The sharpening of circular ripsaw blades is normally carried out on a saw sharpening machine or by hand filing. However, neither of these operations is within the scope of this Unit of Competence.

To ensure true running of a saw blade, it should be fitted in the same position on the saw spindle each time it is used. This can be achieved by always mounting the blades on the spindle with the location/driving peg uppermost and, before tightening, pulling the saw blade back onto the peg.

Resin deposits on saw blades should be cleaned off periodically. They can be softened by brushing with an oil/paraffin mixture and scraped off. A wood scraper is preferable as it will avoid scratching the saw blade.

Machine maintenance

Routine periodic maintenance of the machine will:

- prolong its serviceable life
- ensure all moving parts work freely
- ensure the machine operates safely.

The manufacturer's maintenance schedule supplied with each machine, gives the operator information regarding routine maintenance procedures. The schedule will detail the parts to be lubricated, the location of grease nipples and the type, frequency and amount of grease.

A typical procedure might be:

- Remove all rust spots with fine wire wool.
- Clean off resin deposits and other dirt, using an oil/paraffin mixture and wooden scraper.

- Wipe over entire machine using clean rag.
- Apply a coat of light grade oil to all screws and slides. Excess should be wiped off using a clean rag.
- Clean off grease nipples and apply correct grade and amount of grease using the correct gun. Parts can be rotated manually during this operation.
- Check freeness of all moving parts.

Learning task

Consult BS 6854 Safe Guarding of Woodworking Machines. Answer the following questions.

Define a circular sawing machine in accordance with the Standard.

_____

_____

_____

Name the part that covers circular sawing machines.

_____

What paragraph relates to the thickness of a riving knife?

_____

Describe what the Standard says about training.

_____

_____

Questions for you

1. Produce sketches to show the difference between deeping and flatting.

2. Name a type of saw blade that is most suitable for ripping abrasive timber.

_____

3. Describe the safe working position that the operator of a circular hand fed saw bench should take.

_____

_____

4. The riving knife fitted to a circular saw must have a maximum clearance between itself and the blade of:
(a)   6 mm
(b)   10 mm
(c)   12 mm
(d)   20 mm

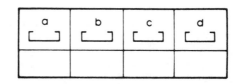

5. The guard on a circular saw that covers the top of a saw blade is known as the:
(a)   shaw guard
(b)   top guard
(c)   crown guard
(d)   bridge guard

6. List **FOUR** general requirements for the safe use of woodworking machines.

_____

_____

_____

_____

7. State one piece of information that must be fixed to every circular saw machine.

_____

_____

8. State the purposes of packings to circular saw blades.

_____

_____

9. State **TWO** reasons for using a hardwood mouthpiece.

_____

_____

10. Label the illustration that shows a portion of a circular saw blade.

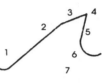

11. State **TWO** reasons for undertaking routine periodic maintenance of woodworking machines.

_____

_____

12. State **TWO** situations where a push stick must be used.

_____

_____

13. List **FIVE** tasks that may be included in the periodic maintenance of a circular saw.

_____

_____

_____

_____

_____

14. Explain why a riving knife thicker than the saw blade should be used.

_____

_____

15. Describe how you would ensure that a saw blade is refitted in exactly the same position after each time it has been taken off for sharpening.

_____

_____

COMPLETE THE
WORD PUZZLE

WORD PUZZLE

Solve the clues to complete the word puzzle. All the answers are associated with *'Woodworking Machining'*. The number of letters in each word is shown in brackets e.g. (6) indicates a six-letter word and (4, 3) indicates two words having four and three letters each.

Across

3. Covers top of saw blade (5, 5)
6. To cut out of vertical (5)
7. Sideways projection of saw teeth (3)
9. Not flat (4)
10. Fitted behind saw blade (5) (second word)
11. Fitted to top of saw tooth (3)
13. Sawing with the grain (7)
14. A component being machined (4, 5)

Down

1. Abbreviation for type of saw (3)
2. Used to provide protection (5)
4. Prevents binding (6) (first word)
5. Cutting timber to the required thickness (7)
7. Not required by tipped saws (3)
8. The width of a saw cut (4)
12. Used to rip timber (3)

6 Maintenance of buildings

READ THIS CHAPTER, WORKING THROUGH THE QUESTIONS AND LEARNING TASKS

In undertaking this chapter you will be required to demonstrate your skill and knowledge of maintaining internal and external timber components along with the associated trade skills of painting, plastering, brickwork, glazing and ceramic tiling.

You will be required practically to:

- Repair timber by splicing
- Remove and replace timber frames
- Remove and replace structural timber
- Replace sash cords
- Paint timber and plaster
- Re-lay brickwork
- Make good plasterwork and rendering
- Cut glass and install glazing with beads and putty
- Re-fix ceramic tiles.

It is an accepted fact that all buildings will deteriorate (develop faults and defects which if not rectified may lead on to failures) to some extent as they age. This deterioration may even start as the individual components are incorporated into the building elements during the construction process. In certain circumstances the deterioration of the components may have started either prior to their delivery to the building site or during the storage, before the commencement of construction operations.

The rate and extent to which a building deteriorates is dependent on one or more of the following main factors: maintenance; the environment; design and construction.

Defining maintenance

This is taken to mean the keeping, holding, sustaining, or preserving of a building and its services to an acceptable standard. This may take one of two forms: planned maintenance or unplanned maintenance.

Planned or routine maintenance

This is a definite programme of work aimed at reducing to a minimum the need for often costly unplanned work. It includes:

- the annual inspection and servicing of general plumbing, heating equipment, electrical and other services, etc.
- the periodic inspection and cleaning out of gutters, gullies, rainwater pipes and airbricks etc.

- the periodic redecoration, both internally and externally;
- the routine general inspection/observation of the building fabric and moving parts.

Preventative maintenance – Finally, also included under this heading, is what is known as preventative maintenance. Basically this is any work carried out as a result of any of the previous inspections in anticipation of a failure, e.g. the early replacement of an item, on the assumption that minor faults almost certainly lead onto bigger and more costly faults unless preventative work is carried out.

Unplanned emergency or corrective maintenance

This is work that is left until the efficiency of the element or service falls well below the acceptable level or even fails altogether. This is the most expensive form of maintenance, making inefficient use of both labour and materials and often also creating serious health/safety risks, and is the type most often carried out. This is because the allocation of money to enable maintenance work to be planned is often given low priority.

Environmental factors

These include:

- the deterioration of components and finishes owing to chemical pollution in the atmosphere;
- the effect of the elements (weather) on the structure, e.g. frost, rain, snow, sun and the wind;
- the effect of these elements when allowed to penetrate into the building;
- the deterioration of components owing to biological attack (fungal decay and insect attack).

Design and construction factors

Faulty design and construction methods can lead to rapid deterioration of a building. In fact over 30% of all maintenance/repair could be avoided if sufficient care is taken at the design and construction stages.

Faulty design

This results from inadequate knowledge or attention to detail on the part of the architect or designer leading to, for example, poor specification of materials/components, structural movement, moisture penetration, biological attack and the inefficient operation of the building services.

Faulty construction

Inadequate supervision during the construction process can result in poor workmanship, the use of inferior materials and the lack of attention to details/specifications. These can all lead to the same problems as those stated for faulty design, resulting in subsequent problems and expense for the building owner.

Agents of deterioration

Apart from the natural ageing process of all buildings during their anticipated life (however well maintained), deterioration of buildings can be attributed directly to one or often a combination of the following agents:

- dampness
- movement
- chemical attack
- biological attack
- infestation.

Dampness

Dampness in buildings is the biggest single source of trouble. It causes the rapid deterioration of most building materials, can assist chemical attack and creates conditions which are favourable for biological attack. Dampness can arise from three main external sources: rain penetration, rising damp and condensation. In addition, leaking plumbing and heating systems and spillage of water in use are also significant causes of dampness.

Rain penetration – This is rain penetrating the external structure either through the walls or the roof and appearing on the inside of the building as damp patches. After periods of heavy rain these patches will tend to spread and then dry out during prolonged periods of dry weather. They will, however, never completely disappear, as a moisture stain and in some cases even efflorescence (crystallised mineral salts) will be left on the surface.

Mould growth (fungi resulting in dark-green or black patchy spots) may occur in damp areas particularly behind furniture, in corners and other poorly ventilated locations. The main causes of rain penetration are shown in Figures 6.1 and 6.2. It can be seen that penetration takes places through gaps, cracks, holes and joints either in, around or between components and elements.

Roofs – Loose or missing tiles or slates including the hip and ridge capping tiles will allow rainwater to run down rafters, causing damp patches on the ceilings and tops of walls. These patches may appear some distance away from the defective area as the water spreads along timbers and across the ceiling, etc. This dampness will also saturate any thermal insulation material making it ineffective. If left unrepaired, saturation of the roof timbers will occur leading to fungal decay in due course. Another major area of penetration is around the chimney stack and other roof-to-wall junctions; this may be due to cracked chimney pots, cracked or deteriorating flaunchings (the sloping mortar into which the pots are set), or corroded or pitted metal flashings (these cover the joint between the stack or wall and the roof) which may be cracked or deteriorated. Poor pointing to the stack can also be a cause of penetration. Any of these defects can cause large patches of damp on the internal wall.

Walls – Clearly rainwater travels downwards and when assisted by high winds it will travel sideways through gaps. But depending on the nature of the material, it can often move unassisted both sideways or upwards because of capillary attraction (the phenomenon whereby water can

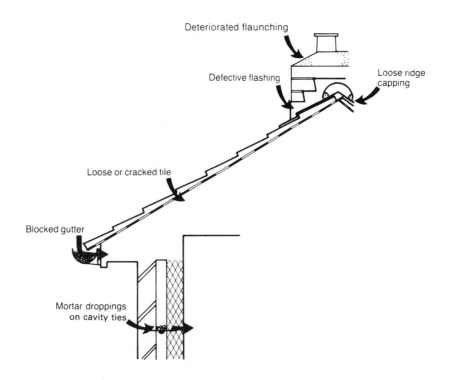

Figure 6.1 *Rain penetration*

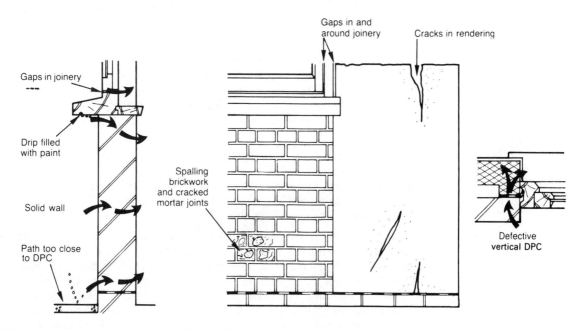

Figure 6.2 *Rain penetration*

travel against the force of gravity in fine spaces or between two surfaces which are close together; the smaller the space the greater the attraction (see Figure 6.3).

There are two main conditions that promote **capillarity** in the external envelope. The fine cellular structure of some materials provides the interconnecting pores through which water can travel. Also

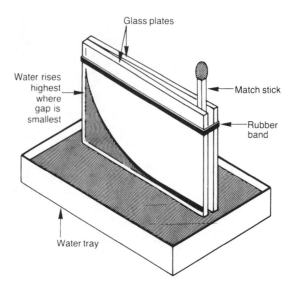

Figure 6.3 *Experiment to show capillarity*

the fine joints between components, e.g. wall and door or window frame, mortar joints between brickwork, close joints between overlapping components. The risk of capillarity is reduced or avoided by either:

- Physically separating the inside and outside surface by introducing a gap (e.g. cavity wall construction).
- Introducing an impervious (waterproof) barrier between components (e.g. mastic pointing, DPCs, DPMs, moisture barriers and flashing, etc.).

Over time, the water resistance of brick/stonework and their mortar joints will deteriorate. This deterioration can be accelerated by the action of frost. Rainwater may accumulate below the surface and freeze. Ice expands causing the brickwork/stonework and their mortar joints to spall (crumble away). The wall then offers little resistance to the weather and should be replaced. This entails either:

- Cutting the surface of the spalled components back and replacing with matching thin components (half bricks) and finally repointing the whole wall.
- The entire wall may be 'hacked off' (cut back to remove spalling) and covered with one of the standard wall finishes, cement rendering, rough cast, pebble dash, Tyrolean or silicone-nylon fibre.

Cracks in cement rendering and other wall finishes can be caused by shrinkage on drying, building movement or chemical attack. Once opened up, deterioration is accelerated by frost action. Small cracks may be enlarged and filled with a cement slurry. Large areas which may have 'blown' (come away) from the surface will require hacking back to sound (firmly adhering) work and replaced. With cavity wall construction, rainwater that does penetrate the outer leaf should simply run down inside the cavity and not reach the internal leaf. The vertical mortar joints of the outer leaf are sometimes raked out at intervals along the bottom of the cavity to provide weep holes through which the water can escape.

However, when the cavity is bridged by a porous material (e.g. the collection of mortar droppings on the wall ties during construction), the water will reach the inner leaf causing small isolated damp patches on the internal wall surface. The remedy for this fault is to remove one or two bricks of the outer leaf near the suspected bridge and either clean out or replace the tie as necessary.

Dampness around door and window frames is likely to be caused by wind-assisted rain entering the joint between the wall and frame, by the action of capillarity or by a defective vertical DPC used around openings in cavity walls, where the inner and outer leaf join. An exterior mastic can be used to seal the joints but where DPCs are defective they will require cutting out and replacing. A check should be made at the sill level of frames. Cracked sills allow water to penetrate and therefore should be filled. The drip groove on the underside of the sill should be cleaned out as it often collects dirt/dust and is filled by repeated painting. The purpose of the drip groove is to break the under surface of the sill making the water drip off at this point and not run back underneath into the building.

Blocked or cracked gutters and down-pipes, dripping outside taps and constantly running overflows can cause an excessive concentration of water in one place which will be almost permanently damp. This will result in an accelerated deterioration of the wall and subsequent internal damp patches etc. The immediate fault can be easily rectified by repairing or replacing the defective component. But if left unattended the resulting damage to the building structure has most serious and costly implications.

Rising damp – This is normally moisture from below ground level rising and spreading up walls and through floors by capillarity. This most often occurs in older buildings. Many of these were built without DPCs and DPMs, or, where they were incorporated have broken down possibly with age (e.g. slate, a one time popular DPC material cracks with building movement, thus allowing capillarity). The visual result on the walls is a band of dampness and staining spreading up from the skirting level; wallpaper peeling from the surface and signs of offlorescence. The skirting, joists and floorboards adjacent to the missing or failed DPC are almost certain to be subject to fungal attack. Solid floors may be almost permanently damp causing considerable damage to floor coverings and adjacent timber/furniture etc. Rising damp can still occur in buildings that have been equipped with DPCs and DPMs (see Figure 6.4).

One of the main reasons for this is the bridging of DPCs; in the case of cavity walls, builders' mortar droppings or rubble may have collected at the bottom of the cavity, allowing moisture to rise above the DPC level; or earth in a flower bed being too high above the DPC. **Note:** DPCs are normally located at least two courses of brickwork (150 mm) above the adjacent ground level. This is because even very heavy rain is unlikely to bounce up and splash the walls much more than 100 mm from the surrounding surface. Thus the splashed rainwater is still prevented from rising above the DPC. Where the surrounding surface is later raised these splashes might bypass the DPC and result in rising damp. Weak porous rendering which has been continued over the DPC is another means by which the DPC may be bypassed.

In solid floors with a DPM, rising damp can only occur if this is defective (see Figure 6.5). For example, it may have been penetrated by jagged hardcore during the pouring of the over site concrete or have been inadequately lapped (permitting capillarity between the lapped joint, or finally it may not have been linked in with the DPC in the surrounding walls (allowing moisture to bypass at this point).

The remedy to rising damp faults will of course vary; bridged or bypassed DPCs can be rectified by simply removing the cause, e.g. lowering the ground level or removing mortar and rubble from the cavity etc. Where

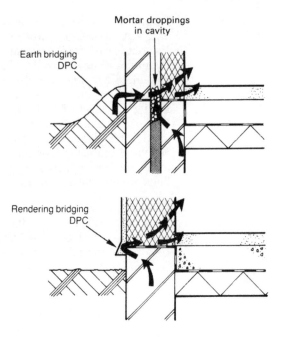

Figure 6.4 Rising damp

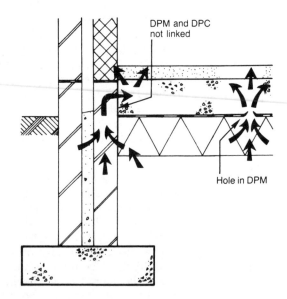

Figure 6.5 Rising damp

the DPC itself is faulty or missing altogether, one can be inserted by either cutting out a few bricks at a time to allow the positioning of a new DPC, sawing away the mortar joint a section at a time and inserting a new one.

Alternatively, liquid silicone may be injected near the bottom of the wall. This soaks into the lower courses which then acts as a moisture barrier preventing capillarity.

Localised faults in DPMs can be remedied by cutting out a section of the floor larger than the damp patch, down to the DPM, taking care not to cut through it. This should reveal the holed or badly lapped portion which can be repaired with a self-adhesive DPM. An alternative method which can also be used in floors without any DPM, is to cover the existing concrete floor with a liquid bituminous membrane or a sheet of heavy-duty polythene sheeting before laying a new floor finish, although, to be effective it should be joined into the DPC.

Condensation – The results of this form of dampness are often mistakenly attributed to rain penetration or rising damp, as they can all cause damp patches, staining, mould growth, peeling wallpaper, efflorescence, the fungal attack of timber and generally damp, unhealthy living conditions. The water or moisture for condensation actually comes from within the building. People breathing, kettles boiling, food cooking, clothes washing and drying, bath water running, etc. Each of these processes adds more moisture to the air in the form of vapour.

Air is always capable of holding a certain amount of water vapour. The warmer the air, the more vapour it can hold, but when air cools the excess vapour will revert to water. This process is known as condensation. Thus whenever warm moist air meets a cool surface condensation will occur (see Figure 6.6). This can only be controlled effectively by achieving a proper balance between heating, ventilation and insulation. The building should be kept well heated but windows should be opened or mechanical ventilators used especially in kitchens and bathrooms to allow the vapour-laden air escape outside and not spread through the building. External walls need thermally insulating to remove their cold surfaces. Both cavity wall insulation and lining the walls with a thin polystyrene veneer help a great deal. Double glazed windows also help reduce condensation by preventing the warm moist air coming into direct contact with the cold outside pane of glass.

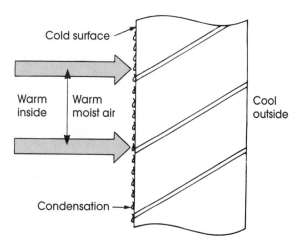

Figure 6.6 *Surface condensation*

In addition to this surface condensation, there is another condensation problem that occurs when wall surfaces are warm. This is known as interstitial or internal condensation. This is illustrated in Figure 6.7. It is caused by the warm moist air passing into the permeable structure until it cools, at which point it condenses, thus leading to the same problems associated with penetrated and rising dampness.

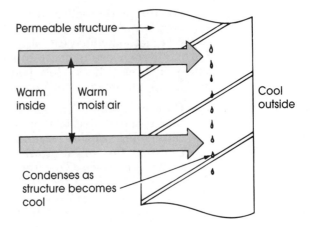

Figure 6.7 *Interstitial condensation*

Interstitial condensation can be dealt with either:

● by the use of a vapour barrier (this prevents the passage of water vapour) on the warm inside of the wall, e.g. a polythene sheet or foil backed plasterboard; or
● by allowing this water vapour to pass through the structure into a cavity where it can be dispersed by ventilation.

Movement

The visual effects of movement (Figure 6.8) in buildings may apparently be of a minor nature, e.g. windows and doors that jamb or bind in their frames; fine cracks externally along mortar joints and rendering; fine cracks internally in plastered walls and along the ceiling line etc. They can however be the first signs of serious structural weakness. Movement in buildings takes two main forms these being: ground movement and movement of materials.

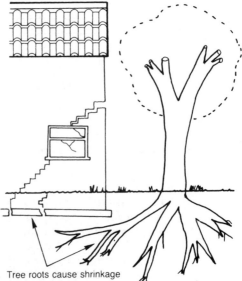

Figure 6.8 *Ground movement*

Ground movement – Any movement in the ground will cause settlement in the building. When it is slight and spread evenly over the building it may be acceptable, although when more than slight or is differential (more in one area than another), it can have serious consequences for the building's foundations and load-bearing members, requiring expensive temporary support (shoring) and subsequently, permanent underpinning (new foundations constructed under existing ones).

Ground movement is caused mainly by its expansion and shrinkage near the surface, owing to wet and dry conditions. Compact granular ground suffers little movement, whereas clay ground is at high risk. Tree roots cause ground shrinkage owing to the considerable amounts of water they extract from it. Tree roots can extend out in all directions from its base, greater than its height. In addition, overloading of the structure beyond its original design load can also result in ground movement.

Frost also causes ground movement. Water in the ground on freezing expands. Where this is allowed to expand on the undersides of foundations it has a tendency to lift the building (known as frost heave) and drop it again on thawing. This repeated action often results in serious cracking. Freezing of ground water is limited in this country to about the top 600 mm in depth.

Movement in materials – All building materials will move to some extent owing to one or more of the following reasons: temperature changes, moisture-content changes and chemical changes. Provided the building is designed and constructed to accommodate these movements or steps are taken to prevent them, they should not lead to serious defects.

Temperature changes – These cause expansion on heating and shrinkage on cooling; particularly affected are metals and plastics, although concrete, stonework, brickwork and timber can be affected also.

Moisture changes – Many materials expand when wetted and shrink on drying. This is known as moisture movement. The greatest amount of moisture movement takes place in timber, which should be painted or treated to seal its surface. Brickwork, cement rendering and concrete can also be affected by moisture movement. Rapid drying of wetted brickwork in the hot sun can result in cracks, particularly around window and door openings.

Chemical and fungal attack

Corrosion – These consist of the corrosion of metals and the sulphate attack of cement. Corrosion causes metals to expand and lose strength. Corrosion of steel beams can lift brickwork causing cracks in the mortar joint. Bulges in cavity brickwork may be caused by corroded wall ties. The sulphate attack of cement is either in the ground or from products of combustion in chimneys. The sulphate mixes with water and causes cement to expand. Sulphate-Resisting Portland Cement (SRPC) should be used in conditions where high levels of sulphate are expected.

Smoke containing chemicals is given off into the atmosphere as a result of many manufacturing processes. This mixes with water vapour and rainwater to form dilute or weak acid solutions. These solutions corrode iron and steel, break down paint films and erode the surfaces of brickwork, stonework and tiles. The useful life of materials in these environments can be prolonged by regular cleaning to remove the contamination.

Ageing – Exposure to sunlight can cause bleaching, colour fading of materials and even decomposition owing to solar radiation. Particularly affected are bituminous products, plastics and painted surfaces.

Biological attack – Timber, including structural, non-structural and timber-based manufactured items are the targets for biological attack. The agents of this are fungi and wood-boring insects. Given the right conditions an attack by one or both agents is almost inevitable.

There are two main types of fungi that cause decay in building timbers, these being dry rot and wet rot.

Dry rot – This is the more serious and is more difficult to eradicate than wet rot. It is caused by a fungus that feeds on the cellulose found mainly in sapwood (outer layers of a growing tree). This causes timber to lose strength and weight, develop cracks in brick-shape patterns and finally to become so dry and powdery that it can easily be crumbled in the hand. The appearance of a piece of timber after an attack of dry rot is shown in Figure 6.9. Two initial factors for an attack are damp timber in excess of about 20% moisture content (MC) and bad or non-existent ventilation.

Figure 6.9 *Timber after dry rot attack*

As the fungus is a living plant, an attack commences with the germination of its microscopic spores (seeds) that send out into the timber hyphae (roots) to feed on the cellulose. Once established, these hyphae branch out and spread through and over the timber forming a matt of cottonwool-like threads called mycelia. At this stage, the hyphae can penetrate plaster and brickwork in search of further timber supplies to feed on. This further timber supply need not be damp as the developed hyphae can conduct their own water supply, thus adjusting the moisture content as required. Finally the fruiting body like a fleshy pancake with an orange brown centre, will start to ripen and eject into the air millions of the rust-red spores, to begin the process elsewhere. Very often in the early stages, apart from a damp musty mushroomy smell, there is little evidence of an attack. It is not until the wall panelling, skirting or floorboards are removed that the full effects are realised, as Figure 6.10 shows.

Eradication and treatment – To eradicate an attack of dry rot, firstly rectify sources of dampness and bad ventilation:

- Remove all traces of decayed timber and at least 600 mm of apparently sound timber beyond the last signs of attack.
- All affected timber including swept-up dust, dirt and old wood shavings etc. must be sealed in airtight polythene bags and arrangements made for their incineration (contact your local authority for information). This prevents spreading and kills hyphae and spores.
- Strip plaster from walls, wire brush brickwork, heat up brickwork with a blow lamp to sterilise, and brush or spray wall with a dry-rot fungicide (this kills any hyphae and spores in the walls).
- Finally, work may be reinstated with preservative treated timber. (**Note:** The idea behind preservative treatment is to poison the food supply of fungi and wood-boring insects, by applying a toxic liquid to the timber.)

Figure 6.10 *Advanced dry rot*

Wet rot – This is also caused by a fungus, but it does not normally involve such drastic eradication treatment, as it does not spread to the same extent as dry rot. It feeds on wet timber (30% to 50% MC) and is most often found in cellars, neglected external joinery, ends of rafters, under leaking sinks or baths and under impervious (waterproof) floor coverings. During an attack, the timber becomes soft, darkens to a blackish colour and develops cracks along the grain. Very often timber decays internally with a fairly thin skin of apparently sound timber remaining on the surface. The hyphae when apparent are dark brown or black; internally hyphae may be white and form

Figure 6.11 *Wet rot in rafters*

into sheets. Its fruiting body, which is rarely found, is of an irregular shape and normally olive green in colour, as are the spores. Figure 6.11 shows the appearance after an attack of wet rot in the rafters of a roof.

Timber treatment – To eradicate an attack of wet rot all that is normally required is to cure the source of wetness and allow the timber to dry out. Replacement of soft timber may be required after an extensive attack particularly where structural timber is concerned. Non-structural timber may be treated with a wet rot wood hardening fluid.

Infestation

Wood-boring insects – This is also known as woodworm, after the larvae which are able to feed on, and digest, the substance of wood. The majority of the damage done to building timber in the UK can be attributed to five species illustrated in Table 6.1, which also includes their identifying characteristics.

The female adult beetle lays eggs during the summer months, usually in the end grain, open joints, or cracks in the timber. This affords the eggs a certain amount of protection until the larvae hatch. The larvae then start their damaging journey by boring into the timber, consuming it and then excreting it as fine dust. The duration of this stage varies between six months and ten years depending on the species. During the early spring, at the close of this stage, the larvae bore out a pupal chamber near the timber surface, where they undergo the transformation into adult beetles. This takes a short period after which the beetles bite out of the timber leaving characteristic flight holes. The presence of flight holes is often the first external sign of an attack. After emerging from the timber the beetle's instinct is to mate, lay eggs and then die, thus completing one life cycle and starting another.

Timber treatment – To eradicate an attack of wood-boring insects open up the affected area (take up floorboards etc.) remove all affected timber and replace with new preservative-treated timber. **Note:** again all removed timber and swept up dust and old wood shavings etc. must

Table 6.1 *Wood-boring insects*

Name	Actual size	Location and timber attacked
Furniture beetle	beetle flight holes	Softwoods and the sapwood of hardwoods; causes considerable damage to timber, flooring and furniture
Death-watch beetle		Mainly hardwoods in old damp buildings (churches); often in association with fungal attack
Lyctus beetle (powder post)		Sapwood of freshly-cut hardwoods; normally in timber yards before use
House long-horn beetle		Sapwood of softwoods; mainly roof timbers
Weevils		Damp or decayed hardwoods and softwoods; often found around sinks, baths, toilets and in cellars

be sealed in airtight polythene bags and arrangements made for their incineration. Brush timber to remove dust, strip off surface coating, e.g. paint, varnish, etc. (wood-worm fluid will not penetrate surface coatings). Apply two coats of a proprietary woodworm killer by brush or spray to all timber, even apparently unaffected timber. Pay particular attention to cracks, joints, end grain and flight holes. Inspections for fresh flight holes should be carried out for several successive summers. A further treatment of fluid will be required if any are found. (Fresh bore dust around the affected area indicates fresh flight holes.)

6 Maintenance of buildings

─────── **Questions for you** ───────

1. Define the term 'building maintenance'.

_____

_____

2. Name two factors that affect the rate and extent to which a building deteriorates.

_____

_____

3. Name three agents to which deterioration in buildings can be directly attributed.

_____

_____

_____

4. Produce a sketch to show two methods by which moisture may bypass DPCs.

5. Define the term 'capillary attraction'.

_____

_____

6. Name two causes of movement in buildings and identify their likely effect.

_____

_____

_____

7. State the purpose of treating timber with preservative.

_____

_____

8. Identify two causes of rising damp and suggest a remedy for each.

_____

_____

_____

9. List two defects under each of the following headings that can lead to the rapid deterioration of a building:

(a) movement

_____

_____

(b) biological attack.

_____

_____

10. Identify the probable causes of the following defects:

(a) small isolated damp patches at intervals on the internal leaf of an external cavity wall;

_____

(b) small holes in the surface of timber with fine dust around them;

_____

(c) damp patch in the centre of a solid ground floor.

_____

WELL, HOW DID YOU DO?

WORK THROUGH THE SECTION AGAIN IF YOU HAD ANY PROBLEMS

Undertaking repairs and maintenance work

Building firms who specialise in maintenance work, will often tend to employ or give preference to operatives, who possess multi-skills, as they will be expected to carry out in conjunction with their main craft skill, a range of basic skills of the other crafts e.g.

- After hanging a replacement door you may be expected to paint it.
- When replacing a window you may be expected to glaze it, re-lay the brickwork under the sill and patch in the plasterwork. If this was in a bathroom or kitchen it may also involve replacing ceramic tiles.

Inspections and repair surveys

Whenever a building firm undertakes major repairs or maintenance it is desirable to undertake a survey of the building. The extent of the measurements, sketches and details taken, will depend on the nature and extent of the work. Clearly a survey prior to replacing windows in a house will be very different to that of one involving structural movement.

Existing information – In many cases, there will already be in existence information that can assist you when carrying out a survey:

- *Drawings* – Make enquiries to the buildings owner to determine whether there are any existing drawings of the building. These may be in their possession from when the building was new or from when an extension was added some time in the past. Figure 6.12 illustrates the typical general location plans from when the house was built, which might be available. If so these can simplify your task by forming the basis of the survey sketches.
- *Previous survey reports* – Often there are existing reports, made by building society surveyors for mortgage purposes, or structural reports made for insurance purposes when a claim is being made. Figure 6.13 shows extracts from a typical schedule of remedial works made following a structural survey of a house, as part of an

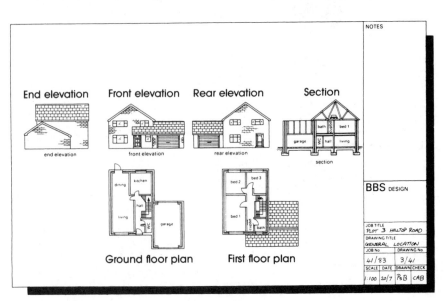

Figure 6.12 *General location plans*

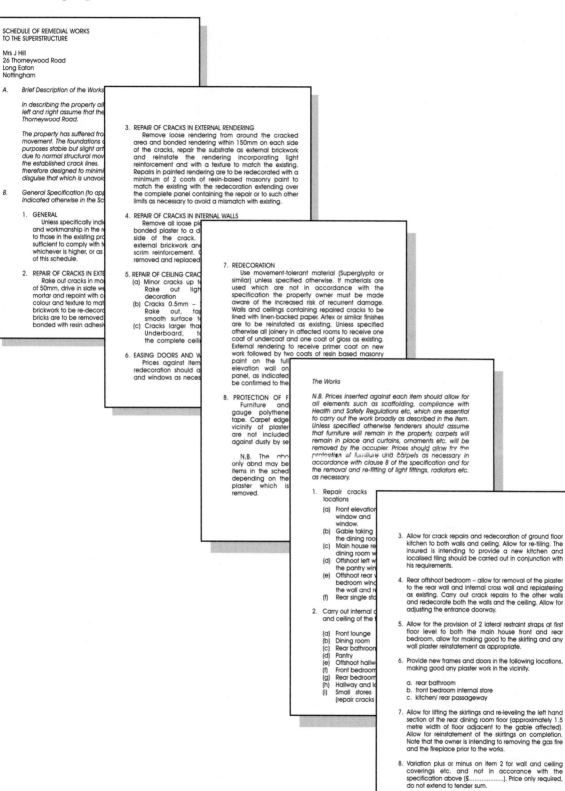

Figure 6.13 *Schedule of remedial work*

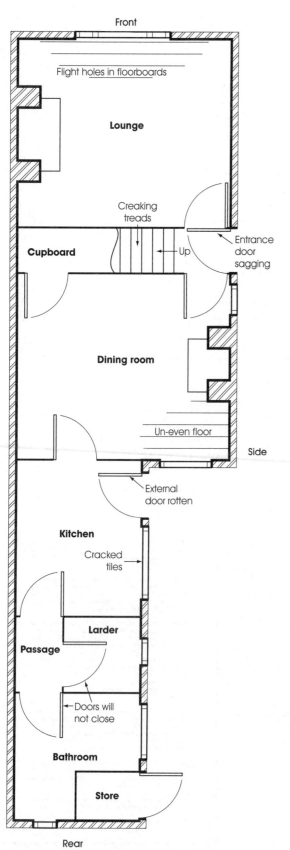

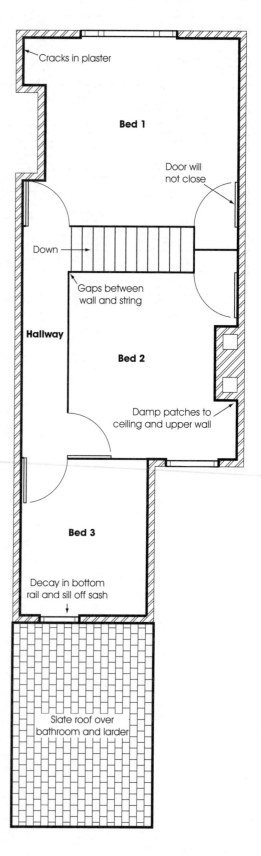

Figure 6.14a *Ground floor plan showing defects*

Figure 6.14b *First floor plan showing defects*

insurance claim. This identifies the main areas of concern. You would concentrate on these points to estimate the precise amount of work involved.

Undertaking the survey – Before you start the actual survey you should provisionally look the building over, both internally and externally, to determine its general layout and any likely difficulties. This will involve making notes and sketches to create a true record of the building's existing condition, including work/defects outside your craft.

Internal survey

Sketch plans are made of each floor or room, starting at ground floor level. You may be guided to the apparent major problem by the building's occupants, or another survey report etc. (e.g. schedule of remedial work). This can be the starting point for adding details to your sketches. Doors, windows, stairs and fitments should be added along with any defects you come across. This work may involve lifting floorboards, partial removal of skirting, panelling or casings and gaining access to the roof space. Figure 6.14 illustrates a typical set of internal survey sketches for an early 1900's built semi-detached house.

Where a lot of detail is required an accompanying list of defects should be made. Table 6.2 shows details of the defects found in the form of a tabled schedule.

Table 6.2 *Internal defects schedule*

Location	Defect	Possible cause	Remedial action
Lounge	• Flight holes in floorboards	• Woodworm	• Expose under-floor space and check remainder of house to determine the extent of attack, then rectify
Dining room	• Uneven floor	• Possible structural movement (subsidence) or fungal attack	• Consult structural engineer • Expose under-floor space to determine extent, then rectify
Lower hall	• Entrance door sagging	• Joints failed	• Dismantle and re-assemble door using external WBP adhesive
Stairs	• Creaking treads • Gap between wall and string	• Shrinkage between tread and riser, glue blocks loose • Moisture movement and/or failure of fixing	• Screw treads to risers. Re-fix glue blocks • Re fix string , cover gap with decorative moulding
Kitchen	• External door rotten • Cracked tiling	• Wet rot • Movement or accidental	• Replace with new door • Replace tiles
Bathroom/ larder	• Doors will not close	• Door twisted • Hinge bound • Defective ironmongery	• Ease rebates or replace door • Scrape off paint, pack out hinge • Adjust or replace tiles
Bedroom 1	• Cracks in plaster • Door will not close	• Structural movement/ shrinkage • As above	• Consult structural engineer • Cut out and repair • As above
Bedroom 2	• Damp patches to ceiling and upper wall	• Condensation • Defective slates • Deflective flashing	• Provide roof space ventilation • Replace • Replace
Bedroom 3	• Decayed window	• Wet rot due to lack of repainting	• Replace window

Where joinery items are to be repaired or replaced, full size details of the sections and mouldings must be made to enable them to be matched up. This task can be eased by the use of a **moulding template** see Figure 6.15. The pins of the template are pressed into the contours of the moulding. It can be placed on the sketch pad, drawn around and dimensions added. The location of where the moulding was taken should be noted as they may vary from room to room.

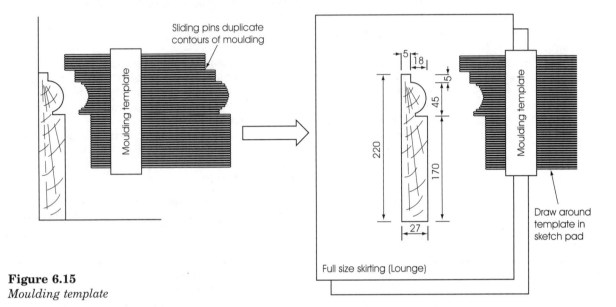

Figure 6.15
Moulding template

External survey

Sketch outline elevations of the building and add any defects found. Photographs of the elevation may be taken as a backup to your sketches, especially where intricate details have to be replaced. Often defects found on the internal survey are a result of external defects. These should be your starting point. As an example a damp mouldy patch in the corner of a kitchen might be the result of surface condensation, due to poor ventilation. Alternatively it may be due to a leaking rainwater gutter or down pipe. Binoculars are useful for viewing higher levels of a building; closer observation might involve the use of a ladder or the erection of a scaffold. Figure 6.16 illustrates a typical set of external survey sketches used for the inspection of an early 1900's semi-detached house.

Your focus of attention when carrying out the external survey should include the following points.

Walls:

● Signs of structural movement: cracks in brickwork joints, rendering and missing pointing.
● Staining: particularly just below the roof eaves, above the damp proof course (DPC) and behind rainwater down pipes.
● Height of DPC above ground level: this should be a minimum of 150 mm.
● Air bricks: ensure they are clear and not blocked by overgrown vegetation.

Window and doors:

● Condition of woodwork: look out for poor fitting doors and casements.

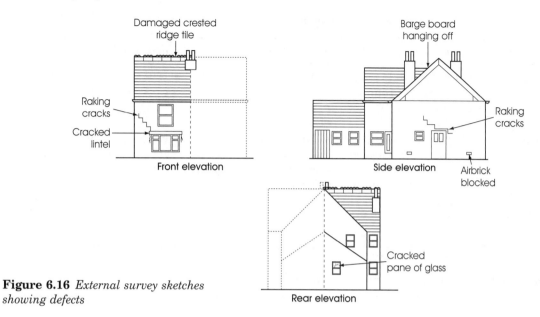

Figure 6.16 *External survey sketches showing defects*

- Condition of paintwork: cracked paintwork at joints will allow water penetration and may lead to wet rot. The easy insertion of a penknife or bradawl may confirm your suspicions.
- Condition and operation of ironmongery.
- Condition of glass, putty and glazing beads.

Roofs:

- Missing, displaced or damaged tiles, slates and flat roof coverings.
- Missing, displaced or damaged flaunching, flashings, valley gutters and verges.
- Barge boards, fascia and soffits: condition of paintwork; look out for signs of decay and distortion. Also check soffits for the presence of any ventilation gaps or grills (these may require cleaning, collected debris or repeated painting may block them).

Guttering, down pipes and drains:

- Check joints are sealed; look out for signs of water staining and moss growth.
- Feel behind cast iron down pipes for corrosion damage due to lack of paint protection.
- Check all brackets and clips are secure.
- Check drain gullies are clear. Look out for signs of them discharging water over their edges onto a path or house wall.
- Check drain gullies are retaining their water seal. If no water is seen in the 'U' bend, it may be cracked or broken and discharging water to undermine the foundations and also causing dampness.

Outside areas:

- Check condition of garden walls, paths and driveways. Look out for signs of structural movement.
- Wooden fences, post and gates: look out for signs of decay. They are particularly susceptible at ground level and joints, where water can be retained.
- Note position of trees and other large plants.

Table 6.3 shows the results of the external survey in schedule form.

Table 6.3 *External defects schedule (Figure 6.16 refers)*

Location	Defect	Possible cause	Remedial action
Front elevation	• Ridge tile damaged • Cracking to ground floor lintel and raking cracks above	• Wind damage/ uncertain • Structural movement	• Replace and make good • Consult structural engineer
Side elevation	• Air bricks blocked • Raking cracks above entrance door • Barge board hanging off	• Build up of dirt, soil and vegetation • Structural movement • Fixings failed	• Clean out, reduce ground level to at least 150 mm below DPC • Consult structural engineer • Re-fix and make good slates if required
Rear elevation	• Cracked pane of glass to bathroom	• Accidental/unknown	• Re-glaze window
Outbuildings and structures		(Not viewed)	

(left margin: 6 Maintenance of buildings)

Timber repairs

When considering timber repairs a great deal of judgement and negotiation with the client is often required. Can it be repaired cost effectively or is it cheaper in the long run to replace it? Each job being considered on its own merits, cost against future service life being the main consideration.

Doors

There are many defects associated with doors. Remedial action will depend on the type and location and may range from a simple adjustment through to complete replacement. Table 6.4 and Figure 6.17 cover the most common defects, causes and recommend remedial action.

In all but minor cases consider/discuss with clients the possibility of renewing the door.

Note: Always wear a dust mask when rubbing down paintwork and eye protection goggles when scraping off. Surfaces painted prior to the 1960's may contain harmful lead within the paint. In these circumstances, rub down using a wet process (with wet and dry paper) to minimise the potential risks.

Door frames – Defects to external door frames can normally be attributed to either wet rot to the lower end of the jambs or breakout damage in the lock striking plate area as a result of an attempt to force the door. Both of these can normally be resolved by splicing in new timber to the area of damage. See Figure 6.18. In the worst cases a new frame may be required. However, this option will cause the most disturbance to the internal plasterwork and decoration.

Timber repairs

Table 6.4 *Door defects*

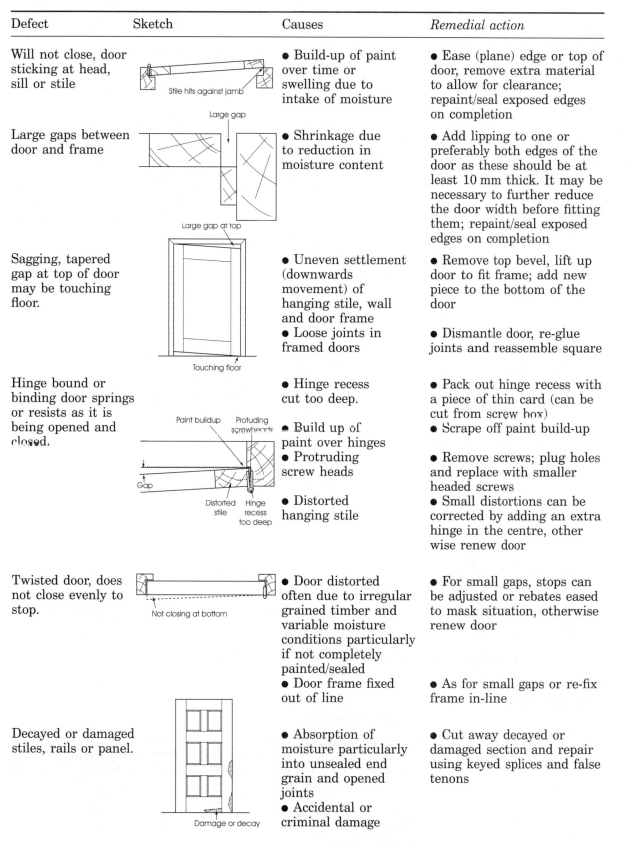

Defect	Sketch	Causes	*Remedial action*
Will not close, door sticking at head, sill or stile	*Stile hits against jamb*	● Build-up of paint over time or swelling due to intake of moisture	● Ease (plane) edge or top of door, remove extra material to allow for clearance; repaint/seal exposed edges on completion
Large gaps between door and frame	*Large gap* / *Large gap at top*	● Shrinkage due to reduction in moisture content	● Add lipping to one or preferably both edges of the door as these should be at least 10 mm thick. It may be necessary to further reduce the door width before fitting them; repaint/seal exposed edges on completion
Sagging, tapered gap at top of door may be touching floor.	*Touching floor*	● Uneven settlement (downwards movement) of hanging stile, wall and door frame ● Loose joints in framed doors	● Remove top bevel, lift up door to fit frame; add new piece to the bottom of the door ● Dismantle door, re-glue joints and reassemble square
Hinge bound or binding door springs or resists as it is being opened and closed.	*Paint buildup* *Protuding screwheads* *Gap* *Distorted stile* *Hinge recess too deep*	● Hinge recess cut too deep. ● Build up of paint over hinges ● Protruding screw heads ● Distorted hanging stile	● Pack out hinge recess with a piece of thin card (can be cut from screw box) ● Scrape off paint build-up ● Remove screws; plug holes and replace with smaller headed screws ● Small distortions can be corrected by adding an extra hinge in the centre, other wise renew door
Twisted door, does not close evenly to stop.	*Not closing at bottom*	● Door distorted often due to irregular grained timber and variable moisture conditions particularly if not completely painted/sealed ● Door frame fixed out of line	● For small gaps, stops can be adjusted or rebates eased to mask situation, otherwise renew door ● As for small gaps or re-fix frame in-line
Decayed or damaged stiles, rails or panel.	*Damage or decay*	● Absorption of moisture particularly into unsealed end grain and opened joints ● Accidental or criminal damage	● Cut away decayed or damaged section and repair using keyed splices and false tenons

Table 6.4 *Door defects (continued)*

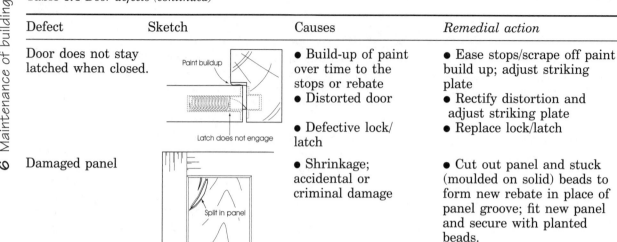

Defect	Sketch	Causes	*Remedial action*
Door does not stay latched when closed.		● Build-up of paint over time to the stops or rebate ● Distorted door ● Defective lock/latch	● Ease stops/scrape off paint build up; adjust striking plate ● Rectify distortion and adjust striking plate ● Replace lock/latch
Damaged panel		● Shrinkage; accidental or criminal damage	● Cut out panel and stuck (moulded on solid) beads to form new rebate in place of panel groove; fit new panel and secure with planted beads.

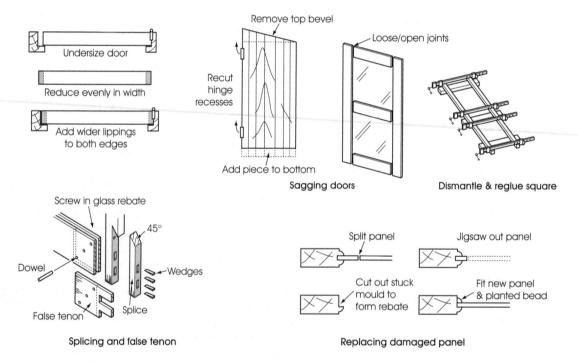

Figure 6.17 *Remedial treatment to doors*

Window frames

Defects to wooden windows are similar to those of doors and door-frames. They will either be associated with poorly fitting opening parts (sashes and casements) or decayed/damaged frames. These can be rectified using the methods previously outlined for doors e.g. scraping off the paint build-up, easing leading edges, dismantling and re-assembly of sagging casements and splicing of new timber to decayed or damaged areas. In the worst cases the installation of a new window should be considered.

Figure 6.18 *Repairs to door and window frames*

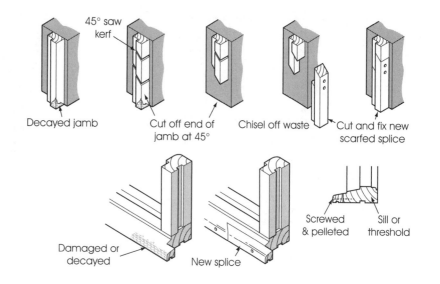

45° saw kerf

Decayed jamb

Cut off end of jamb at 45°

Chisel off waste

Cut and fix new scarfed splice

Damaged or decayed

New splice

Screwed & pelleted

Sill or threshold

Boxed frame sash windows – This type of window is the traditional pattern of sliding sashes and for many years has been superseded by casements and solid frame sash windows. This was mainly due to the high manufacturing and assembly costs of the large number of component parts. An understanding of their construction and operation is essential as they will be met with frequently in renovation and maintenance work.

The double-hung boxed window consists of two sliding sashes suspended on cords that run over pulleys and are attached to counter-balanced weights inside the boxed frame.

Figure 6.19 shows an elevation, horizontal and vertical section of a boxed frame sliding sash window. It shows the make-up of this type of window and names the component parts.

Re-cording sashes – The maintenance carpenter is often called upon to renew a broken sash cord (Figure 6.20). It is good practice to renew all four cords at the same time, for the remaining old cords will be liable to break in the near future.

Figure 6.19 *Boxed frame sliding sash window details*

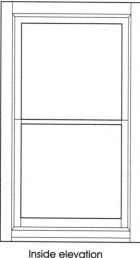

Inside elevation

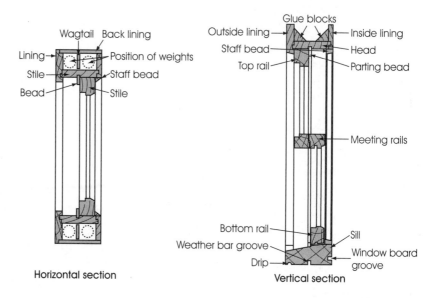

Wagtail   Back lining

Lining

Position of weights

Stile

Staff bead

Bead

Stile

Horizontal section

Glue blocks

Outside lining

Inside lining

Staff bead

Head

Top rail

Parting bead

Meeting rails

Bottom rail

Sill

Weather bar groove

Window board groove

Drip

Vertical section

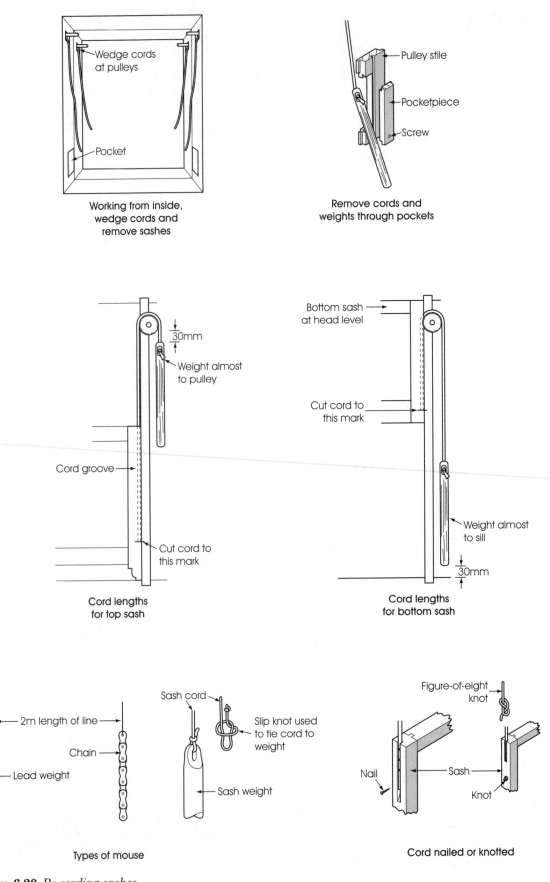

Working from inside,
wedge cords and
remove sashes

Remove cords and
weights through pockets

Wedge cords
at pulleys

Pocket

Pulley stile

Pocketpiece

Screw

Cord lengths
for top sash

30mm

Weight almost
to pulley

Cord groove

Cut cord to
this mark

Cord lengths
for bottom sash

Bottom sash
at head level

Cut cord to
this mark

Weight almost
to sill

30mm

Types of mouse

2m length of line

Chain

Lead weight

Sash cord

Slip knot used
to tie cord to
weight

Sash weight

Cord nailed or knotted

Figure-of-eight
knot

Nail

Sash

Knot

Figure 6.20 *Re-cording sashes*

236

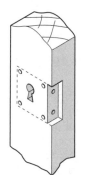

Old lock removed

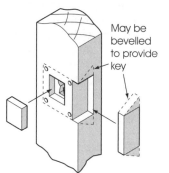

Filling pieces cut, holes
and recesses enlarged

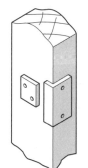

Oversize filling pieces glued
and pinned in place

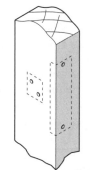

Filling pieces planed off flush,
pin holes filled and sanded off flush

Figure 6.21 *Making good
holes and recesses*

The sequence of operations for renewing sash cords is as follows:

- Carefully remove staff beads.
- Carefully remove pockets, (access pieces cut towards the bottom of pulley stiles).
- Take out bottom sash. The sash cords should be wedged at the pulley and removed from the groove in the sash.
- Carefully remove parting beads. Break paint joints first and carefully prise out with a chisel.
- Take out top sash in a similar manner to the bottom sash.
- Remove the weights and cords through the pockets. The wagtail will move to one side to give access to the outside weights.

Note: the weights may not all be the same, so ensure they are returned to their original positions.

- Thread new cords over pulleys and down to the pockets. A 'mouse' can be used to thread the cords easily. A 'mouse' is a small lead weight that is attached to a 2 m length of string that in turn is tied to the cord. The mouse is inserted over the pulley and drops to the bottom of the frame. The sash cord can now be pulled through. Many carpenters use a length of small chain instead of a mouse.
- Fasten sash cords to weights. To obtain the length of cord for the top sash, rest the sash on the sill and mark on the pulley stile the end of the sash cord groove. Pull the weight up to almost the top and cut the cord to the position marked on the pulley stile. Wedge the cord in the pulley to prevent the weight from dropping. To obtain the length of cord for the bottom sash, place the sash up against the head of the frame and mark on the pulley stile the end of the sash cord groove. With the weight just clearing the bottom of the frame cut the cord to the position marked on the pulley stile. Wedge the cord in the pulley.
- Fix sash cords to the top sash and insert the sash into the frame. The cords are normally attached to the sashes by nailing them into the cord grooves. Alternatively the cord can pass through a closed groove and end in a knot.
- Replace the parting beads. Where these have been damaged new ones should be used.
- Fix the sash cords to the bottom sash and insert the sash into the frame.
- Replace the staff beads and check the window for ease of operation. Candle wax can be applied to the pulley stiles and beads to assist smooth operation.

Door and window hardware

The moving parts of locks, latches, bolts and hinges require regular lubrication and need to be kept free from paint build-up, in order to ensure their trouble-free operation. Inevitably they will eventually begin to wear and require replacement. In general these should be replaced with like for like or the nearest alternative. However proposed replacement does provide the opportunity to upgrade hardware, particularly locks for increased security.

When replacing or upgrading hardware it is often necessary to make good holes and recesses. Figure 6.21 illustrates a typical situation. In general all follow the same procedure:

- Cut oversize filling pieces of a similar material. These are often bevelled to provide a key.

- Mark and cut out enlarged hole and recesses to receive filling pieces.
- Glue and pin filling pieces in place.
- Punch in pins, plane off flush, fill pinholes with wood filler, sand off smooth and repaint or seal the area.

Frame replacement – When extensive repairs are required it is often more cost effective in the long run to consider a complete replacement. This should be discussed with the building owner. It should be emphasised that although the replacement may be more expensive than the repair initially, the replacement would last a lot longer and also provide the opportunity of upgrading fittings, etc. and modification to suit their requirements.

Before removing frames, always check the wall above for signs of support. See Figure 6.22. Newer building may have a concrete or steel lintel, older properties a stone lintel, brick arch, or soldier course or sometimes none at all apart from the frame. Also look out for cracks in the brickwork mortar joints above the opening, which could be indications of structural movement, possibly leading to collapse on removing the frame.

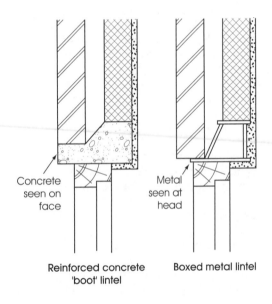
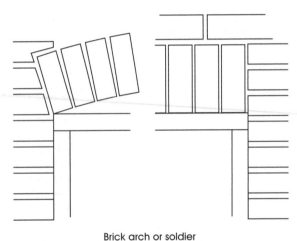

Reinforced concrete 'boot' lintel

Boxed metal lintel

Concrete seen on face

Metal seen at head

Brick arch or soldier course seen on face

Figure 6.22 *Means of support over openings*

Do not proceed if a means of support is not evident or there are signs of movement. Seek the advice of a structural expert, as arrangements may have to be made for temporary support, the insertion of a lintel and structural repairs to be carried out by others before the frame replacement itself.

Once you are sure the opening is correctly supported, the frame can be cut out and removed in sections in sequence as shown in Figure 6.23. When the frame has been removed, clean off any projecting mortar and previous fixings. Make good any damaged brickwork and holes previously occupied by 'built-in' horn fixings. Finally fix in position the new frame. See Figure 6.24.

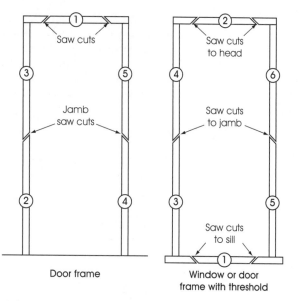

Figure 6.23

Door frame

Window or door
frame with threshold

Cut out and remove in sections using numbered sequence

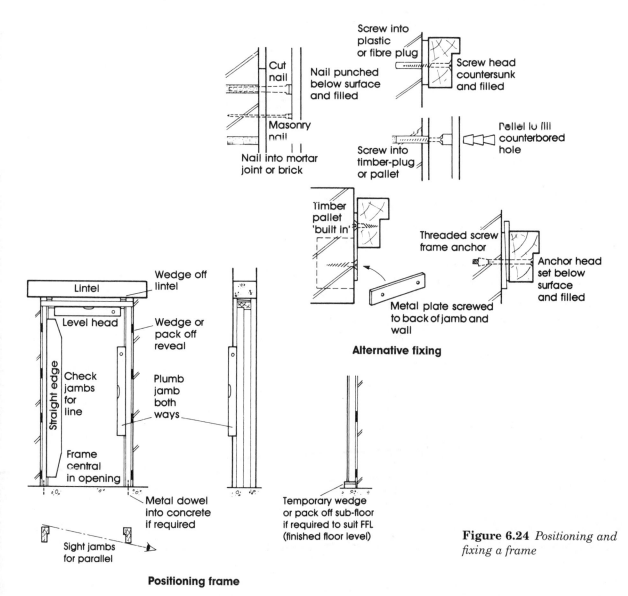

Figure 6.24 *Positioning and
fixing a frame*

- Cut off horns and seal cut ends (paint or preservative).
- Place frame in the opening, temporarily holding with wedges at head or sill if required.
- Check head and sill with a level and adjust wedges as required.
- Check jambs for line with a straight edge, plumb one jamb with level, 'sight in' the other, adjust position and wedge as required.

Floors and roofs

If the defect is the result of fungal decay or wood boring insect damage, the procedure outlined previously should be adopted. Use Figures 6.25

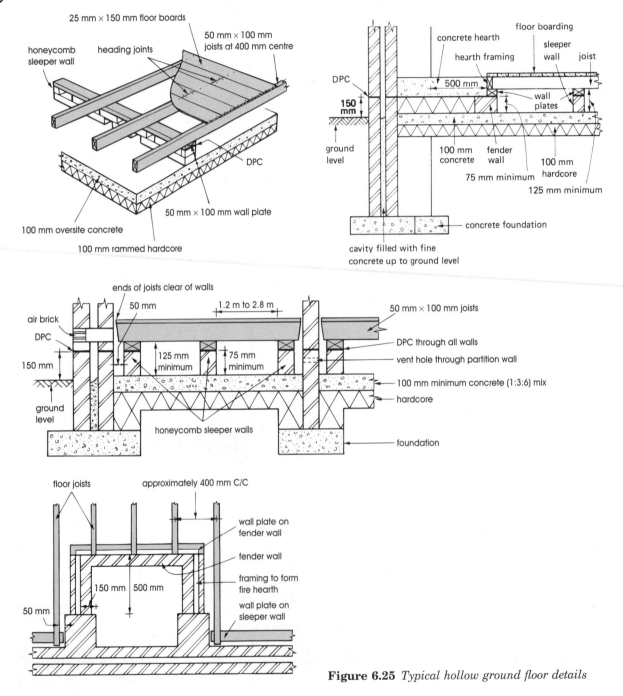

Figure 6.25 *Typical hollow ground floor details*

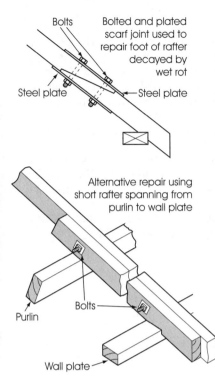

Bolts

Bolted and plated scarf joint used to repair foot of rafter decayed by wet rot

Steel plate

Steel plate

Alternative repair using short rafter spanning from purlin to wall plate

Bolts

Purlin

Wall plate

Figure 6.26 *Typical roof details*

and 6.26 as a guide to replacing timber components like for like. However, where the work is extensive, especially in circumstances where structural timber is affected, e.g. upper floor joists, rafters and purlins, etc. it is often wiser and more cost effective to have this work referred to a specialist contractor who will be fully equipped and experienced to undertake it.

Floorboards – Again where the defect is the result of fungal attack or wood boring insects, the procedure explained before should be adopted. If due to movement (loose fixings), wear or damage, one or more boards can simply be re-fixed or replaced.

Note: Care must be taken when re-fixing or replacing floorboards as there is always the possibility of services (water, gas and electricity) running below.

The surface of the area to be worked on can be scanned before starting work, with a metal/live electric circuit detector. As an added precaution it is wise to turn off all service supplies at their meter/stop valve before any re-fixing or cutting out operations commence.

Loose boards are best re-fixed by screwing down into the joists rather than nailing, especially at upper floor levels in older properties, where significant amounts of nailing causing vibration, may damage the lath and plaster ceiling.

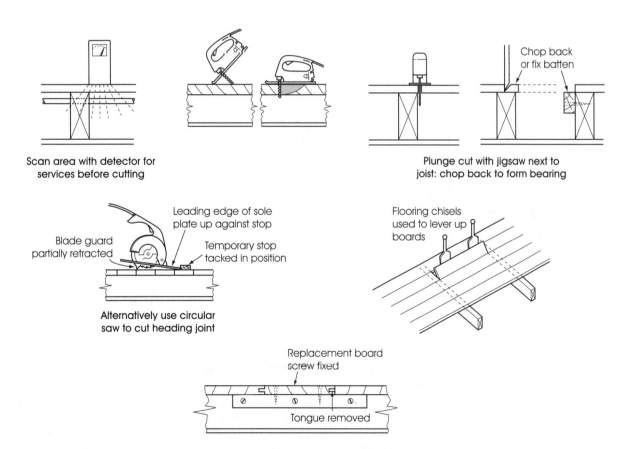

Scan area with detector for services before cutting

Plunge cut with jigsaw next to joist: chop back to form bearing

Chop back or fix batten

Blade guard partially retracted

Leading edge of sole plate up against stop

Temporary stop tacked in position

Alternatively use circular saw to cut heading joint

Flooring chisels used to lever up boards

Replacement board screw fixed

Tongue removed

Figure 6.27 *Removing and replacing floorboards*

241

Removing a floorboard:

- A jigsaw can be used to cut the ends of a floorboard next to a joist. The ends can then be chopped back to form a bearing (for heading joints) using a wood chisel, or fix a batten to the edge of the joist.
- Alternatively a small circular saw may be used to cut the heading joints over the joists. The blade should be set to the floorboard thickness.
- A sharp knife, padsaw or jigsaw can be used along the length of the board to separate the tongue.
- Punch the fixing nails through the board. Insert two wide blade flooring chisels in one of the edge joints and lever up the board.
- Where more than one adjacent boards are to be replaced the heading joints should be staggered over different joists.
- Finally, cut the new boards to length and re-fix in place. Where more than one board wide a folding technique should be used.

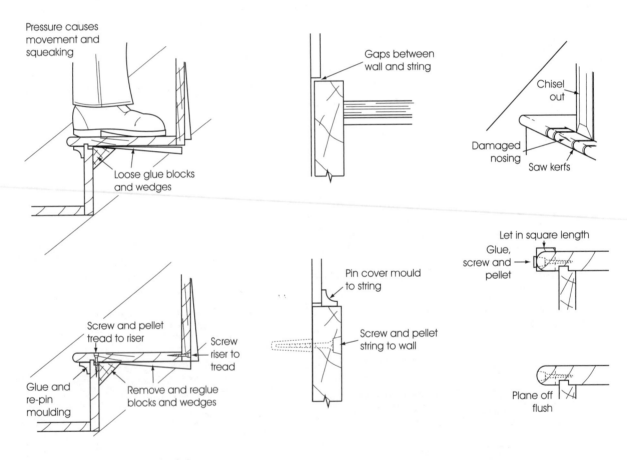

Figure 6.28 *Common stair defects*

Stairs – The most common defects encountered are illustrated in Figure 6.28.

- *Creaking treads* – This results from movement between the tread and riser joint when walked on. Where access to the underside of the flight is possible (in cases where it has not been plastered over) the creaking can be remedied by renewing the glue blocks at the tread to riser junction and re-gluing/re-wedging the treads and risers in their string housings. Where access to the underside is not possible, the problem can be remedied by gluing and screwing the tread down into the top of the riser. Small gaps, normally the result of shrinkage, may be apparent at the tread-to-string housing. These should be filled by gluing in thin strips of timber veneer.

● *Gaps between the wall and string* – This may be the result of either shrinkage or movement, or a combination of both. Shrinkage gaps can be masked by the application of a cover mould. Movement gaps are normally the result of the fixings between the wall and string becoming loose or failing, causing the string to move away from the wall when using the stairs. Re-fix the string back to the wall by plugging and screwing. Any gap or damage between the string and plasterwork can again be masked by a cover mould.

● *Damaged nosings* – These can be repaired by cutting out the damaged section and splicing in a new piece. A square length should be 'let-in'. Cut at 45° at either end for additional support and glue line. This is fixed by gluing and screwing. Finally planing and rubbing down to match the nosing profile. Where a scotia mould is used at the underside of the tread to riser junction, it is best to renew the whole length, gluing and pinning the new one in place.

Brickwork, plastering and tiles

You may be required to replace one or two bricks which have been removed or damaged during other work, or even lay several courses to fill in, say under the sill of a reduced height replacement window.

Replacing bricks

The first task is to attempt to match the pattern, size and make of the original. Measure the brick size and take a small piece to the brick supplier for them to identify. Brick sizes vary slightly due to the way they are made. New metric size bricks are a little smaller than the old imperial ones. When working on older property matching bricks may be difficult to obtain. Try suppliers who specialise in reclaimed building materials. If imperial bricks cannot be obtained, matching metric ones can be bonded into the existing work by slightly increasing the mortar joints.

Figure 6.29 illustrates the procedure to follow when replacing a single brick. In this case the brick previously cut around is the built-in horn of a sill or threshold.

● Using a bolster and club hammer (do not forget to wear eye protection goggles) cut out the old brick and clean away the old mortar joints. Brush out all dust particles, taking care in modern buildings to ensure nothing is allowed to enter the cavity.
● Cut the brick to size if required. First gently score a line around the brick using a bolster and club hammer, finally use a heavier blow on the lines to sever it.

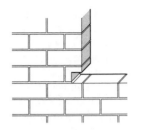

Old 'built in' horn position

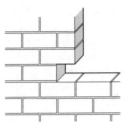

Cut out to nearest joint

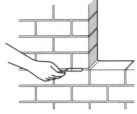

Cut replacement brick
to size

Lay bed joint, 'butter' up
end and top edge of brick

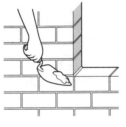

Place brick in position and
clean off excess mortar

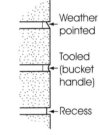

Rake out adjacent mortar
joints and point up to match
existing pointing

Weather
pointed

Tooled
(bucket
handle)

Recess

Figure 6.29 *Replacing a brick*

- Prepare a mortar mix, typically 1:6 (1 part Portland Cement to 6 parts bricklaying sand). Sufficient water is added so that the mix has the consistency of soft butter (firm enough not to collapse when heaped, but easily compressed with a shovel). One part lime or a mortar plasticiser may be included in the mix for improved workability. Alternatively, pre-packed bricklaying mortar mixes are available. **Note:** The colour of the sand used should match the existing mortar joints. Red and yellow sands are commonly available.
- Lay the bed of mortar into the prepared hole.
- Butter up (apply mortar) to the end and the top edge of the brick. Place it in position and then remove the surplus mortar.
- Fill any gaps in the mortar joint. When it has started to go off, rake the joints out below the brick surface.
- After about 24 hours rake out the adjacent mortar joints.
- Re-point the joints with a mortar mix that matches the original in colour and finish.

Repointing – The most common methods are:

- weather pointed, which is done with a pointing trowel;
- tooled, a concave finish (bucket handle) created by working along the drying mortar with a special jointing tool, or alternatively a metal bucket handle (hence the name) or a piece of 15 mm copper pipe may be used;
- recessed, created by brushing out the drying mortar with a stiff bristle hand brush; alternatively a more consistent depth can be achieved by working the joint with a piece of timber having a protruding countersunk head screw.

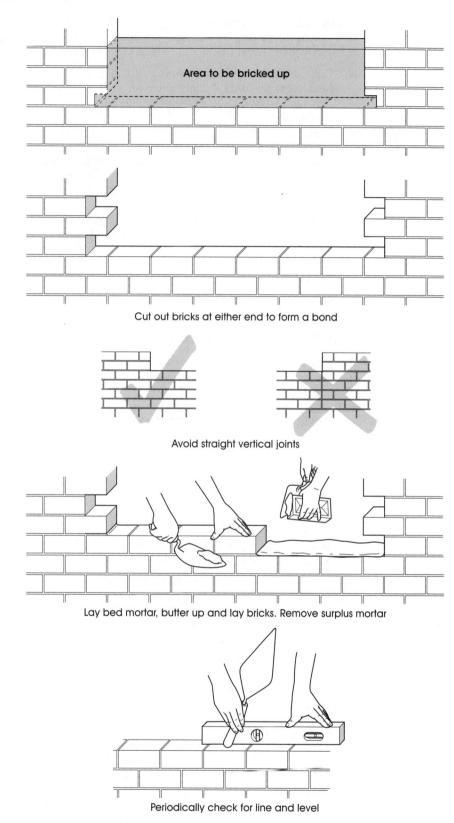

Figure 6.30 *Laying brick courses*

Re-laying brick courses – Figure 6.30 illustrates the procedure to follow when relaying or building whole courses of bricks. Refers in this case to under the sill of a reduced replacement window.

- Cut out bricks at either end to form the bond between the adjacent vertical joints. Clean away any old mortar and dust particles.
- Dry lay the bricks to determine the pattern. Cut the bricks to size if required.
- Prepare a mortar mix as before, using a 10 mm joint. Approximately 1 kg of mix is required for each brick.
- Apply a bed of mortar to the existing brick course, approximately 10 mm thick. Furrow the surface to a 'V' shaped groove with the point of a trowel. Butter up and lay bricks, removing surplus mortar as you go.
- Repeat the process to lay the subsequent brick courses. Periodically check the bricks are being laid horizontal and in line with a spirit level. Use the end of the trowel to tap the bricks into place if required.
- Complete the job by raking out the mortar joints and finally pointing them as before.

Repairs to plasterwork

Modern buildings – The internal brick and blockwork walls, will have a hard plastered finish. This is normally applied in two layers, a 9 to 12 mm thick backing coat and a 2 to 3 mm thick finishing coat. Ceilings and stud partition walls are surfaced with sheets of plasterboard. These may be finished by a 2 to 3 mm coat of board finishing plaster applied on to the plasterboard, which acts as the backing. Alternatively the plasterboard joints may be taped up and filled to provide a 'dry lined' finish, ready for decoration. Ceilings which have been 'dry lined' were often decorated using a textured coating, worked to create a repeating pattern or stipple finish.

Older buildings – The wall plaster may be much softer. This is still normally two coats. A thick lime-based backing coat followed by a thin finishing coat. Ceilings and stud partition walls were then finished using 'lath and plaster'.

This is a system using thin timber laths nailed to the undersides of joists and faces of studs. Wet plaster was pressed up against them and allowed to squeeze between the gaps in the laths forming a key to hold this backing plaster in place. This was finally finished using again a thin coat of finishing plaster.

External walls – The external walls of both modern and older buildings may be covered in rendering. This is a surface coat of sand and cement mortar applied to a wall for decorative and/or waterproofing purposes.

All of these finishes may crack due to structural movement, damage by accidental impact or be disturbed during renovation work, therefore requiring repairs that the maintenance carpenter and joiner may be asked to undertake.

Patching plasterwork – The first thing to do when patching plasterwork on any background is to protect the floor, by covering with a dustsheet. Figure 6.31 shows the procedure to follow when patching a 'blown' or damaged area of plasterwork to a brick or blockwork wall.

- Tap plaster around the damaged area to 'see' (hear) if any part sounds hollow or loose.

'Hack off' existing
loose plaster

'Brush off' to remove
dust and loose particles

'Damp down'
with water

Mix plaster
in a bucket

Scoop up plaster from
hawk and apply to wall
in an upward sweep

Reinforce large
areas with repair
mesh or scrim

Comb or scratch area
to provide a 'key'

Brush off and apply
finishing plaster

'Rule off' using a sideways
sawing action,
working upwards

Trowel up to a
smooth finish

Repeat trowelling up whilst
splashing with water

Figure 6.31 *Patching plasterwork*

- Use a club hammer and bolster to hack off all existing loose plaster until the surface is sound.
- Brush down the surface to remove all loose particles and dust, using a stiff bristle or wire brush.
- Damp down the wall surface by brushing or spraying with water. This prevents the wall suction from drying out the plaster too quickly, which could result in cracking on drying. Some surfaces such as concrete, shiny or glazed bricks and impervious engineering bricks do not help the plaster to stick. In these cases brush on a PVC bonding agent before plastering to ensure good adhesion.
- Add a small amount of backing plaster into clean cold water in a bucket. Stir with a timber stick until a thick creamy consistency is achieved.
- Transfer some of the plaster to your hawk. With the hawk tilted away from the wall scoop up a small amount of plaster on the edge of the steel trowel and press the plaster against the wall using an upward sweep of the trowel. The trowel should be used at an angle to the wall, with the angle reduced as you sweep it up the wall. Take care not to allow the trowel to lay flat against the wall, as the suction will pull the fresh plaster off the wall.
- Continue adding plaster to the wall until the whole area to be repaired is covered, to within 2 to 3 mm below the surrounding wall finish. Larger areas may be reinforced by pushing into the backing coat a repair mesh or scrim.
- Before the backing plaster is completely set, scratch the surface with a comb. This provides a 'key' to help with the adhesion of the finishing coat.

6 Maintenance of buildings

- After about 3 to 4 hours the backing coat surface will be hard, but not dry. It is then ready for finishing. If allowed to dry further, it will require damping down again with water before finishing.
- Brush down the surface to remove any loose particles. Mix up a small batch of finishing plaster, by adding to a little water as before, except this time it should be a runnier consistency. Trowel on the plaster, aiming to leave it slightly proud of the surrounding area.
- Rule flat the surface, using a timber or metal straight edge. Start at the bottom of the patch, move it up the wall with a side-to-side 'sawing' action keeping it tight against the existing sound plaster as a guide. Trowel on more plaster to fill any hollows before ruling off again.
- The plaster will start to set within 30 to 45 minutes. At this stage smooth the surface with a plastering trowel. Again using upward sweeps with the trowel held at an angle. After 15 or so minutes lightly splash the surface with clean cold water, whilst trowelling up and over the surface, to provide a smooth hard finish. Ensure the trowel is kept clean and damp during this process, to prevent damaging the newly plastered surface. Regular brushing off in a bucket of cold water is ideal. **Note:** Small patches in rendering can be repaired in one or two coats, using the above procedure, except that a sand and cement mix is used in place of plaster.

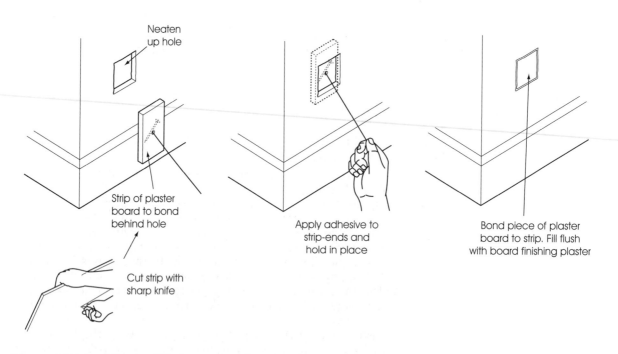

Figure 6.32 *Patching small holes in plasterboard*

Patching damage to plasterboard or lath and plaster surfaces – to repair small holes caused for example by striking the surface with the corner of a piece of furniture when moving it. The procedure to follow is illustrated in Figure 6.32.

- Neaten up the jagged edges using a sharp knife for plasterboard or a pad saw for lath and plaster.
- Cut a strip of plasterboard about 1½ times the length of the neatened hole and just narrower than it in width. Make a hole in its

centre, pass through a piece of string and knot it behind on a nail. **Note:** Plasterboard is simply cut by scoring on the face with a sharp knife, break along the line by applying pressure along from the scored side. Run the knife along the paper on the other side to separate.

- Mix up some plasterboard adhesive and apply to both ends of the strip. Feed the strip into the hole, using the string to pull it tight against the inner face of the board or laths. Tie off the string to a scrap of timber positioned over the face of the hole.
- When the adhesive has set, cut off the string. Cut another piece of plasterboard. This time to fit the hole and again bond in place using plasterboard adhesive. Press in until it is just below the surrounding wall surface, leave to set.
- Fill the patched hole using board finishing plaster and trowel up as before.

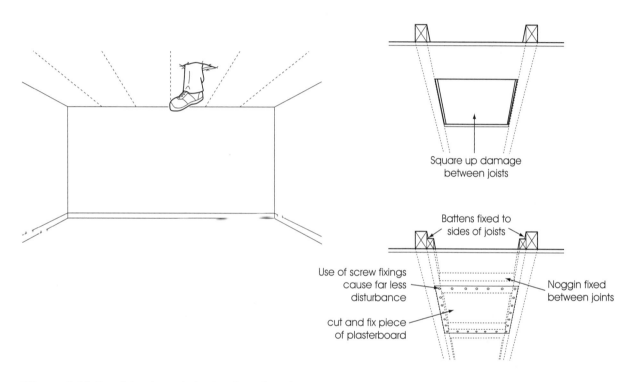

Figure 6.33 *Repairing large holes in plasterboard*

To repair large holes for example caused by a foot slipping through the ceiling when working in a loft, the procedure to follow is illustrated in Figure 6.33.

- Mark on the ceiling two lines at right angles to the joist direction and enclosing the damaged area.
- Use a pad saw to cut along these lines until the adjacent joists are reached after first checking for the presence of cables and plumbing.
- Again using the pad saw cut along the joist edges. Remove the damaged area, leaving a neat rectangular hole.
- Cut battens; fix to the sides of the joists.
- Cut and fix noggins between the battens at either end of the hole, ensuring the noggins centre lines straddle the cut line, to provide a bearing for both the existing sound ceiling and new plasterboard.

- Cut a piece of plasterboard 2 to 3 mm smaller than the hole in both directions. Fix in place using plasterboard nails or plasterboard screws into the noggins and battens.
- Use a sharp knife to cut away the finishing plaster about 25 mm all round the hole. Bed lengths of plasterer's scrim over the joints between the patch and existing sound ceiling, using a thin (runny) mix of board finishing plaster as an adhesive. This is to reinforce the joint and reduce the risk of later cracking.
- Fill the patched area using board finishing plaster and trowel up as before.

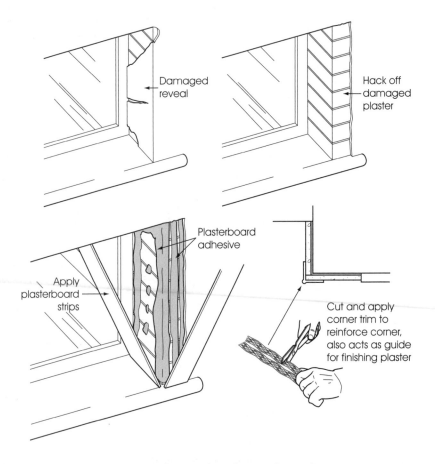

Figure 6.34 *Making good plasterwork to damaged reveals*

To make good the plaster work around the reveals of a replaced door or window: in most circumstances these can be patched using the two coat backing and finishing plaster method as before. Where there is extensive damage, or the plaster is loose, the entire reveal should be hacked off and replaced. Figure 6.34 illustrates the procedure to follow using plasterboard and board finishing plaster:

- Hack off plaster reveal back to the brick or blockwork surface and extending around the corner by about 75 to 100 mm.
- Cut two strips of plasterboard, one for the reveal and the other for the return.
- Brush down the wall surfaces. Mix up some plasterboard adhesive. Using a trowel or special caulker, apply dabs of adhesive up the centre of the reveal and continuously around the perimeter.

- Press plasterboard strips in place and check for plumb with a spirit level. The return strip should finish 2 to 3 mm below the adjacent plaster, to allow for a coat of board finish.
- Reinforce the corner with a length of metal plasterboard bead, (this also acts as a guide for the later board finishing plaster coat). Apply a bed of plasterboard adhesive or board finish to the corner. Press the bead in place, check with spirit level for plumb. Also ensure it is in line with existing wall surface. Remove excess adhesive and allow too dry for 2 to 3 hours.
- Reinforce the joint between return plasterboard strip and existing wall plaster, using a length of scrim as before.
- Complete repair by applying a coat of board finishing plaster and trowel up in the normal way.

Ceramic wall and floor tiles

You may be required to replace damaged tiles individually or lay a much larger area such as a whole wall or floor.

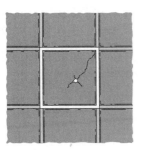
Rake out grout joint

Drill holes around centre

Break out from centre

Scrape off old adhesive

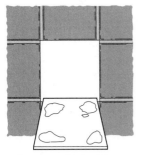

Press new tile in place

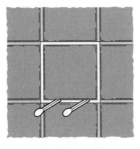
Insert spacers

Apply grout, then point

Polish to remove haze

Figure 6.35 *Replacing a damaged tile*

Replacing damaged tiles – Probably the hardest task is to find a good match for replacement. The building owner may have spares left over from the original work. Alternatively take a damaged piece to a tile supplier for them to find a match. Figure 6.35 illustrates the procedure to follow.

- Prepare the surrounding area and yourself. Cover the floor and surrounding units or bath and sanitary ware with dustsheets to protect from dust and possible scratching by the small sharp particles of broken tiles. Protect yourself by wearing eye protection goggles, gloves and a dust mask.

- Rake out grout joint around damaged tile, to relieve the perimeter stresses.
- Drill a series of holes around the centre of the tile and break out using an old chisel, working progressively towards the edges. Do not try to break out the tile by trying to prise it off from the edge joints, as almost inevitably you will damage the adjacent tiles. Masking tape can be applied when drilling out the centre, to prevent the masonry drill skidding across the ceramic surface.
- Scrape or chip off the old tile adhesive back to the surface, taking care not to damage the plaster base.
- Apply four dabs of tile adhesive to the back of the tile, or use a notched comb to provide a uniform ribbed layer.
- Press the tile in place, so that it lies flush with the surrounding ones. Insert tile spacers or matchsticks in the joints to position or support the tile. Adjust the tile as required to ensure a uniform gap all around.
- Allow the adhesive to set for about twenty-four hours and then remove the spacers.
- Fill the gap around the tile with grout, working in with a rubber squeegee. Point the joint with a finger tip or piece of wood dowel with a rounded end point.
- Finally when dry polish up the surface to remove the grout haze, using a clean dry cloth. **Note:** The long-term success of tiling

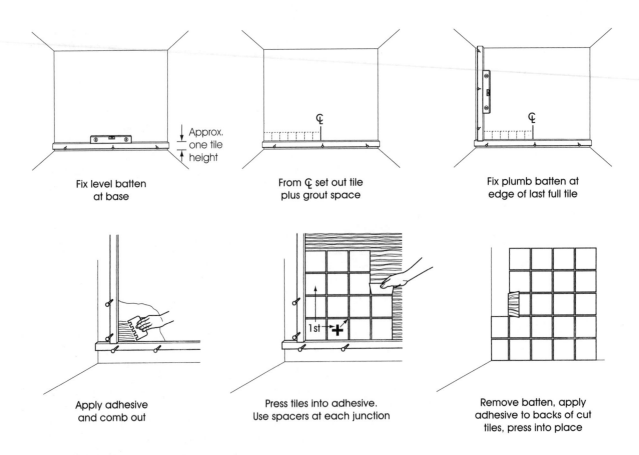

Fix level batten
at base

From ₵ set out tile
plus grout space

Fix plumb batten at
edge of last full tile

Approx.
one tile
height

Apply adhesive
and comb out

Press tiles into adhesive.
Use spacers at each junction

Remove batten, apply
adhesive to backs of cut
tiles, press into place

Figure 6.36 *Ceramic wall tiling*

depends on the adhesive and grout used. Most are available either in ready mixed or powder form for mixing with water to a creamy paste with water. A standard type mix is only suitable for dry areas. It may also tolerate a little condensation or occasional splashing with water. In areas subject to more prolonged condensation or extensive wetting such as a shower area, always use waterproof products.

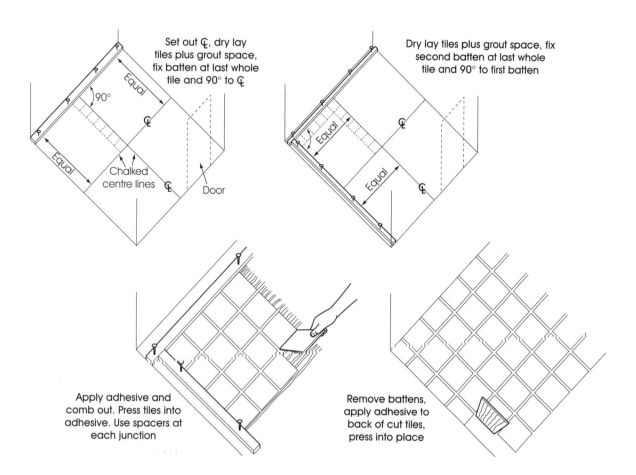

Set out ₵, dry lay tiles plus grout space, fix batten at last whole tile and 90° to ₵

90°

Equal

Equal

₵

Chalked centre lines

Door

Dry lay tiles plus grout space, fix second batten at last whole tile and 90° to first batten

Equal

Equal

₵

₵

Apply adhesive and comb out. Press tiles into adhesive. Use spacers at each junction

Remove battens, apply adhesive to back of cut tiles, press into place

Figure 6.37 *Ceramic floor tiling*

Re-tiling a whole wall or floor – In circumstances where a match for a damaged tile is not possible, you may be required to replace the whole area. Figures 6.36 and 6.37 illustrate the procedures to follow.

Surface preparation – Protect yourself and the surrounding area as before.

- *Walls:* Remove all existing tiles and traces of the old adhesive back to a sound, level base. Walls not previously tiled should be thoroughly cleaned to remove all traces of dirt, grease and old wallpaper. Make good any holes or loose plaster
- *Floor:* Remove all existing tiles and traces of the old adhesive back to a sound, level base. Ensure the surface is clean and dry (there should be an effective damp proof membrane below the surface to prevent rising damp). Uneven or damaged surfaces can be repaired with a floor levelling compound to provide a level and smooth surface for tiling.

Setting out –

- *Walls:* Temporarily fix a straight timber batten to the wall surface, horizontally level with its top edge a little more than one tile height above the floor, skirting, worktop or bath. Check with a spirit level. This will ensure the tiling is straight and level even if the underlying surface runs out. **Note:** Where the underlying surface is way out of level, the batten should be positioned so that maximum distance is one tile in height. Cut tiles are then used to infill when the batten is removed. Measure the length of the wall to determine the centre point, mark along the batten from the centre a series of distances equal to a tiles width plus a 2-mm grouting space. Ensure you are not left with a narrow strip to tile as they will be difficult to cut. If this is the case re-mark, this time straddling the middle tile over the centre point. The aim is to end up with more or less a half tile at either end of the wall. Temporarily fix a straight batten to the wall surface, vertically plumb, with its edge next to the last full tile mark.

- *Floor:* Measure the length and width of the room to determine the centre lines. Mark in both directions using a chalk line. Dry layout tiles using 4 mm or 6 mm grout joint spacers from the centre point. Fix temporary batten at last whole tile position. This must be at 90° to one centreline and parallel with the other. Dry layout tiles plus grout space, from centre line along batten. Fix second temporary batten at last whole tile position. This must be at 90° to the first batten and again parallel to the centre line. This will determine the cut tile sizes around the perimeter. Again if either of these are narrow strips straddle the centre tiles over the centre lines.

Score along line with
tile cutting point

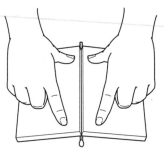

Place matchsticks under
score, press down to snap
tile in two

Figure 6.38 *Cutting ceramic tiles*

Laying tiles –

- *Walls:* Starting at the junction of the battens, apply adhesive to about 1 m² of wall and comb out. Press tiles into ribbed adhesive, with spacers set in between them. Continue working sideways and upwards about 1 m² at a time to lay all of the whole tiles. Allow to set for about 24 hours. Carefully remove battens. Cut tiles to fit around the perimeter and fix them in place, using adhesive dabbed or combed onto their backs. Use spacers or matchsticks to ensure even grout joints. Tiles are best cut using a proprietary tile cutter, or diamond tipped wet saw. However, small amounts can be cut by scoring the surface with a carbon tipped tile cutting point and snapping the tile along the scored line. Place two matchsticks under scored line. Press down firmly on either side to snap in two, see Figure 6.38. Corners and curves can be cut out of tiles to fit around projections using a tile saw blade in a coping saw frame. Alternatively the lines of the area to be removed may be scored and the waste nibbled away with a pair of pincers.

- *Floor:* Tiling starts at the junction of the two battens, working away from there in both directions. Trowel on the adhesive and comb out again working about 1 m² at a time. Press tiles into ribbed adhesive with spacers set in between them. Continue laying tiles, working out from the corner, aiming to lay the last whole tile next to the doorway (do not trap yourself into a corner as you will not be able to walk the freshly laid area). Allow to set for about 24 hours. Cut tiles to fit around the perimeter and fix them in place with adhesive. **Note:** Floor tiles are often thicker than those for walls and may require the use of a heavy duty tile cutter or diamond tipped wet saw to cut them.

Grouting – When all cut tiling is complete allow to set for about 24 hours. The joints between them can then be grouted. Working grout with a rubber squeegee, point up with finger or a rounded end dowel. Allow to dry and polish off the haze with a dry clean cloth as before.

Finishing off – The joint between tiles and horizontal surfaces such as kitchen worktops, baths and sanitary ware will require sealing with a silicone sealant to prevent moisture penetration. Figure 6.39 illustrates the procedure to follow, which ensures a neat bead of sealant to these locations.

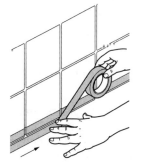
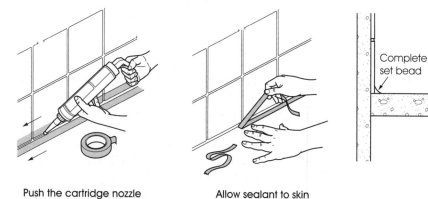

Apply masking tape along angle to be sealed

Push the cartridge nozzle along the angle

Allow sealant to skin over, peel off tape

Complete set bead

Figure 6.39 *Sealing tiles to a worktop*

Apply masking tape to both the vertical and horizontal surfaces, 2 to 3 mm away from the internal angle. Trim the cartridge nozzle off at an angle of 45° to give a bead just wide enough to fill the gap between the two taped edges. Gently squeeze the cartridge gun trigger until the sealant is just seen at the tip. Place the nozzle at one end of the angle to be filled, with the gun held at 45° to the wall. Apply steady, even pressure to the trigger whilst pushing the gun along the angle. The nozzle will form the sealant into a neat concave curve. To stop the flow at the corners and on completion, release the metal tag adjacent to the trigger. Any unevenness in the bead can be smoothed using a small paintbrush dipped in water. Leave sealant for a short while to skin over, then peel off the tape to leave a well-formed neat bead.

Glazing and painting

Maintenance of glazing work involving sealed double-glazing units and large window panes is best undertaken by specialist glaziers, who will be kitted up to undertake the work efficiently and safely.

Re-glazing

Re-glazing of small single-glazed panes can be undertaken by the carpenter and joiner. Wherever possible glass should be pre-cut to size by the glass supplier. Measure the timber rebate sizes and order glass 3 mm undersize in both directions. For example, a piece of glass for a rebate opening size of 150×250 mm should be ordered as a cut size of 147×247 mm. If necessary pieces of glass can be cut to size by scoring along the required line using a glass-cutting wheel. Lay the glass on a flat surface with matchsticks placed under the scored line at either end. Apply pressure on both sides to snap in two along the line. Never attempt to cut narrow strips and always wear eye protection and gauntlets.

The first stage is to remove the broken pane. Where practical, sash or casements should be removed from their frame so that broken glass can be removed and replaced with a new piece with relative safety, at ground level.

When replacing broken glass at high level ensure that the area below is cordoned off so that no one can enter the area below. Before starting to hack out the broken pane and hardened putty, ensure you are wearing eye protection goggles and gauntlets to protect hands, wrists and lower arms. These should be worn during the whole process as inevitably shards of glass and fine splinters will be created as the pane is removed and the rebates cleaned up.

Start at the top of the pane removing the old putty or glazing beads with a wood chisel or hacking knife. Remove glazing sprigs (flat or square nails) with pliers and then lever out remaining glass from behind again using a wood chisel. Finally continue hacking out remaining back putting to rebates.

The procedure for re-glazing is illustrated in Figure 6.40.

- Check glass is correct size.
- Ensure rebates are primed with paint.
- Work a bead of putty around the back of the rebate.
- Position plastic seating blocks in the bottom of the rebate to support the glass.
- Position the bottom edge of the glass on seating blocks. Gently push the glass into the rebate, applying pressure evenly around the edge until a back bed putty thickness of 1 to 2 mm is achieved.
- Use glazing sprigs to secure the glass in place. These may be driven in using a pin hammer or the edge of a firmer chisel. (Panel pins should not be used to secure the glass in place, as their round point of contact results in pressure points, which can lead to the formation of cracks.)
- Work a bead of putty all around the rebate in front of the glass. Only a small bead is required when using glazing beads to secure the glass.

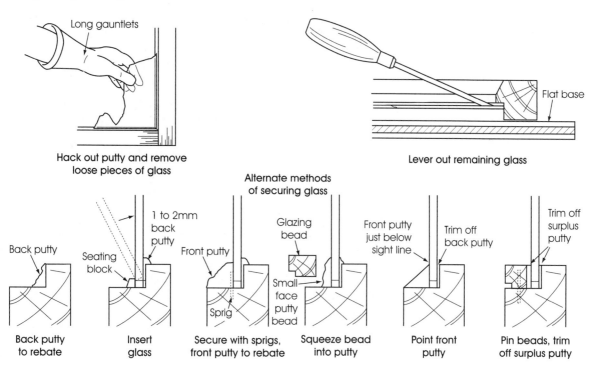

Figure 6.40 *Re-glazing procedure*

- Replace glazing beads squeezing putty into glass, or point up the front putty bead using a putty knife or chisel to form a bevelled fillet. Its upper edge in contact with the glass should be just below the rebate sight line. Slight imperfections in the putty fillet can be improved by running over with a wetted paint brush.
- Trim off the surplus putty to beads and then trim off the back bedding putty on the inside of the glass.
- Clean the glass to remove oil and putty marks before it dries.

Painting woodwork

Woodwork is painted to provide a decorative finish. However, more importantly it serves also to protect it from the elements. As a carpenter and joiner carrying out maintenance work you may be required to paint new replaced items as well as repaint existing items that have been eased or repaired. The paint system for wood normally consists of a primer to seal the surface and provide a bond for later coats, an undercoat which provides a smooth opaque covering coat and finally a decorative gloss or satin top coat.

Preparation – The key to a successful paint system is careful preparation. Paint will not last long on a defective surface.

Bare wood – should only need an initial rub down with glass paper to remove any roughness and sharp arrises. Knots in bare soft wood can be full of resin and may later 'bleed' through to the finished paint surface if not sealed. Firstly wipe over the surface with a cloth soaked in white spirit to remove any stickiness and excess resin. Then coat all knots with a knotting solution. On resinous hardwoods that are to be painted, wipe off excess resin using white spirit and seal the entire surface with an aluminium wood primer.

- Apply wood primer to all surfaces and edges taking particular care to achieve full penetration of any end grain. This is best undertaken prior to fixing in order to ensure full protection. For example, the backs of skirtings, architraves, door frames and linings etc. are inaccessible when fixed. This is particularly important for external timber.
- Fill any defects and open end grain with a wood filler. Always select a waterproof type for external use. Rub down flush with the surface using glass paper
- As priming tends to raise the grain of woodwork resulting in a felt-like hairy surface, the whole job will require rubbing down (de-nibbing) prior to over painting.
- Wipe off surface with a 'low tack' cloth to remove any surface dust; apply undercoat.
- When undercoat is dry, apply the topcoat. Refer to paint manufacturer's information with regard to minimum and maximum over-coating times. If the top coat is applied too soon, the undercoat will tend to bleed into the top coat causing defects; too long and it may not bond successfully to the undercoat, resulting in early breakdown and peeling off.

Previously painted wood – If in good condition, lightly rub down with glass paper or clean off using a sugar soap solution. This cleans the surface dirt or grease deposits and removes some of the gloss. New coats of paint will not key well on a gloss surface and will easily chip and peel, if not rubbed down or cut back.

- Knot and prime any eased edges or repairs. When dry, rub down to blend in primer to existing paint surface.
- Fill and rub down any minor defects and imperfections.
- Remove surface dust, apply undercoat followed by the top coat within recommended over-coating time.

When the old system has broken down, it is best to completely strip off the old paint, make good and start again from scratch using the same procedure as for bare wood.

Small areas showing signs of deterioration, may be repaired without fully stripping the area.

- Treat any minor areas of soft timber caused by wet rot with a wood hardener.
- Rub down the surface to remove all loose defective paint. **Note:** Always wear a dust mask when rubbing down paintwork. Surfaces painted before the 1960's may contain harmful lead within the paint. It is best in these circumstances to rub down using a wet process (wet and dry paper) to minimise the potential risk.
- Apply the paint system as before.

Painting procedure

Internal painting – Protect carpets and furniture with dustsheets. Doors to other rooms can be sealed with masking tape prior to any rubbing down. Open the window to ensure adequate ventilation. This is both for you and to help the paint dry. Always wear a dust mask when rubbing down and eye protection goggles when scraping off.

- Primers and undercoats are applied by brushing out along the grain.
- Top coats are initially applied along the grain, brushed out across the grain and finally 'laid off' finished with gentle brush strokes along the grain. The aim is to produce a thin, even paint film, which does not 'sag' on vertical surfaces or 'pond' on horizontal ones.

External painting – In general the same procedure for internal painting can be adopted, except for adverse weather conditions and taking extra care to ensure full paint coverage to avoid the possibility of moisture penetration.

- Do not work in strong sunlight, as this prevents paints drying properly and likely to cause it to 'blister'. Wait until the area is in shade before painting.
- Do not paint if rain is expected.
- Do not paint first thing in the morning or last thing in the evening, when there might be a 'dew'. The resulting moisture will spoil the paint finish.
- Do not paint when there is a risk of frost.
- Do not use paint intended for interior use only.

In these circumstances it is best to aim to paint from mid morning to just after lunch. This will allow the air to dry before starting and the paint film to dry before the early evening dampness starts to form.

Sequence of operations – A logical approach is required when painting framed joinery. The aim is to keep a 'wet edge' blending in adjacent areas of paint, so that joints are not seen when the paint dries.

Figure 6.41 illustrates typical numbered sequences for a range of joinery.

Doors: remove handles, paint in sequence shown. Leading edge should be painted to match the woodwork of the room it opens into

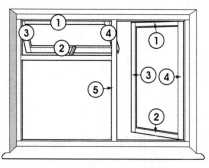

Casement window: paint opening parts before frame and interior sill

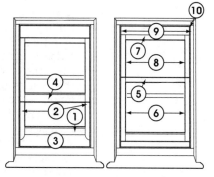

Sash window: from inside open sashes as far as they will go, paint all accessible surfaces, reverse sashes and complete painting

Figure 6.41 *Sequence for painting doors and windows*

Painting plasterwork

Walls and ceilings are normally painted using emulsion paint. Newly plastered and repaired surfaces should be left for seven to ten days to dry and then treated with a coat of plaster sealer before decoration. This prevents the new plaster showing through the paint finish as a kind of 'patchiness'. Alternatively, a thinned emulsion can be applied as a primer, before at least two full strength coats are put on. The priming coat should be about one part water to about three parts emulsion paint.

Before starting work, arrange for any furniture in the room to be removed. Protect carpets and fixtures with dustsheets. Wear a dust mask and eye protection goggles when rubbing down and scraping off.

The procedure to follow is illustrated in Figure 6.42

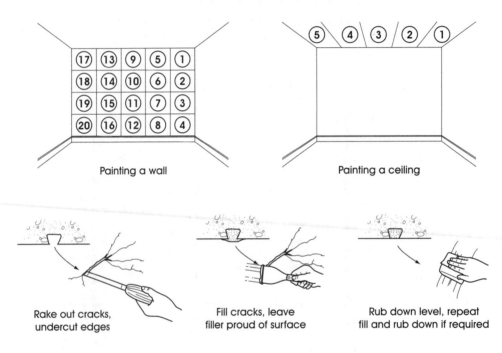

Figure 6.42 *Painting plasterwork*

- Remove all loose material such as dirt, dust and flaking paint.
- Rake out any minor cracks in the plaster surface, using the end of an old slot blade screwdriver. The raking out is to make the crack a little deeper and wider with undercut edges.
- Fill cracks with a plaster filler. Ensure filler is pressed well into the cracks in order for it to key on the undercut edges.
- Leave filler slightly proud of surrounding surfaces. Rub down level when dry. Fill the area again and rub down if required.
- Rub down the entire wall or ceiling surface.
- Wash down the surface and allow it to dry.
- Ceilings should be painted before walls. A small brush is used to cut into the corners and up to the frames and skirtings etc.
- Use a roller or large brush to cover an area of about 1 m² at a time. Apply paint in one direction, spread it out by brushing or rollering diagonally. Finally finishing off using light pressure only, in the same direction as you started.

- Using the numbered sequence continue painting the subsequent squares or strips, blending in the paint application of one with another whilst the paint is still wet. Otherwise pronounced lines will be apparent in the finished work, if wet paint is applied over a drying one.
- Clean all brushes/rollers and equipment in water on completion.

Paint coverage

This depends upon the absorbency of the surface to be painted and the quality of the paint. Typically:

- Primers and undercoats cover 12–14 m² per litre per coat;
- Gloss or satin top coats cover 14–16 m² per litre per coat.
- Emulsions cover 10–12 m² per litre per coat.

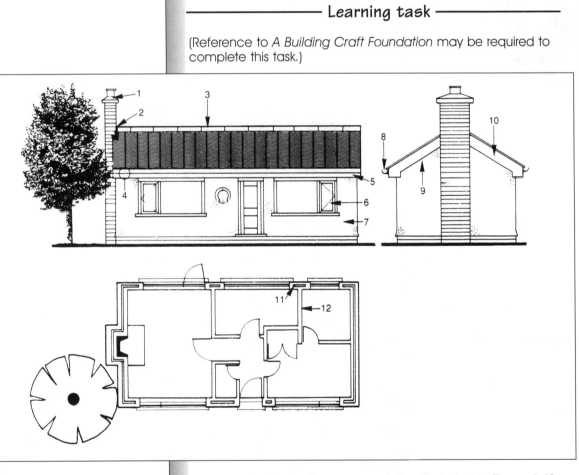

─── **Learning task** ───

(Reference to *A Building Craft Foundation* may be required to complete this task.)

Figure 6.43 *Plan and elevation*

1. Name the type of accommodation illustrated in Figure 6.43

2. Using the following items, identify the numbered features shown in Figure 6.43; not all of the items are applicable: gable, ridge, sash, hip, verge, eaves, parapet, cavity, partition wall, cladding, lintel, flashing, casement, barge board, fascia board, gutter, rendering, casement, flaunching.

_____

_____

_____

_____

_____

_____

_____

_____

_____

_____

_____

_____

3. Define the following terms and indicate an example of each of them on the section shown in Figure 6.44:

(a) substructure

_____

(b) superstructure

_____

(c) primary element

_____

(d) secondary element

_____

(e) finishing element

_____

(f) component

_____

4. Name the type of foundations illustrated in Figure 6.44

_____

5. Sketch an alternative type of ground-floor construction

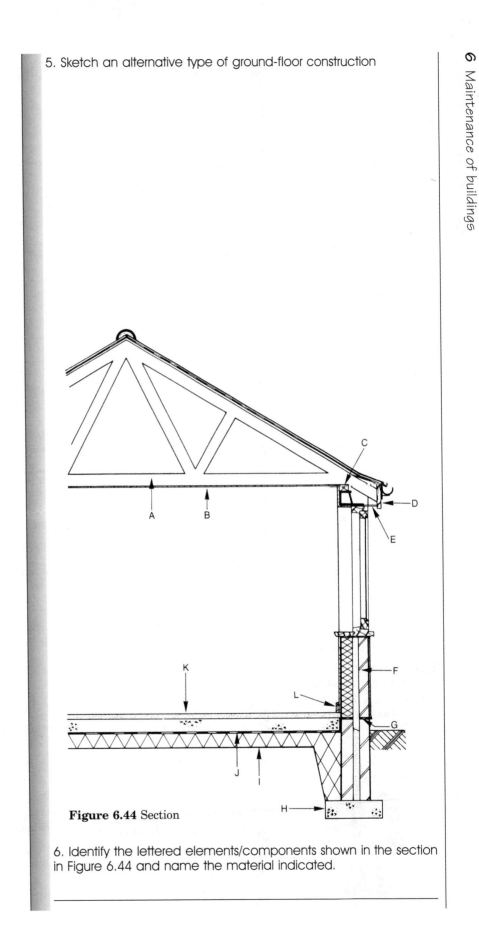

Figure 6.44 Section

6. Identify the lettered elements/components shown in the section in Figure 6.44 and name the material indicated.

_____

_____

_____

_____

_____

_____

_____

_____

_____

_____

_____

_____

7. During a close inspection of the building in Figure 6.43 you notice the following defects. State for each a possible cause and remedy:

(a) Small damp patch in the centre of the lounge floor.

_____

_____

(b) Rafters next to chimney stack are wet and show signs of fungal attack.

_____

_____

(c) Vertical cracks both internally and externally in walls down the side of the chimney and under the lounge window.

_____

_____

(d) Soft woodwork to external kitchen window sill.

_____

_____

(e) Front door has dropped at head, sticks on the threshold and shows signs of open/loose joints.

_____

_____

REFER BACK TO THE INDICATED SOURCES IF YOU HAVE ANY PROBLEMS

8. Write a letter to the building owner, informing them of the defects you identified during your survey visit and suggest appropriate remedial action.

_____

_____

_____

_____

_____

_____

_____

_____

_____

_____

_____

_____

_____

_____

_____

_____

_____

_____

_____

_____

_____

_____

_____

_____

_____

_____

_____

_____

6 Maintenance of buildings

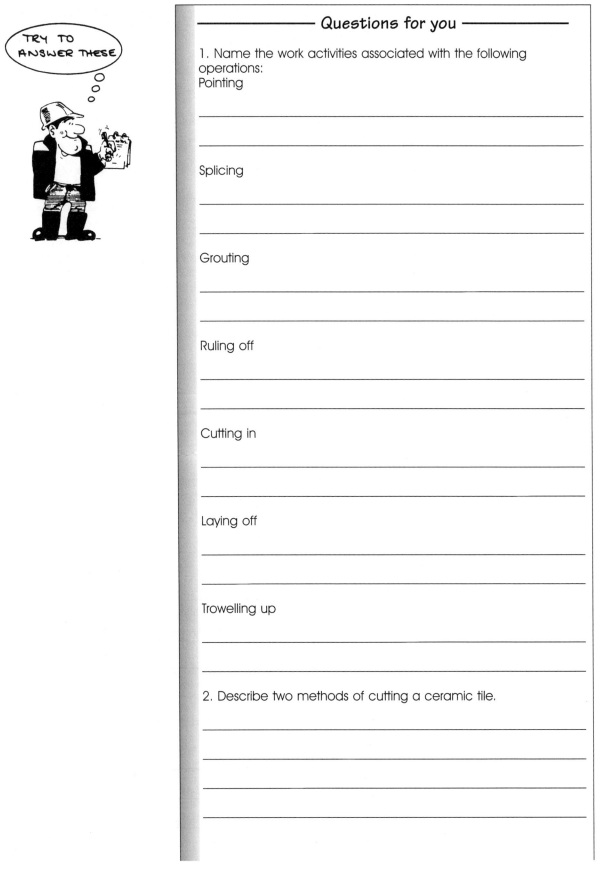

————— **Questions for you** —————

1. Name the work activities associated with the following operations:

Pointing

_____

_____

Splicing

_____

_____

Grouting

_____

_____

Ruling off

_____

_____

Cutting in

_____

_____

Laying off

_____

_____

Trowelling up

_____

_____

2. Describe two methods of cutting a ceramic tile.

_____

_____

_____

_____

3. State why screwing of plasterboard when repairing a ceiling is preferable to nailing.

_____

_____

4. A high level sash window requires re-glazing. Describe a safe method of work.

_____

_____

_____

5. You are asked to replace a badly decayed window frame with a new one. However, on examination there is no lintel or other means of support evident above the opening. Outline the procedure to follow.

_____

_____

_____

_____

_____

6. On lifting a floorboard, the underside is found to be soft, powdery and full of small holes. The most likely cause is:
(a) Wet rot attack
(b) Dry rot attack
(c) Wood boring insects
(d) Excessive floor load

a	b	c	d
⊏ ⊐	⊏ ⊐	⊏ ⊐	⊏ ⊐

7. A maintenance carpenter has a 'mouse' in their tool bag. State what it would be used for.

_____

_____

_____

8. State or sketch the sequence of operations required to keep a 'wet edge' when applying the finishing coat of paint to a six panel door.

9. State the precautions to be taken before removing unsound plasterwork in a carpeted room.

_____

_____

_____

_____

10. Describe the procedure for disposing of old timber, shavings and swept up dust during the eradication of a dry rot attack.

_____

_____

_____

_____

WELL, HOW DID YOU DO?

WORK THROUGH THE SECTION AGAIN IF YOU HAD ANY PROBLEMS

COMPLETE THE WORD SQUARE

WORD-SQUARE SEARCH

Hidden in the word square are the following 20 words associated with *'maintenance'*. You may find the words written forwards, backwards, up, down or diagonally.

Brick	Plaster
Paint	Splicing
Back putty	Scrim
Pipe	Fungi
Batten	Ceramic
Pointing	Plumb
Bonding	Level
Glazing	Sashcord
Trowel	Mortar
Mixing	Grouting

Draw a ring around the words, or line in using a highlight pen thus:

(EXAMPLE)

EXAMPLE

A	C	O	U	N	N	T	P	F	B	S	B	P	I	P	I	P	S
B	R	O	M	R	G	R	O	U	T	I	U	G	L	L	L	C	A
O	A	T	B	G	R	O	U	T	I	N	G	U	A	A	R	A	S
N	E	A	B	L	E	W	E	A	L	G	B	N	S	I	A	F	S
S	C	R	M	O	T	W	M	E	T	E	R	S	U	M	M	I	G
A	M	I	R	C	S	E	V	D	B	Q	I	O	W	F	O	R	N
S	O	C	O	K	A	E	U	R	R	U	C	G	U	U	R	F	I
C	R	R	B	N	L	L	B	O	T	A	K	N	A	T	T	U	Z
O	T	O	O	S	P	L	I	C	I	N	G	L	A	S	T	N	A
R	A	R	T	I	N	G	L	H	P	E	N	N	P	P	A	N	L
D	R	A	O	T	W	L	L	S	A	T	I	U	O	L	R	N	G
S	T	R	O	W	E	L	H	A	N	T	D	I	I	O	U	N	P
A	D	H	E	S	E	Y	O	S	Z	A	O	U	N	U	I	M	J
S	R	Y	T	T	U	P	K	C	A	B	N	F	T	X	I	R	B
H	E	A	D	I	N	I	G	P	R	A	B	N	I	P	A	N	T
C	E	R	A	M	I	P	A	I	N	T	G	M	N	O	I	N	T
O	C	I	M	A	R	E	C	P	N	N	R	O	G	R	I	P	P
R	D	D	P	O	E	K	E	I	I	G	O	T	E	A	S	L	A

Index